The Economic Development Process in the Middle East and North Africa

Offering a comprehensive analysis of the development of economies in the Middle East and North Africa over the past half century, this book charts the progress of these countries through an examination of Muslim societies, socio-demographic conditions, international relations and economic challenges.

Far from being a simple process, economic development in the Middle East and North Africa is the result of the interaction of a set of changing systems including international relations, political regimes, economic resources endowment, and social conditions. By analysing these interdependent factors, *The Economic Development Process in MENA* seeks to provide answers to the most pressing issues facing the economies in this area.

Providing an interpretation of regional economic development in light of dialectics between state and society, this book will be of value to students and scholars with an interest in the Middle East, Economics, and International Relations.

Alessandro Romagnoli is Associate Professor in the Department of Economics at the University of Bologna.

Luisa Mengoni is Contract Professor and International Relations and Projects Officer at inter-university consortium AlmaLaurea.

Routledge Studies in Middle Eastern Economies

This series provides up to date overviews and analysis of the region's economies. The approaches taken are not confined to a particular approach and include analysis of growth and future development, individual country studies, oil, multinational enterprises, government policy, financial markets, and the region's role in the world economy.

The Egyptian Economy
Performance Policies and Issues
Khalid Ikram

The Turkish Economy
The Real Economy, Corporate Governance and Reform
Edited by Sumru G. Altug and Alpay Filiztekin

Economic Co-Operation in the Gulf
Issues in the Economies of the Arab Gulf Co-Operation Council States
Badr El Din A. Ibrahim

Turkish Accession to the EU
Satisfying the Copenhagen Criteria
Eric Faucompret and Joep Konings

Turkey and the Global Economy
Neo-Liberal Restructuring and Integration in the Post-Crisis Era
Edited by Ziya Öniş and Fikret Şenses

Industrialization in the Gulf
A Socioeconomic Revolution
Edited by Jean-François Seznec and Mimi Kirk

The Israeli Central Bank
Political Economy, Global Logistics and Local Actors
Daniel Maman and Zeev Rosenhek

Human Development in Iraq
1950–1990
Bassam Yousif

State Reform and Development in the Middle East
Turkey and Egypt in the Post-Liberalization Era
Amr Adly

Political Economy of the Gulf Sovereign Wealth Funds
A Case Study of Iran, Kuwait, Saudi Arabia and the UAE
Sara Bazoobandi

The Economic Development Process in the Middle East and North Africa
Alessandro Romagnoli and Luisa Mengoni

The Economic Development Process in the Middle East and North Africa

Alessandro Romagnoli and
Luisa Mengoni

LONDON AND NEW YORK

First published 2014 by Routledge

2 Park Square, Milton Park, Abingdon, Oxfordshire OX14 4RN
52 Vanderbilt Avenue, New York, NY 10017

Routledge is an imprint of the Taylor & Francis Group, an informa business

First issued in paperback 2019

British Library Cataloguing in Publication Data
A catalogue record for this book is available from the British Library

Library of Congress Cataloging-in-Publication Data
Romagnoli, Alessandro, 1950-
The economic development process in the Middle East and North
Africa / Alessandro Romagnoli and Luisa Mengoni.
pages cm. -- (Routledge studies in Middle Eastern economies)
Includes bibliographical references and index.
1. Economic development--Middle East. 2. Economic development--
Africa, North. 3. Middle East--Economic conditions. 4. Middle
East--Economic policy. 5. Africa, North--Economic conditions.
6. Africa, North--Economic policy. I. Mengoni, Luisa E. II. Title.
HC415.15.R66 2014
338.956--dc23
2013012118

ISBN: 978-0-415-59405-9 (hbk)
ISBN: 978-0-367-86571-9 (pbk)

Typeset in Sabon
by Saxon Graphics Ltd, Derby

Contents

List of figures

List of maps

List of tables

Acknowledgements

We would like to gratefully acknowledge Professor Adel Beshai (American University in Cairo), Professor Giuliana Campanelli (William Paterson University, NJ) and Professor Giovanni Guidetti (University of Bologna) for their valuable guidelines and advice. We also want to thank the students of our courses on MENA economics who, by reading some chapters of the book, provided us with useful suggestions. We are, of course, responsible for all the errors and omissions.

The map on the 'Expansion of the Ottoman empire' is reprinted with permission from Encyclopedia Britannica © 1997 by Encyclopedia Britannica, Inc., which we acknowledge for the use of copyright.

An honourable mention goes to our families and friends for their understanding and support throughout the writing process.

Introduction

For 50 years like no other world area, the Middle East and North Africa (MENA) region has caught the attention of the media reporting political, economic, and social events, and of the scholars of different disciplines studying the issue of political instability (due, for instance, to recurring conflicts or revolts), provision of the world's energy, and religious integralism. Sometimes these observers, although specialists, have not been fully capable of dealing with such matters, because they only had a partial understanding of the area or due to biased evaluations or ideologies. In other respects, the complexity of the socio-political reality of the region, its distance from Western standards and distinctive social habits made (and still make) difficult to cope with. Economists do not represent an exception, especially when the disciplinary framework they develop to study a specific phenomenon is based mainly on the experience of Europe and North America and on its theorization, as is the case of development.

For all these reasons to propose a book centred on the development process in the Middle East and North Africa, which aims to provide the reader with an instrument to understand the outcomes of the regional economies and the problems they are facing, is a cultural challenge. To accept this challenge we must go beyond the economic field and employ some innovative methodological tools in order to handle these topics, with respect to the few existing volumes on this argument. Our first challenge stays in the framework used to analyse the process, that is, in the adoption of a dynamic institutional view that sees socio-cultural and historical specificities as central explanatory variables. A similar approach is adopted in *A Political Economy of the Middle East* by Richards and Waterbury (Westview Press, 2008, third edition): an outstanding classic that, however, betrays its 30 years of planning. To this feature can be attributed, among others, the lack of new subjects (like institutions), and of a unifying methodology, but also by its nature a handbook is not concerned with an adopted theoretical idea of development. On the contrary, in the recent *Arab Economies in a Changing World* (Peterson Institute for International Economics, 2007) by Noland and Pack, a more updated set of problems is presented, yet using a too restrictive methodological approach (the 'international political economy') that makes development appear as nothing but an imitation.

The second challenge of our book is that these regional economies are considered to be 'latecomer' countries approaching development, intended as a path introducing a new socio-economic system. In so doing a revision of the theoretical setting of another classic on the topic is proposed, *The Economic Development in the Middle East* (Routledge, 2012, first edition 1995) by Wilson, a well-structured subject-oriented study related mainly to the economic thought of 1960s and 1970s.

The third challenge faced in planning this new book on the MENA economies is to give a comprehensive and multifaceted reading of the development process in the area, consistent with that supplied in other fields of study (for example, international relations) and complementary to that offered by some books that mainly examine the economic outcome of single countries of the region, like *Economic Policy and Performance in the Arab World* (Linne Rienner Publishers, 2001) and *Arab Economies in the Twenty First Century* (Cambridge University Press, 2009), both by Paul Revlin, and the volume *Explaining Growth in the Middle East* (Elsevier, 2006), edited by Nugent and Pesaran, which are all recent collections of good essays.

The present volume is, first of all, a book on development, where this process consists of a shift from an old to a new socio-economic system (namely from a traditional society to 'capitalism') creating new subjects and organizations, making new goods and services available, empowering new social and political actors, in a framework of old established states of affairs outside and inside the country. Together with new economic forces and technologies, a central explanatory power of the phenomenon is thus recognized in the international environment in which this process evolves and in the domestic condition and institutional heritage on which new rules and habits are built: while the country's potential for managing its own economic capacity depends on the first, the speed of change of social activities and rules is affected by the second. Thus the economic development of MENA countries (like that of any other country) doesn't emerge as the result of a textbook example, but as the interaction among different social domains, like economy, political regime, international relations, social norms and skills. On this stance, the book will linger on the geostrategic position of the regional economies and on their historic evolution, on the interplay between state and society in shaping the change process, on the traditional role of Muslim institutions in arranging economic activities and in building the welfare systems, on the progress in achieving reforms and economic integration.

A methodological framework based on a systemic approach and on some analytical concepts (the geographical unit, a socio-economic interpretation of the clan, a definition of capitalism and of development, a dynamic concept of institution, etc.) is required both to implement such an interpretation of development, and to review the last 50 years' experience of the MENA countries searching for a proper path of development between the evolution of the international relations framework and the rapid change of an ancient, well-established society. In this framework some specific topics will be examined: the development process of 'latecomers' and the institutional change, the development of policies and macroeconomic performance, the structure of the economies, oil and gas challenges, the cycles and waves of the MENA economic transition process, demographic dynamics, the labour market, migration and the new role of the family, the openness of the economies and economic integration, the social contract and the welfare system, poverty and inequality, and the relationship between Muslim societies and capitalism.

Considering both the theoretical base for the economic analysis of development in MENA and the connected methodological premises, the dialectic between a weak state and a powerful society arises as a relevant guideline to explain regional outcome, also providing an answer to the main and most recent issues faced by these economies. The strain between the two different social domains (economic and political systems) succeeds in producing development only when it displays a sort of co-evolution of both fields, that is a shared, coordinated and consistent path toward a change.

The starting point for the analysis of the economic development process in the Middle East and North Africa is the awareness that an appropriate geographical unit is needed in order to understand the phenomenon in its distinctive nature and authenticity. This problem will be faced in Chapter 1. Although there are different concepts of region as well as divergences in defining the extension of the Middle East and North Africa, colonial legacies, international relations and geopolitical perspectives, jointly with language, culture and economic ties enable the identification of a single geographic unit. This region, homogeneous in most respects but free from regionalism (because of the colonial experience), has shifted in the last century from a geo-political periphery of the international relations to a geo-economic core, as a consequence of its strategic role for political and economic world relations. For all these reasons the Middle East and North Africa can be considered as a suitable geographical entity when discussing the problems of development of the whole area.

In Chapter 2, the economic foundations of the analysis will be set up, assuming that development represents a crossing from an old socio-economic system to capitalism, in a distinctive and historical environment. In fact, the appraisal of the outcomes and of past and future challenges of low-income economies has to take into account both the general features of the development and the environmental context in which it has been carried out. Starting from this premise the chapter will review the features of capitalism, the characteristics of the successful experience of the 'first comers', and the economic and political world context in which a new 'latecomer' implements its own path. As to the last item, a 'new development paradigm' (recently proposed by outstanding economists) will be deepened by stressing, in particular, the need for a concept of development not restricted to economics, the importance of the institution building process along the development path, and the impact that the world social, political and economic contexts have on this process. The emerging result is that the replication of the path of development by 'latecomers' is greatly different with respect to the process experienced by the 'first comers'.

The following chapter (Chapter 3) completes the analytical framework of the book by introducing a model of institutional change and a systemic representation of capitalism based on it. If institutions can be conceived as behavioural rules embedded in social activities, the transition towards a new socio-economic system presents the need for a change in behavioural regulations of some social domains (the polity, the economy, and so on) potentially conflicting with traditions in other fields of social activities more resilient to the change (like habits and religion, for example). The problem of the emergence of capitalist institutions is thus crucial in any development process, especially in the case of the MENA region, where the coexistence of capitalism with principles of Muslim societies had been questioned. In such respect, the debate among historians on the failed update of 'Maghribi traders' commercial rules and the discussion among economists on the institutional quality in the region, are representative. The institution building process carried out within dialectics between weak states and strong societies can thus be considered as an additional guideline to the interpretation of MENA region economic development.

The demographic dynamics represent an important phenomenon affecting each development process by means of population changes (in quantity and in age structure) and movements (rural-urban migration), and by worsening economic values like the rate of food self-sufficiency and of income inequality. Yet the demographic changes that have occurred in the MENA region in the last decades have resulted also in a decrease of the 'dependency ratio' and in a considerable rise of the 'working age population', thus opening new perspectives of development. The window of opportunity is highlighted by the lower fertility rates, the increasing participation of women in the labour force, and the rising number of smaller families tending to invest more in the education of fewer children. All these matters are reviewed along the developing path of the region in Chapter 4 focusing, in particular, on the policies some Arab countries have successfully implemented to reduce their population growth, and on the increasing pressure on the labour markets, in the presence of high unemployment, due to rising participation rates. As the intraregional migration movements (from labour-abundant to the oil-rich countries with low population growth) no longer represent a mechanism for achieving demographic balance, the present situation calls into question the sustainability of the development strategies adopted by the regional economies, emphasizing the need for appropriate economic and social policies.

The economic outcomes of MENA countries in the last 50 years are presented in Chapter 5: economic cycles and trends are identified to explain why the region experienced first a boom and then bust and periods of stagnation. Although these macroeconomic phases are common to all regional economies, they present different intensity in groups of countries with similar economic structures and policies. Such a phenomenon thus calls for the consideration of various aspects that may represent growth constraint: the specific features of the economy determine the region performance (like population growth, natural resources endowment and productive diversification) together with structural factors (economic role of the state, bureaucracy, political instability and uncertainty). Past and present challenges of the development process will thus be reviewed in order to identify the future policies to be adopted.

The appraisal of the performance of MENA economies cannot be independent from the policies adopted, in general, to implement the development path and, in particular, to improve human conditions. This issue will be tackled in Chapter 6, starting with a review of state policies implemented to promote development and to manage the economies during the three phases previously presented. Both the development policies and the programmes used to address poverty and inequality are embedded in the 'social contract', that is, the institutional arrangements and the social policies about education, housing, health care and food subsidies committed to the state for a long time. Until the 'Arab Spring', the social contract represented an instrument legitimating specific forms of state-society relations. The increasing rate of growth of the economies experienced by MENA regions until the mid-1980s, allowed an improvement in all these social fields by providing services that were lacking, while religious communitarian spirit, religious organizations and NGOs' social activism promoted gains in human indicators in critical economic periods, thus sustaining social cohesion. The chapter will focus on trends in human indicators according to the different periods, on the new social actors providing welfare system, and on the consequences of the new course of the social contract. Poverty reduction policies and the growth-inequality nexus in the MENA region will be, in particular, deepened as a challenge for these economies in the future.

Together with the demographic dynamics, the human capital quality affects the labour supply and so too does the structure of the economy with respect to the demand for labour. Thus the MENA region's labour markets, despite their countries' variations, are generally characterized, by the particular segmentation between public sector jobs (with more guarantees in terms of insurance and wage) and the private jobs, and by a dominant role of the State in terms of employment creation. Nevertheless, in recent decades, with growing unemployment and overstaffing of the public sector, the MENA informal labour market has become so active that today it represents one of the main sources of employment for the regional labour force. Another important feature of the Arab labour markets is the structural imbalance between demand and supply of skills, with a surplus of highly-educated people waiting for a job, and a lack of a labour force with firm-specific technical skills. As a result, empirical studies show how, on the one hand, human capital is not contributing much to growth, and why on the other hand, the low productivity of the region can be attributed to the low quality of the educational system and to the misallocation of labour across sectors: the underutilization of the highly skilled is thus a main concern. Such issues will be explored in Chapter 7, where the future of the labour market also questions the possibility of relying on 'a quality' self-employment in the informal sector (accountable, regulated and able to attract skilled labour) as a viable solution for employment creation.

Since the the 1970s intra- and inter-regional migration flows have represented one of the main strategies of development for the Arab countries, although it has not been expressly adminted. With the insufficient perform-ance of MENA economies in foreign trade, labour migration played a unique role in promoting regional development through market integration, thus suggesting complementarities with respect to foreign aid. Despite the repatriation of Arab migrants following the 1991 Gulf War, the implementation of policies to prevent naturalization of Arab migrants by MENA-receiving countries and the move to a restrictive regime in the EU, the flows are still consistent. For these reasons the phenomenon will be analysed in Chapter 8 both in respect to its spatial features (south-north flows vs. south-south flows), to its temporal duration (permanent migrants vs. temporary migrants), and to its trends (the shift from permanence to temporary). The impact of massive return (of a different nature according to migration trajectories) for the local development of migrants' origin countries will be then discussed, fostering 'brain gain' dynamics, diversification of economic activities and availability of labour force with skills demanded by the market. Nevertheless the implementation of restrictive policies, both in the western recipient countries and in the Gulf ones, question the possibility of migration to be a feasible solution in the future for structural labour market problems, especially for the labour-abundant countries.

There is a wide consensus among researchers on the lack of integration in international markets for MENA countries. Empirical studies show that Arab trade with the rest of the world is low and remains below the foreign trade of countries with similar levels of development. The reasons behind the poor integration of MENA in international markets have been attributed to market distortions and insufficient institutional development, inward-oriented policies and protectionism, high tariff barriers, polarized market structure and bottlenecks in the transport sector, the lack of cooperation on procedures and on harmonization of policies. But considering the labour market's openness, a special role is played by migration flows, emerging as one of the more dynamic features of regional integration, and also as an assessment of the relation between trade and migration as a balance to, or a complement for, trade. In recent years, several initiatives have been taken to increase trade, as the participation to multilateral trade agreements and the joining of WTO, the unilateral trade liberalization and the signing of trade agreements with individual countries or with group of countries (as between EU and individual MENA). In this direction, the creation of trade agreements among MENA countries (resulting in sub-regional trade blocks as GAFTA, AMU, GCC and the Arab Common Market) has proved to be a viable pathway: as a matter of fact, the proportion of trade within subgroups has been significantly higher than overall intra-Arab trade. In Chapter 9 all the previous topics will be developed to question if the institutional change created by the international trade regime is suitable to support the internationalization of the MENA economies.

A lot of interesting topics about the development of Middle East and North Africa could be included in the book, yet we present the most relevant ones, suitable to understand why the region still draws the world's attention on issues related to the youth unemployment, the Arab Springs and oil provision. Postgraduate students and scholars who are interested in economics can find in our treatise useful theoretical digressions justifying the chosen point of view in explaining the arguments, while those concerned with international relations or political and social sciences (as well as the readers willing to go deep to the heart of MENA region' affairs) can appreciate the interplay between social and economic variables in an actual, discussed development process.

1 The Middle East and North Africa

A 'harmonizing geographic region' without a complete regionalism

'For over 50 years the Middle East and North Africa (MENA) have been seen as a single unit of analysis' assuming, their 'political, socio-economic and cultural aspects [...] as a distinct subsystem of the international system' (Ehteshami 2007:47). Despite the fact that this representation is widely accepted and is, on the whole, believed to be self-evident, this world area presents both divergent extents (according to the scholars of different disciplines), and little shared political and economic aims. As to the latter argument, in most recent decades, contrasts and conflicts among the states involved followed one another, preventing political co-operation: by way of example can be mentioned the division between Arab republics and the conservative bloc in the 1960s; the upgrading of Arabian Peninsula states because of the petroleum diplomacy in 1970s; the fragmentation of the Arab world first in 1978 when the Camp David Accords were signed and then again during Iraqi invasions both of Iran and of Kuwait in the 1980s and 1990s, and yet again during the third Gulf War. Not even economic collaboration occurred, and the evidence of this failure is the fact that the integration of the MENA economies is far from comparable with that of other developing areas (Akhtar and Rouis 2010). In this context, we must question in what sense the Middle East and North Africa can be considered a region and how such a representation is consistent both with the previous historic evidence, and with the International Economic Organization's belief that it is a suitable tool to discuss the problem of the development in this particular part of the world.

Though the nature of region of the Middle East and North Africa can be disputed theoretically without unquestionable conclusions, a methodological investigation on this unit of analysis (the regional entity) and on the assumptions retained in it is needed as a first step to research an aggregate of economies. On one hand, the review of the literature on the topic highlights the controversial concepts of 'region' and of 'regionalism' (words usually employed to categorize a world area) and on the other hand, it highlights the fact that their use for the MENA countries goes beyond some aspects (like Islamic religion, Muslim societies, Arab language, etc.) assumed as common and as uniformly spread between the Atlantic Ocean and the

Gulf. In fact, an historical digression can demonstrate that, in addition to cultural and religious traditions, the element homogenizing the area is a common twofold identity, based on strong local traits (reinforced by a society cell as the clan) and on a universal belonging spirit connected to religious, social and language sharing.

This common belonging, built on a decentralization of the political power as well as on socio-cultural and psychological components, survived unchanged throughout the centuries. It was sometimes supported by invader policies (like during the Ottoman empire), sometimes offset by institutional transfer and by the economic activities of colonizers (like during the Mandates period), and sometimes channelled for state reasons (occurring since independence). The presence of this sense of belonging, which was evident in various forms during the last two centuries, opposed the dismantling of regionalism carried out by the colonial policies and the geo-economic strategies set up by the industrial powers searching for energy resources.

All the issues sketched thus far will be discussed in this introductory chapter, aiming to present the environment in which the economic development process of the MENA countries took place, paying particular attention to the political and economic interventions enacted by the world economic powers because of the growing importance of the region.

A regional setting as an analytical unit

The concept of 'region' has been deeply analysed by different disciplines, mainly during the 1950s and the 1970s, but without reaching a common theoretical framework. Geographers and regional scientists, international political scholars and economists tried to set up theoretical meaning and the features of the term to analyse the different problems concerned with the concept. The first group of researchers was essentially interested in the characterization of a territory to arrange a well set geographical unit for applied studies. The international political scientists investigated the process of 'regionalization', that is, the reason why regional arrangements are created and the conditions necessary to manage them. Economists, who approached the problem from the perspective of the international trade, were first keen on the welfare effects connected to a regional trade area, and then on the rise of regional trade agreements in the context of an increasing globalized world. If geographers pointed out the physical meaning of the term 'regionalism', political scientists and economists deepened its institutional framework, arriving to discuss the regionalization path and its steps.

In their pioneering works on geography, Herbertson (Herbertson 1905) and Hartshorne (Hartshorne 1939) proposed the concept of 'formal region' as a natural manifestation of the relationships between a territory, physically and environmentally categorized, and its long-standing population.

Configuration, climate, vegetation, and population density represented the environmental dimensions of this geographic unit, completely determining the territorially organized systems of social activities and habits included in it (Cloke, Philo and Sadler 1991: 3-13). On this basis, the mapping out of a certain number of typical regions was then elaborated, achieving the systematic identification and description of this geographic unit of analysis.[1] But this theoretical representation appeared too deterministic to the regional scientists who used a less restrictive concept of region, simply characterized as a 'meaningful and significant unit[s] for a number of topical geographical studies, as well as for a number of problems studied by regional science' (Wrobel 1962:41). In this 'geographic region' boundaries and differences (mutual geographic distinctions) on one side, common identity, homogeneity, uniformity and cohesion (internal consistency) on the other, were the main geographic and socio-cultural features that must present for an area to be considered a region, i.e. the geographic framework for the disciplinary investigation.

An attempt to categorize the concept of region was made, as well, in the field of international political studies by Thompson, who, in a 1973 methodological paper written to assess the use of systemic analysis for regional investigations, first collected a list of 21 attributes of the analytical unit discussed in the literature, and then on that base built a set of necessary and sufficient methodological conditions (named structural conditions) for the existence of a regional subsystem, including the interaction, the regularity, the proximity, a distinctive theatre of operations and a multiplicity of actors (Thompson 1973).[2] In so doing he changed the theoretical representation of the region put forward by the geographers, shifting from a uniform, self-contained entity to an open-system organism, and from the methodical account of a container to the methodological report of relational contents emerging in a geographic space ('systemic region').

With the passing of time, international political scholars widely shared the opinion that the political actors (states) perceive and interpret the idea of region, and that the international agreements creating regional subsystems are one among the instruments bringing to life this image. Accordingly, given that 'all regions are socially constructed and hence politically contested' (Hurrell 1995: 38-9), there are good reasons to study, independently from the existence of a geographic region, how and why the states organize their international relations in more or less enduring and comprehensive arrangements. This approach converged the interest of researchers on 'regionalism', that is on the process creating an uniform entity on a geographic area ('harmonizing region') by a set of distinct but interrelated elements: on one hand some real, perceived or created socio-cultural conditions like 'regional awareness, identity and consciousness' (belonging to a particular community sharing culture, history, and habits), on the other hand, some institutional processes like the integration of social activities in a territory, 'regional interstate co-operation' (whose variety is the 'economic integration'), and 'regional cohesion' arrangement (the institution building to give rise to a consolidated regional unit).[3] As the regionalism was perceived as a response to the pressures exerted from outside the states or as a balancing instrument to manage the interdependence inside a group of countries,[4] the main ties of the alliances created to cope with them are the external hegemonic power in the first case and the institutional building process in the second, both working in the theatre of operations of the international politics or economics. Supported by these unleashing forces, the concept of region that lies behind the idea of regionalism drops the determinism of the geographic characters (even though it preserves the socio-cultural features of the populations as an important condition for the outcome of the international cooperation policies of the states), and introduces the state as primary regional subject.

But in applied studies, in spite of the wide range of conditions, elements and processes considered in defining the theoretical meaning of regionalism, the basic concept used by the international political scientists to review the phases of the phenomenon is minimal: in fact, they consider only the 'regional interstate co-operation' (and, sometimes, the regional process of integration of social activities) implemented both by the states wielding their external hegemonic power or promoting agreements and institutional building processes, and by the international organizations of all kinds (firms and NGOs included).[5] Thus the resulting unit of analysis is a 'virtual region', a space experiencing a process of regionalization consisting in the implementation of institutions or of agreements to manage the international relations among the states. Thanks to this result, despite the variety of methodology used, a large consensus was achieved in scheduling these four waves of regionalism during the past two centuries (Fawcett 1995; Mansfield and Milner 1999):

1   The former upsurge of regionalism, in the sense just discussed, occurred in the second half of the nineteen century, when the idea of a regional security regime was spread as a means to create a sphere of influence of powers (the Monroe Doctrine), or when custom unions (like the German Zollverein introduced in 1850) and bilateral trade agreements (such as the Anglo-French commercial treaty set up in 1860) were implemented mainly in Europe (Mattli 1999: 1-2; Mansfield and Miller 1999: 596);

2   A similar tendency appeared in the period between the First World War and the Second World War, when the clause of 'regional understanding' was included in the Covenant of the League of Nations to reflect the interests of the US in the Americas (Fawcett 2004: 436), or when France (in 1928) and Great Britain (with the Commonwealth agreement starting in 1932) consolidated their powers by creating trade preferential systems with their colonies (Mansfield and Milner 1999: 596);

3   A third wave of regionalism spread out at the end of the Second World War as a signal of (and as a response to) the new international order (characterized both by the Cold War and by the decolonization process), or because of mutual trading interests of some fast-growing economies (such as the Western European countries). It embedded, generally, the creation of multipurpose agreements and the development of international organizations in all the fields of politics and economics;

4   The so-called 'new regionalism', starting at the end of the Cold War, is the symptom of a changed international scenario, whose main facts are a long-lasting presence of one pole in international politics, new conflicts and new entries in the international arena, and a new process of globalization more profound and more pervasive than before. The interpretation of this phase presents the institutional building as the more apparent explanatory key, but also hegemony is necessary to make clear particular tendencies in international relations. In addition, regionalism (but in this case it would be better to use the term regionalization) is conceived as a partial way of promoting international co-operation, if compared to the universal one supported by the world agencies providing security (UN and NATO, for example) or economic welfare (like WTO): just this dispute between globalization and regionalism gives rise to the question if the best international interstate co-operation can be reached by universalism or by bilateralism.

As to the last dispute, the economists, whose main interests in the subject are the international trade agreements and the institutional building process creating free trade areas, argued the existence of a trade-off between the universal way of promoting the co-operation among the states and a more limited way: they consider the trade liberalization at world level the best condition for the international economic co-operation because it determines the structural convergence of the economies and the maximization of their welfare (Baldwin 1952), while they judge 'regionalization' as a process producing a sub-optimal equilibrium because the preferential trade areas implemented by regional economic agreements discriminate third countries, may be more efficient.[6] Given these theoretical implications, we can summarize that, in the view of economists the geographic area experiencing a process of regionalization through the building of an international market tends to take the shape of a homogeneous super-national (may be not necessarily land-continuous) 'virtual region'. This conclusion can be supported by the fact that the economic theory of regional integration traditionally deepens the flow of goods (although international exchanges concern goods, workers, and financial assets)[7] and examines overall welfare and trade effects on the structure of the economies experiencing the integration of markets, alongside the degree of harmonization created in a free trade area. Thus economists perceive the 'virtual regions' as entities endowed by different cohesion (that is a variety of regionalization), according to the different levels of integration,[8]

Table 1.1 Taxonomy of region concepts

Concept of region	Definition of region	Regional features		Methodological features	Institutional arrangement
		Geographical features	Socio-cultural features		
Formal region	A natural manifestation of the relationships between a territory and its long-standing population	Environmental dimensions (configuration, climate, vegetation, and population density)	Social activities and habits	None	None
Geographical region	A significant unit for topical geographical studies, and for regional science problem analysis	Mutual geographic distinctions (boundaries and differences)	Internal consistency (regional awareness, identity and consciousness)	None	None
Systemic region	A geographic space with emerging relational contents	None	None	Structural conditions (regularity, proximity, distinctive theatre of operations, multiplicity of actors)	None
Harmonizing region	A synchronizing area where some processes of state co-operation operate on a set of distinct but interrelated elements	None	Real, perceived or created conditions (regional awareness, identity, consciousness)	None	Regionalism (regional interstate integration in social and institutional fields, regional interstate co-operation)
Virtual region	A space beyond the nation state experiencing the same set of institutions and of functioning conditions	Super-national area (may be not necessarily continuous)	None	Functioning conditions (homogeneity, efficiency, quality, legitimacy, compliance)	Regionalization (regional institutions, state compliance with them, regional institutional depth and cohesion)

Source: Authors' elaboration.

so siding with the New Regionalism Approach searching for 'factors that promote (or inhibit) the emergence of regional political economic formations and/or the impact that greater regionalization is likely to have' (Lawson 2008: 13).

The review just presented shows that both the nature of the concept of 'region' has been tweaked (see Table 1.1), and interest of scholars has shifted from the study of a specific population living and operating in a world area to the analysis of the implementation (by a group of states) of an international co-operation and integration project. As these aims are different, divergent images of region are necessary: a real complex entity in the first case, and a theoretically efficient model of political and economic co-operation in the second. In some applied analyses (but also in the Hurrell theoretical framework, see Hurrell 1995: 41), the two elements and their respective methodological approaches are not substitutes but complements for the recognition and/or the implementation of a sustainable regional space, given that the first refers to the socio-cultural cohesion of countries and the second to the level of political and economic co-operation among the states. This methodological approach is useful for our analysis, because it explains to what extent MENA countries constitute a far-back region, and why they presented difficulties of co-operation and different aims in international politics and economics, thus why Middle East and North Africa countries have been identified and analysed as a geographical region with a limited regionalism (El-Erian and Fischer 1996; Aarts 1999; Harders and Legrenzi 2008; see also Binder 1958; Thompson 1970). But, in order to validate both the socio-cultural cohesion and the limited integration in international politics and economics, and to understand why the first element did not automatically produce the second, it is necessary to refer to the history of the populations living in this part of the world to look for the roots of both aspects.

Shared legacies and common identity from the Hercules Pillars to the Silk Route

The origins of the common sense of belonging for the communities living in Middle East and North Africa – the shared history, culture and habits representing the most important conditions for the 'regional awareness, identity and consciousness'– must be brought back to the spread of Arab language and of Islam. Although spoken Arabic (a Semitic subgroup of Afro-Asiatic languages diffused among some Bedouin tribes of the Arabian Peninsula) dates back to the eighth century BC, and despite the fact that written documents appeared since the first century, it was only in the seventh century AC when the Arabs expanded outside of the Levant, that this language spread, reaching over the Mediterranean sea in particular. Such a diffusion was due both to the administrative needs of the Arab empire and to the conversion to Islam of the dominated people: with reference to the last matter, the Quran was influential not only for the diffusion of the new, unified and well-structured Arabic script used to write it, but also for the integration of residents living in the occupied territories because it propagated religious principles as well as social norms. In addition, Islam acted as an important instrument for the political identity of all inhabitants of the empire since the converted, soon considered equal to the Arabs as they were Muslims, became supporters of the government. Thanks to a common language and to a shared religion, since the middle of the eighth century BC, a wide territory extending itself from the Atlantic to the Indian Ocean was militarily contended and culturally unified in the course of 800 years of long-lasting Arab domination. Despite the quick land occupation, the conversion to Islam grew by a slow process, and the same applies to the diffusion of Arabic: in North Western Africa, for example, it was habitually spoken only since the eleventh century, while in some occupied territories such as Iran, Pakistan, Afghanistan and Caucasus it was soon replaced by the previous languages, because of the fusion of the Arabs with the native populations (Lapidus 2002: 42-43). So, the Muslim world expanded beyond both the Arab-speaking world (Maps 1.1 and 1.2), and beyond the Arab dominion.

The Ottoman conquest of the Arab territories, between 1512 and 1683, represented a sort of continuity with respect to the socio-cultural characters of the previous historical period. The common background, although transformed, maintained its basic features and in some cases was also reinforced as, for example, 'Ottoman sovereignty consolidated North African politico-religious institutions as variations upon Middle Eastern Islamic themes' (Lapidus 2002: 321). Most Arab lands, although provinces of the new Muslim empire (except Morocco, an independent state since 788 BC), kept their traditions, habits and religion, strengthening some previous socio-political organizations (i.e. the clan) in the following centuries of Turkish dominion. So, in 1798, when the French Expedition envisaged the age of colonization in the Mediterranean, they had to deal with another legacy, in addition to the language and to the religion, shared in the core of Muslim world: the organization of society as a set of local fairly independent communities, whose socio-political and economic cells were the clans.[9]

To explain what it is meant by this term, and to understand the importance of this feature not for the political development of this world area (an issue that a large, specialized literature has been devoted to, see Khoury and Kostiner 1990) but for its identity formation and for its economic progress, a short digression from the subject is needed. Every organization, a purposive group of interdependent individuals acting for a common shared aim, survives when endowed with an efficient co-ordination of the activities. The co-operative behaviour of its members is due to the expectation both of 'reciprocity' in the contribution/reward evaluation and of 'impartial application' of this principle to each partner. When there is some ambiguity in evaluating a member performance, owing to functional or technical reasons, the co-operative spirit can be supported by a certain degree of

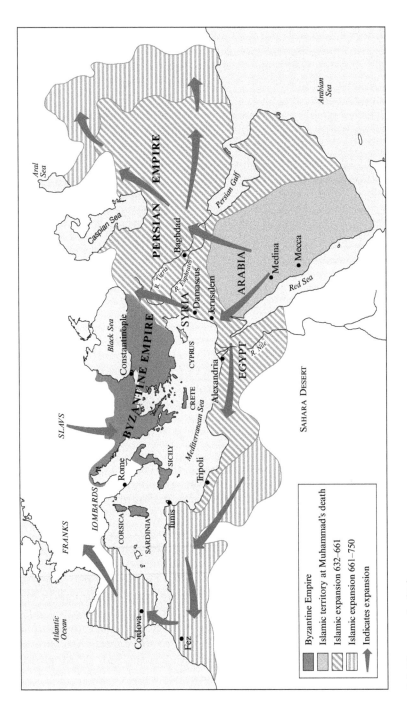

Map 1.1 The spread of Islam

Byzantine Empire

Islamic territory at Muhammad's death

Islamic expansion 632–661

Islamic expansion 661–750

Indicates expansion

Atlantic Ocean

FRANKS

LOMBARDS

Cordova

Fez

Tunis

CORSICA

SARDINIA

Rome

SICILY

Tripoli

Mediterranean Sea

CRETE

BYZANTINE EMPIRE

Constantinople

Black Sea

SLAVS

CYPRUS

Alexandria

R. Nile

EGYPT

SAHARA DESERT

Jerusalem

Damascus

SYRIA

R. Euphrates

R. Tigris

Baghdad

PERSIAN EMPIRE

Caspian Sea

Aral Sea

Medina

Mecca

ARABIA

Red Sea

Persian Gulf

Arabian Sea

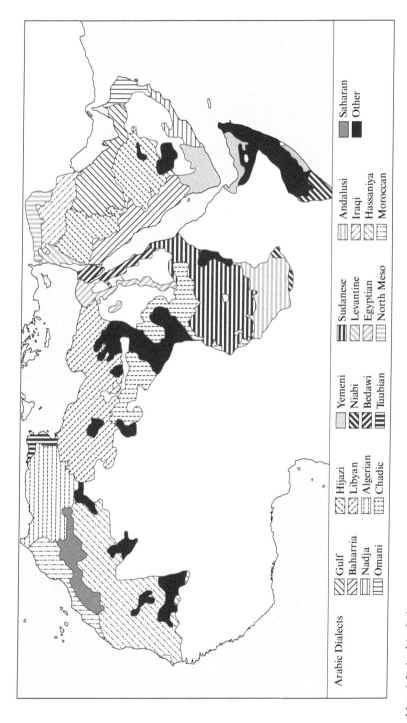

Arabic Dialects

Gulf	Hijazi	Yemeni	Sudanese	Andalusi
Baharria	Libyan	Niabi	Levantine	Iraqi
Nadja	Algerian	Bedawi	Egyptian	Hassaniya
Omani	Chadic	Tuubian	North Meso	Moroccan

Saharan	
Other	

Map 1.2 Arabic dialects

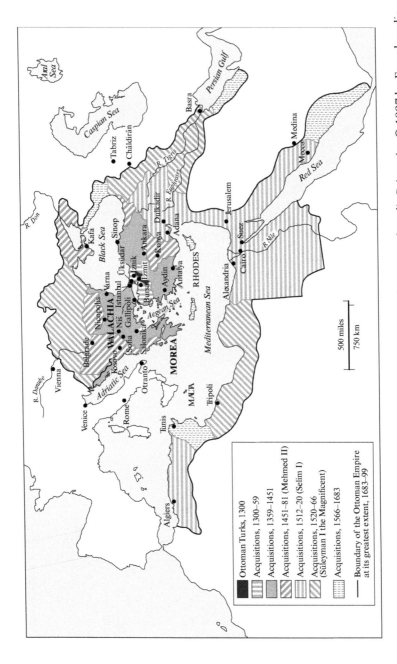

Map 1.3 The expansion of the Ottoman Empire. Reprinted with permission from Encyclopedia Britannica © 1997 by Encyclopedia Britannica, Inc.

Legend:
- Ottoman Turks, 1300
- Acquisitions, 1300–59
- Acquisitions, 1359–1451
- Acquisitions, 1451–81 (Mehmed II)
- Acquisitions, 1512–20 (Selim I)
- Acquisitions, 1520–66 (Süleyman I the Magnificent)
- Acquisitions, 1566–1683
- Boundary of the Ottoman Empire at its greatest extent, 1683–99

Labels: Aral Sea, Caspian Sea, Tabriz, Chāldirān, R. Don, Kafa, Black Sea, Sinop, Basra, Persian Gulf, Medina, Mecca, Red Sea, R. Tigris, R. Euphrates, Dulkadir, Jerusalem, Ankara, Konya, Adana, Suez, R. Nile, Cairo, Alexandria, Üsküdar, İznik, İzmit, Bursa, İzmir, Aydın, Antalya, RHODES, Nicopolis, Varna, WALACHIA, Niš, Istanbul, Gallipoli, Aegean Sea, Belgrade, Kosovo, Sofia, Salonika, Mediterranean Sea, Adriatic Sea, MOREA, Vienna, R. Danube, Venice, Rome, Otranto, MALTA, Tripoli, Tunis, Algiers, 500 miles, 750 km 'congruence' between the collective goal (the purpose of the organization) and the individual's wishes. So, 'in order to mediate transactions efficiently, any organizational form must reduce either the ambiguity of performance evaluation or the goal incongruence between parties' (Ouchi 1980:135). This is done by ensuring contractual relations involving self-co-ordinating behaviours (in the case of market goal incongruence) or fair authorities inducing confident cooperation (in the case of bureaucratic performance ambiguity), that is by bearing 'transaction costs' for communication, for incentives, or for monitoring.

It is generally agreed among economists that market organization provides a diffused perception both of equity and of reciprocity at lower transaction costs than bureaucracy, unless a sense of community (together with a legitimate authority) generates a certain degree of involvement of individuals in the organization's goals: in this case, opportunism and rent seeking decrease, enabling the bureaucracy to lower its transaction costs under the market level.[10] But a bureaucracy experiencing a complete congruence between its own and individual goals (because of cultural elements, like traditions or religion) cuts down the payments for incentives and monitoring up to the lowest transaction costs. This organization is the clan, that is an arrangement of social activities carried out by 'informal identity networks based on kin or fictive kin bonds' (Collins 2004), where on one side 'a variety of social mechanisms reduces differences between individual and organizational goals and produces a strong sense of community', and on the other 'opportunism is unlikely and equity in rewards can be achieved at a relative low transaction costs' (Ouchi 1980: 136). Thus, the nature of the clan is 'the obverse of the market relations since it achieves the efficiency under the opposite conditions: high performance ambiguity and low opportunism.'[11]

The general features of such an organizational unit are as follows:

1   the hierarchical co-ordination of the networks of social activities:
2   the trust in the authority, due to its (traditional, religious, social, economic or technical) reputation;
3   the mutual cooperation and aid, assured as a consequence of the common belonging to the clan;
4   the assurance of security, that is economic, social, and political protection ('patronage');
5   the strong identity, that is due to kinship, to culture, or to other social reasons.

The concept of clan, inspected recently by the new institutional economists in the light of the efficiency principle of lower transaction costs, provides a fruitful research instrument away both from the ambiguity of the term[12] used in anthropology or in history (whose synonyms sometimes are tribe, clients and family), and from the idea that this organizational form is only an historical set of institutions inconsistent with a modern society. It supports the recently developed theory of clan politics well, focusing on the main features of this organizational form (kinship, network, and trust), to explain the state formation in Asian and Middle East countries (Collins 2006; Khoury and Kostiner 1990), as well as the study of the economic organization of Asian capitalism[13] (Hamilton and Biggart 1997).

The organizational clan form of the traditional Arab society has been discussed by and large both by historians searching for its origins in cultural, religious and political rationales (Lapidus 1990), and by political scientists coping with old and new theoretical problems about the corporatism, or with the Asiatic mode of production.[14] According to these investigations the clan was not only an element of continuity in the social structure of Arab societies during the Ottoman Empire, but also a powerful basic component, because of the political weakness of the empire, and because of its economic needs. The 'Ottoman government in Arab provinces was primarily concerned with the task of maintaining military preparedness, preserving urban and rural security and raising [public] revenue' (Owen 1981:10). As the domain was huge and the empire authority weak and sometimes irregular, the direct collection of taxes by a group of officials soon became difficult, avoiding all the appointed aims (security and administrative system financial support included). In addition, after a century of agricultural expansion (due to the rural security provided early by the Ottomans) and of increasing trade (caused by the removal of domestic barriers), the economic revival stopped, reducing the taxable income. Thus, at the end of the sixteenth century, a new tax collection mechanism was introduced, based on the sale of the right of collecting taxes to men of authority and influence inside rural and urban communities. This public sale, made before the achievement of taxable income on production and distribution of goods and services, reinforced the traditional structure of the society and empowered the clan with a strong political role because the social order was an assignment (in addition to the tax collection) for the tax collectors, because the political power of mediating between communities and governors was attributed to them, and because the authority they exerted on people and on military troops used to carry on their job raised a sort of antagonism between them and the state authorities (Ottoman governors).

But the new tax-collecting system also strengthened the economic role of the clan, giving it a central place in the organization of the economy. As the right to tax collection was sold at auction and as tax collectors had to deliver, in advance, to the governors the taxes later earned by paying a reasonably corresponding money value, the recipients belonged to the influential families of a community endowed with financial assets, that is, they belonged to clans. The resources necessary to be competitive in the public sale, also constituted the working capital to implement the economic activity of tax collection, whose profitability depended on the agricultural production and on the farmers' trust. So, the social group constituting the clan (the tax collector and the farmers) acted as a sort of economic unit that jointly produced an output (yield) and a collecting service that received as a reward for these activities the difference between the revenue obtained by the production and the money paid to the governor for the right to collect taxes. In this situation an entrepreneurial aptitude appeared: to maintain trust in rural areas and also production tools, the tax collectors provided the farmers economic insurance in addition to security. They sometimes protected the 'peasant from being ruined because of huge tax-demand by lending them the money himself' (Owen 1981:17) to pay taxes during harvest crisis. In addition, tax collectors tried to maximize their revenues by a direct involvement in rural production: they invested to cultivate directly lands and to sell their produce[15] or they lent money for investments to farmers to increase yields.[16] In this way the tax system promoted the surplus extraction.

The same economic empowerment of social groups engaged in the tax-collection appeared in towns where, as crafts and trade represented the main economic activities, the guild or corporation chiefs and the merchants were awarded with the right to collect custom duties by sell at auction. But in contrast to what happened in the rural areas, when they shared the economic interests of taxed people they didn't reorganize the taxed production processes to increase the profit. As time went on, tax-collecting rights became hereditary both in rural and in urban areas, and tax collectors were more and more often located in towns and more involved in local and international trade, in particular in the markets for agricultural goods where the crops obtained as taxes were supplied. As a consequence of this involvement, continuous market speculation and rising prices occurred.

This tax system, introduced to consolidate the revenue of the Ottoman empire, actually increased the power of local authorities causing the flare up of political disorder, the rise of fiscal pressure for the surplus withdrawal by the clans, and the decline in the empire revenues, which, together with the change in the pattern of international trade of the Middle East, contributed to the economic weakening of the communities. Despite reforms introduced by the Ottomans in the nineteenth century ('Tanzimat') to challenge these problems as well as new technological and philosophical threats, the economic and political role of the clan survived and created, alongside the universal cultural and religious identity embedded in the Islam, a local socio-political identity.

This twofold identity makes the Middle East and North Africa an exceptional case, revealing a 'unique combination of both strong sub-state identities and powerful supra-state identities', due to the fact that the populations tend, one after the other, to 'focus [...] on the sub-state unit – the city, the tribe, the religious sect – or on the larger Islamic community or *umma*' (Hinnebusch 2005: 153). Thus, since identity (together with awareness and consciousness) can be considered one of the socio-cultural features necessary (in conjunction with geographic features) to recognize 'a geographic region', the area under consideration satisfies the requirements to be defined as such (El-Erian and Fischer 1996). But, since supra-state identities and trans-state policies in social and institutional fields have been present in the countries placed between Hercules Pillars and the Silk Road during the last half century, the most apt definition could be 'harmonizing geographic region'.

European colonialism and the dismantling of the MENA region

In spite of the presence of these unique conditions, political and economic cooperation in the Middle East and North Africa spread out much less than elsewhere in the past two centuries.[17] As economic activities and political conditions were in some way integrated in the area in advance, the reasons why the regionalism worsened instead of improving can probably be traced back to the policies the rulers implemented to face the political and economic threats coming from Europe. The response to the pressures exerted from outside and to the needs of an assessment of the intraregional powers by the independent states that existed there up to the twentieth century (the Ottoman Empire and the two brother kingdoms of Morocco and of Persia), did not strengthen the unity of the area, but, ironically, issued the opposite. As a matter of fact, the attempts to restate the ruler authority (by introducing the modern centralized state in a background where the spread of power on the territory was the rule) fostered political instability, and the strategies to reorganize the economy (in order to support this restructuring) led to bankruptcy. So, the political reforms and the economic policies carried out by these states during the nineteenth century alone brought about a process of de-regionalization, as they caused the integration of the area in the political and economic defensive buffer ring of some European powers: France, Great Britain, and Italy.

The so-called 'defensive developmentalism' (Gelvin 2005), or 'defensive modernization' (Richard and Waterbury 2008), promoted by Ottoman sultans (as well as by Persian shahs, and by Egyptian dynasts) after Napoleon's Egyptian military campaign, consisted of a set of 'deliberate policies to reverse the process of fragmentation, [...] to centralize and expand the authority', and 'to make governments more proficient in managing their populations and their resources' (Gelvin 2005: 73). These policies included military reform, the centralization of the state by the establishment of an educated bureaucratic administration, the expansion of the central authority in the fields of education and of social welfare and a uniform legal practice that was pursued by publishing new codes. The core of these policies was represented by some reforms to control and expand the internal revenues of the state: a land property reform (the right to register the land worked in as a private ownership) to pick out who owed the farm tax, the support to cash crop cultivations, sold mainly in international markets, to increase the taxable income, and the substitution of the at auction tax-collecting system with an administrative apparatus to make the tax collection more efficient by reducing intermediary costs.

In the long run, these reforms produced unexpected results, opening the Middle East and North Africa to political instability and to economic dependence. As for the political domain, the change in the social structure (caused by the reform guiding principles in administrative, legal, and economic activities) gave birth to claims and to dissents all over the region. Everywhere the new classes created to centralize the state (professional soldiers, educated bureaucrats, and intellectuals) were dissatisfied because they did not have any powers in decision-making. Thus they refused to accept the new order, sometimes participating in revolts, as did both the local notables who lost economic and political prestige and the *ulama* who were limited in their educational and judicial roles. In addition, in rural areas the peasants, suspecting that a land property reform could both increase their tax burden and favour the conscription of the young people of the community, refused to accept the reforms. Whenever they registered the land worked, they worsened their conditions getting into debt because of the land taxes and/or being obliged to become landless tenant farmers working in huge agricultural estates of absentee landowners, often living in towns. Furthermore, to this social unease was added political disorder and fragmentation of power, both in Persia where the particular conditions at the advent of the Qujar dynasty prevented the reduction of power of the local communities,[18] and in the Ottoman empire where the state-building process in some provinces issued political subjects largely independent and prone to military adventures. This is the case of Egypt where Mehmet Alì, a commander of the Ottoman army who was appointed governor of the country at the beginning of the nineteenth century, put into operation the 'defensive developmentalism', by which he centralized the political and economic power (which was also thanks to the physical elimination both of Mameluk tax farmers and of local authorities, and to the confiscation of their lands in favour of the state). Moreover, to supply the economy with the resources necessary for Egyptian development, he invaded Sudan where gold and slaves were taken from, Lebanon, which secured timber and silk, Arabia and Greater Syria – where he established trade monopolies by the control of the ports and of the long-distance trade routes (Gelvin 2005: 76-8).

It was this antagonistic policy and the social revolt leaded by the Colonel Urabi in Egypt that convinced the Ottoman rulers in 1840 (and Egyptian khedive in 1881) to ask the British army for help (who were always eager to hold the commercial passage towards India), and to deliver them the control of the political order in the area. This event was matched with the French colonization of the North Africa, which began in 1830 with the annexation of Algeria (a virtually autonomous territory ruled by an Ottoman governor) after a long period of unpaid grain imports and under the pretext of an outrage to its government, and continued in 1881 with the occupation of

Tunisia because of the debt that this independent monarchy owed to French banks (Gelvin 2005: 89). So, unable to avoid the political threats by the European powers, the 'defensive developmentalism' produced their interference in the political and economic affairs of the Ottoman Empire and broke the cohesion of the Arab world by establishing preferential links between the European colonizers and each specific territory of the MENA region. Although the failure in the homogenization of the region with respect to the administrative centralization (only Egypt, Anatolia and Greater Syria for a short period achieved it, but not Persia and other regions of the Middle East), the defensive developmentalism succeeded in introducing some elements of the state's internal authority (centralization, bureaucracy, conscription) and in spreading both the principles of the modern state and of its authority in some matters that were previously under societal or religious jurisdiction. As a result, the Arab communities, which never felt that each other was living in different states, were brought into distinct administrative and political conditions.[19]

The economic menace was not tackled successfully by the 'defensive developmentalism', if it is true that this policy produced both the bankruptcy and the complete dependence of the MENA economies from the European industrialized countries. But the European economic influence in MENA territories started a long time before 'defensive developmentalism' was put into effect, that is, when the commercial courses of East Asian exports began to round the Cape of Good Hope and upset the pattern of trade in Mediterranean against Arab and Turkish merchants. During the seventeenth century the traditional commercial transit of pepper, spices and silk from the Indian Ocean to the Mediterranean carried out by these merchants stopped, substituted with the sale of Middle Eastern primary commodities (cash crops like cotton, silk and coffee) in exchange for European manufactured woollen cloths (Owen 1981: 83). Although this incident 'affected only some aspects of economic activity in some areas, and then often only for a short space of time' (Owen 1981: 10), it provided France with the monopoly power of the sea-borne European trade in the Mediterranean, leaving the Middle East with a subordinate trade partnership.

The 'defensive developmentalism' worsened this position in the medium-long run because it made the regional economies both structurally dependent on industrialized European countries and indebted to European bankers. In fact, as all the reforms introduced were functional to the building of a centralized and powerful state, they were designed to provide increasing tax revenues to sustain the costs supported for this project, and not to develop the economy by endorsing the private entrepreneurship and the structural change in agriculture, crafts and commerce. Thus the rulers tried to boost the cash crops in agriculture (especially in cotton, silk, and tobacco) and to introduce state monopolies in international trade. As land reforms created an unproductive agriculture, based on impoverished peasants and on absentee landowners, huge estates were put under the army's control and

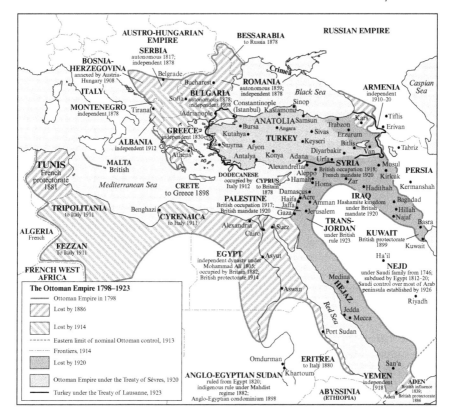

Map 1.4 Partition and colonization of Ottoman Empire regions

reorganized in order 'to establish a system of economic management designed to ensure that the government was able to appropriate the bulk of the rural surplus [...] combining regulations, price fixing and taxation by state officials' (Owen 1981: 66). So, the state-managed production of cash crops required by European factories (like cotton and silk, generally cultivated in Egypt and in Greater Syria) was supported by the rulers introducing new techniques, or financing the cultivation of new crops (like the Mako), or providing cultivators with loans, tools and equipment. The village activities were rearranged to sustain efficiently innovative rotations,[20] new settlements of nomadic tribes populated the abandoned lands (like in Greater Syria) and factories (like, for example, spinning mills, tanneries, etc.) were built to process the agricultural raw materials.

The temporary success of this production policy increased the agricultural output as well as the exports to Europe, giving rise to tax revenues and, consequently, to the imports of weapons. But, because of this restructuring, the economies of some MENA territories became integrated in the international market system, and thus their export revenues were subject to the international price fluctuations and/or to fortuitous causes, as happened in the 1860s when the international price of the cotton increased as the American Civil War cut off the supply, and declined when US exports returned. Furthermore, since the international competition also required infrastructure (railways, roads, ports, canals) to supply the ships sailing Mediterranean and Red Sea, the rulers worked hard to realize these investments. Given that all the state revenues were spent buying weapons and paying civil servants, the state borrowed to invest. But this borrowing led to bankruptcy (because of the weakness of MENA exports in international markets), and bankruptcy led to European colonization. Neither the efforts to increase Ottoman Empire revenues by setting monopolies nor the introduction of duties could stop the failure, because Britain forbid the Ottoman Empire the first policy (in return for its help to restore order in Greater Syria) with the treaty of Balta Liman in 1838, and would later accept only a five per cent tax on its exports to the area. Tax revenue from crafts produced in Ottoman towns was declining too, as the factories producing for home demand experienced a shortage of both agricultural raw materials and financial assistance (the last because of the support to exports), and that led to their collapse (the Egyptian case is the most representative).

The historical process just presented dismantled the traditional economic regionalism characterizing Middle East and North Africa without laying the foundations for a new one. While this horizon was prevented in economics by the preservation of preferential trade relations with colonial powers after independence (a kind of regionalization process), it was prohibited in politics, on one hand, by the incompleteness of Arab states before the independence, and on the other, by the incompatibility between the concept of regionalism and the twofold identity of Arab communities. In fact, during the Mandates period (between the First and Second World Wars) the Arab states were lacking a complete sovereignty (because they were merely endowed with the internal privileges of statehood), so they could not implement the international activities connected to the regionalism. As this process was characterized by international cooperation in politics and in economics among sovereign states, the implementing device is a nation-state that partially sacrifices its own national identity and interest (elements legitimating its sovereignty) to attain 'social capital in terms of a collective identity and a deliberative culture' (Ruiz and Zahrnt 2008). So, regionalism is theoretically consistent with a nation-state identity imagined at the supra-national level and inconsistent with both 'strong sub-state and powerful supra-state identities' diffused in the MENA region: in fact, as to the second identity, 'Pan-Arabism' is a trans-state feeling and 'Pan-Islam' represents a state belief.

Few opportunities to build a new regionalism have occurred since the independence, as 'the incongruence between state and mass identity does generate continuous attempts, by both states and opposition trans-state movements, to bridge the gap' (Hinnebusch 2005: 170) between governments and populations. On one side, regimes that are trying to overcome weak sovereignty (due to the lack of national identity), to promote the citizen loyalty to rulers, and to keep state control over the territory and over the population, were interested (often under Western pressure) in containing the popular identity (rather than in representing it) by strengthened distributive policies and coercive bureaucracies. In some cases 'state élites attempt to reconstruct popular identity by pointing to "realities" of external constraints – Israel's power, economic dependence on the West – as requiring a deflation in the normative expectations of Arabism and Islam', or in some other moral principles (Hinnebusch 2005: 170).[21] On the other side, the masses, trying to overthrow rulers because of their discontent due to material needs (like wealth and security) or to ethnic or tribal repression, fell back upon the supra-state (Arabism or Islam) or a moral identity to aggregate people.[22] Paradoxically, in this way only a local 'national feeling' is spread and intraregional and international relations in the area appeared both discontinuous and state- or identity-biased, rather than oriented towards a process of creating a complete new regionalism.

The MENA region from a geopolitical periphery to a geo-economic core

The colonization of the MENA region, although initiated under the pretext of protecting European economic interests from the threats that the 'wicked' policies of some partner countries of the area caused, had a more extensive aim, as it was a deliberate, assertive instrument to support national capitalism. In fact, by this outward projection of expanding the boundaries of the nation states, the European powers provided both their own economies and their societies with security (that is with inputs and output markets) and with welfare. For the British economy the first source of such a support was India, so the Middle East was mainly a peripheral part of its provision system and of its strategic world scenario, while North Africa was for France an important region to cope with economic problems of raw material supply and of domestic unemployment.

But the support for domestic capitalism needed a consistent international order, thus colonialism (and its variants of protectorate and of mandate) was also the way by which the states embarked on such an international policy could show to other nations their supremacy and their idea of the political organization of the world space. The Middle East arrangement that emerged after First World War is probably the most emblematic manifestation of this international order envisioned and then implemented, as the European powers assumed the privilege to partition the area, creating new states and drawing the boundaries of others. In fact:

> [The entire MENA region became] almost exclusively an Anglo-French preserve. Algeria was a French full colony, Morocco and Tunisia

protectorates, and Syria and Lebanon were held as League of Nations mandates. Egypt gained nominal independence in 1922 but continued to be under British influence through a restrictive treaty [...]. Aden, or South Yemen, was a British colony, Palestine, Transjordan and Iraq were held as mandates, and Britain's interests in Persian Gulf were upheld through treaty arrangements with the ruling families in Kuwait, Bahrain, Qatar [...]. Muscat and Oman were similarly under British control. Libya, an Italian colony since 1911, was an exception to this Anglo-French division of the region.

(Rogan 2005: 29-30).

Such an international political behaviour of powers, centred on their international authority and rule, on their occupation of territories, and on the support to domestic capitalism, was the acting out of a doctrine connecting political power and geographic space in an ideological system (including national culture and society) representing a 'territorial division of the world'. This doctrine is 'geopolitics', that is a 'simultaneously ideology and technology of state power, [that] embodies a range of assumptions that entwine political power to the territorially demarcated system of national states' (Cowen and Smith 2009: 23). This geo-strategy, implemented by France and by Great Britain in the MENA region, reached its highest point during the period of Mandates (roughly the years between the First and Second World War), when they established in the area both state lines and administrative bureaucracies (but not an independent diplomacy), and when European companies began extracting oil from the territories of those states giving rise to a new resource-furnishings policy intended to provide economic powers with energy security.

While the Middle East was led to the ultimate allocation of its communities to separate states, the Arab world acted to gain the liberation from colonizers. But this aim, reached by the independence, was obtained by Iraq in 1932, by Syria in 1943, by Lebanon and Jordan in 1946, while British troops left Palestine in May 1948. In North Africa, Egypt acquired its independence in 1932, Libya in 1951, Tunisia and Morocco in 1956, and Algeria in 1962 after an eight-year liberation war. Moreover, three other states emerged in the area outside of the decolonization process. The treaty of Losanna (1923) recognized the sovereignty and the independence to Turkey, the modern state built on the Ottoman ruins after the First World War. In 1927, Abdul Aziz Al Saud, having unified the Arab peninsula, was recognized by Great Britain as king of the state that was named Saudi Arabia after 1932 (see Table 1.2). Finally, in 1925 the Qujar dynasty was dethroned by a military rebellion that declared Reza Khan Pahlevi as Shah.

While this political process was growing, the Middle East was led to the allocation of its resources. The first step in the direction of resources grant must be probably traced back to the policies of financing the 'defensive

Table 1.2 European rule and actual independence of MENA region countries

Country	European rule	Actual independence
Algeria	French Territory since 1830	July 5, 1962
Bahrain	British Residency[a] of the Persian Gulf since 1880	August 15, 1971
Egypt, Arab Republic	British Occupation and Protectorate[b] since 1882	February 28, 1922
Iraq	British Admin. and Mandate[c] since 1918	October 3, 1932
Israel	British Admin. and Mandate since 1917	May 14, 1948
Jordan	British Admin. and Mandate since 1917	May 25, 1946
Kuwait	British Residency of the Persian Gulf since 1899	June 19, 1961
Lebanon	French Admin. and Mandate since 1918	November 22, 1943
Libya	Italian Occupation since 1911	December 24, 1951
Morocco	French Protectorate since 1912	March 2, 1956
Oman	British Residency of the Persian Gulf since 1892	December 16, 1971
Qatar	British Residency of the Persian Gulf since 1916	September 3, 1971
Saudi Arabia		September 23, 1932
Syria	French Admin. and Mandate since 1918	April 17, 1946
Tunisia	French Protectorate since 1881	March 20, 1956
United Arab Emirates	British Residency of the Persian Gulf since 1892	December 2, 1971
West Bank and Gaza Strip	British Admin. and Mandate since 1917	Oslo Accord, 1993[d]
Yemen	British Influence and Protectorate since 1839	1967 (South Yemen)

[a] A residency is a varying degree of political and economic control by one state over another

[b] A protectorate is a territory, not formally annexed, where a state has power and jurisdiction by treaty.

[c] A mandate is a legal status according to which the control of one country is attributed to another.

[d] The Declaration of Principles on Interim Self-Government Arrangements, signed in 1993 in Oslo by the Government of Israel and the Palestine Liberation Organization (PLO), gave to the Palestinian Authority the exclusive control over security and civil issues in urban Palestinian areas (zone A) and partial administrative control on Palestinian rural areas (zone B), being the remained part of the territory under Israeli control (Zone C).

Source: Authors' elaboration.

developmentalism' in Persia, where in 1901 the government granted William Knox d'Arcy 'the right "to obtain, exploit, develop, render suitable for trade, carry away and sell" petroleum and petroleum products from all of Persia for forty thousand pounds cash and stock and 16 percent of its annual profits' (Gelvin 2005: 86). But it was later in 1929 that the British mandate in Iraq favoured the birth of IPC (Iraq Petroleum Company), the cornerstone of oil production and distribution in Middle East up to 1972 and the model for all the consortia built in the other oil countries of the region.

Five of the eight major international companies were present in IPC, whose equity was carefully divided: 50 percent to British interests, represented equally by Anglo-Iranian and Royal Dutch-Shell; 25 percent to American interests, represented equally by Standard Oil New Jersey [...] and Mobil [...]; and 25 percent to French interests, represented by the Compagnie Française des Petroles [...]. The internal rules of IPC were designed to discourage competition between the IPC partners in the downstream markets as well as upstream elsewhere in the region.

(Luciani 2005: 83-84)

Such a protection of the domestic private economic interests practised by the colonial authorities in the MENA region during the Mandates, continuing after the independence thanks to the persuasive treaties imposed by powers to the new states, was important in some respects. Regarding the future of the region, this strategy represented the building of the economic framework of those new political entities and the allocation of their resources (to foreigners). This has been crucial for the development of an area that, thanks to the increasing importance of oil production and reserves (until now the area owned two third of gas and oil world reserves), marked a turning point in the role played in the world theatre, because it shifted from being on the geopolitical periphery of the colonial powers to being at the geo-economic core of the world economy. Finally, as to the colonial powers' strategy, it opened to a phase of international relations where the security of national capitalism and the welfare of their nation states were no longer ensured by the enlargement of state boundaries, but by guaranteeing the control of international markets and of important resources or goods.

By definition, 'the market' is a landless entity expanding itself in a virtual space limited by the domain of the exchange rules agreed by contractors. National security and welfare are warranted on the market (thus also on the territory of other nation states) when the international market power is held by domestic suppliers or buyers. So the market, extending itself irrespective of the state borders, on one hand is more powerful than territory occupation in promoting the interests of a national economy, and on the other is more influential in endorsing the expansion of international trade agreements. This change in the strategy of powers, enabling them to govern the world scenarios and to gain security and welfare without occupying territories, marks the shift from geo-politics to geo-economics,[23] that is to 'the interaction of economics and finance with global political and security considerations' (Cowen and Smith 2009: 38).

The practising of this doctrine in international relations is particularly evident in the political state of affairs in the MENA region after the Cold War. In the period between the end of Second World War and 1990 the countries of the region took advantage of the rivalry between the USSR and US to pursue their own aims.[24] After 1990 they begun to be part, consciously or not, of a regional order implemented by the US enjoying 'the unprecedented

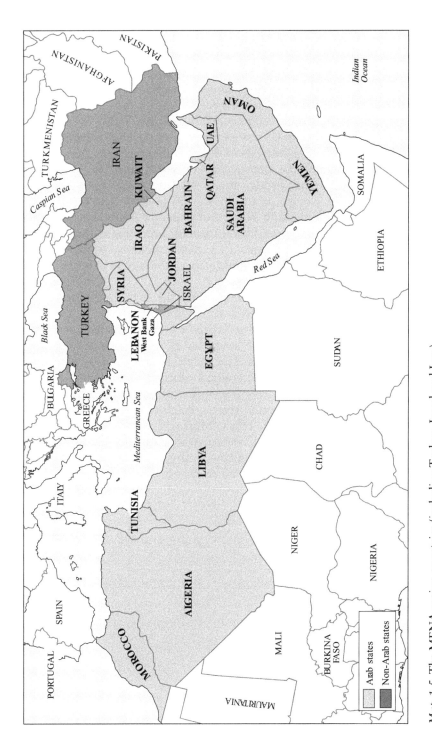

Map 1.5 The MENA region countries (including Turkey, Israel and Iran)

advantage of unipolarity' (Halliday 2005: 134). In fact the big power, being aware of the possibility of attaining its traditional aims (a guaranteed oil supply and the protection of Israel) as well as the promotion of good governance, human rights and a complacent regional order,[25] strengthened the relations with old allies and reorganized its policies. The starting point was the network, created in previous decades by a fragmented and unsettled policy, allocating to each partner of the region specific targets: Turkey kept up the frontiers of the Western military alliance joining NATO in 1950, Iran (where, in 1953, Britain and US restored the rule of the Shah bringing down the republic) protected the interests of Western oil companies up to 1979, Saudi Arabia moderated the international oil prices since the 1970s, and Israel, after resisting to the Egyptian attack of 1973, became a pro-American power of the region. But the post Cold War US policies went further with military intervention in the Gulf Wars, promoting the peace between Israeli and Palestinians, supporting un-liberal regimes, becoming '...the object of intense, often divided sentiment, [...] Simultaneously ostracised *and* dominated, the first in lifestyle and imagination, the second in terms of raw power' (Halliday 2005: 139).

The historic path just presented constitutes the environment where the development process of the MENA region moved along. As the main features issued from it are a shared social and cultural continuity, a political and economic dependence on the strategies of world powers, a lack of shared political and economic aims of the states, the anarchy as a constitutive principle of the regional system of political relations and the multipolarity of the intraregional relations (the distribution of power on the area), the challenge faced by the Arab world (Algeria, Bahrain, Egypt, Arab Republic, Iraq, Jordan, Kuwait, Lebanon, Libya, Morocco, Oman, West Bank and Gaza Strip, Qatar, Saudi Arabia, Syrian Arab Republic, Tunisia, United Arab Emirates, Yemen, Republic) and by Turkey, Iran Islamic Republic and Israel (see Map 1.5) during the last half century had been certainly tricky.

2 The economic development of 'latecomers'

As a point of principle, development isn't just an economic phenomenon. In fact, since in addition to changes in production, consumption and trade, it transforms institutions, administrative organizations, social customs, beliefs and structures, 'it must encompass more than the material and financial side of people's lives [...]. Development should therefore be perceived as a multidimensional process involving the reorganization and reorientation of entire economic and social systems' (Todaro and Smith 2012: 109). As to these sets of activities, moreover, the arrangements mostly shared by the developing countries before the big push reveal pre-capitalist[1] (or pre-industrial) features (Todaro and Smith 2012: 38). Hence it can be deduced that development represents a crossing from a pre-capitalist system to a capitalist system occurring in a distinctive geographic, historical and cultural environment, and that the improvements of economic conditions are changes related to these socio-political and cultural institutions. In the light of these statements, the economic appraisal of the outcome achieved and the analysis of past and future challenges faced by the states approaching this multidimensional context-specific process cannot ignore the socio-political and historical environments in which the improvement of the economy has been carried out, as the explanatory variables affect the economic ones.

Such a methodological context helps the analysis of the economic development of the MENA countries, but at the same time brings to light the need for a debate on some aspects of the theoretic framework used to assess the economic performance of developing societies. As to the socio-economic structure preceding the take-off of development, for example, the countries constituting the region (having common legacy and destiny, as argued in Chapter 1) are both at greater distance from the pre-industrial Western societies taken as a model of the requirements for the development. In addition, considering the historic context, the economic and political world situation in which the MENA countries implemented their own transformation path is greatly different with respect to that of the 'first comers'. These environmental specificities bring the mainstream pre-conditions for the economic development and the path of the process up for discussion, as the regional experience shows in the case both of the institutional framework and of the social principles necessary to implement capitalism (see Chapter 3).

Economic theory imaged the development as a transition process to capitalism since the classical school detected that both the market structure (Smith 1776) and the improving of productive forces (Marx 1867) were engines moving the feudal economy towards a new socio-economic system (Nunes and Valèrio 2001). Some of these suggestions were deepened later in the twentieth century by outstanding scholars (Weber 1930; Sombart 1951; and Polany 1944) who studied the support the process received by the change in institutions (habits, customs and organizations). The debate was enriched when some authors elaborated Smith's propositions (Hicks 1969) and Marx's concepts (Dobb 1946; Sweezy et al. 1976 and Wallerstein 1986), and when Maddison (Maddison 1991) provided macroeconomic data revealing the decisive variables characterizing this process, at least in the Western experience. In all these studies the paths followed in pursuing the capitalist advent, the forces pushing this process, and the features of the capitalist system were highlighted, thus pointing out the structural elements differentiating capitalism from the previous economic system, and portraying the features that the developed countries ('first comers') generally presented. But little attention had been paid on the transition path of societies different from those existing in pre-industrial Western countries, and on the environment in which 'latecomers' develop.

As to the carrying out of the economic development process in particular, on one hand the classic theories of economic growth highlighted the constituents necessary to promote the structural change and the improvement of economic conditions (capital accumulation, population/labour force growth, and technological progress), while on the other hand, more recent approaches find the main threats in market and government failures that cause the mechanism to run aground.[2] Side by side with this theoretical progress are both new economic phenomena (like globalization and transnational corporations), and deepening research (about the historical, technological and institutional transformations, and about the meaning of development), which have enlarged the number of influential variables to political and administrative aspects, giving rise also to the measurement of the degree of economic growth.

To highlight why the MENA region's economic development needs an explanatory approach that takes the specificities of Muslim societies, their recent history and the new frontiers of the world economies into account, all the suggestions deriving from the advances of the economics of development will be reviewed.

The development process as a transition path towards capitalism

The traditional mainstream economics considered development, at least until the beginnings of 1980s, as an economic process that improved the material life conditions of a country moving from a situation characterized by persistent low levels of economic performance, by endemic poverty, and by high death and birth rates. In this definition the environment experiencing the implementation of the process was regarded to be in an endless situation of deprivation and devoid of any influential social order. The ends to be pursued were defined in terms of a quantitative variation of the values of reasonable economic indicators, and the arrival point was presumed to be the convergence of such economic values with those of developed countries. Moreover, there was no awareness that the development process is a transition path from a 'traditional' socio-economic system towards a new organization of social activities (realized by the stressful dismantling of an old order and by the uncertain building of a new one), nor that economic development represents a subset of this process. Finally, nothing was said about the impact that the socio-economic system of departure could have on the course, has it had been considered at most a simple constraint.

However, development is a comprehensive process resulting in the works of classical economists, who studied the 'great transformation' as it emerged and also as it was replicated later, asking themselves how and why this phenomenon appeared. In so doing they examined both the economic and social reality of the time (in relation to that of the past too) for the causes originating the change. Adam Smith attributed the increase of the 'wealth of nations', experienced by the British Isles in the eighteenth century to the implementation of two behavioural principles in the working activities carried out at the time: self interest in an economic environment where agriculture presented a surplus,[3] and the aptitude to exchange in a geographic space where distant sales supported foreign commerce. Once these virtuous processes produced the accumulation of stocks,[4] the division of labour[5] first pushed the commercial markets (Smith 1776: I.3.1) and then spread all over the other socio-economic activities, pulling the society out of the 'rude state [...] in which there is no division of labour, in which exchanges are seldom made, and in which every man provides everything for himself' (Smith 1776: II.1.1). The mechanism of development of different industries fed by the town/country economic exchange and by the exports (as well as by the state laws creating a favourable legal setting) was thus described by Smith in this way:

> England, on account of the natural fertility of the soil, of the great extent of the sea-coast in proportion to that of the whole country, and of the many navigable rivers which run through it and afford the convenience of water carriage to some of the most inland parts of it, is perhaps as well fitted by nature as any large country in Europe to be the seat of foreign commerce, of manufactures for distant sale, and of all the improvements which these can occasion. From the beginning of the reign of Elizabeth too, the English legislature has been peculiarly

attentive to the interests of commerce and manufactures, and in reality there is no country in Europe, Holland itself not excepted, of which the law is, upon the whole, more favourable to this sort of industry. Commerce and manufactures have accordingly been continually advancing during all this period. The cultivation and improvement of the country has, no doubt, been gradually advancing too; but it seems to have followed slowly, and at a distance, the more rapid progress of commerce and manufactures. [...] The law of England, however, favours agriculture not only indirectly by the protection of commerce, but by several direct encouragements. Except in times of scarcity, the exportation of corn is not only free, but encouraged by a bounty. [...] Those who cultivate the land, therefore, have a monopoly against their countrymen for the two greatest and most important articles of land produce, bread and butcher's meat. These encouragements, though at bottom, perhaps, as I shall endeavour to show hereafter, altogether illusory, sufficiently demonstrate at least the good intention of the legislature to favour agriculture. But what is of much more importance than all of them, the yeomanry of England are rendered as secure, as independent, and as respectable as law can make them.

(Smith 1776: III.4.20)

A lot of items are considered to be features of the development process in this analysis: the physical and environmental resources (land, agricultural surplus/stock of capital, transport infrastructures and geographical conditions), the institutional variables (division of labour, laws ensuring the full availability of resources – as the protection of property – and policies supporting sectors like monopoly licences and import duties), as well as triggering elements (human behavioural principles). Even some non-economic effects of this transformation were discussed, like the importance of a nation's wealth for political quality. In fact, Smith declared that:

> [...] commerce and manufacturers gradually introduced order and good government, and with them, the liberty and security of individuals, among the inhabitants of the country, who had before lived almost in a continual state of war with their neighbours and of servile dependency upon their superiors. This, though it has been the least observed, is by far the most important of all their effects. Mr. Hume is the only writer who, so far as I know, has hitherto taken notice of it.
>
> (Smith 1776: III.4.4)

Although the mechanism by which Smith explains the increase of the wealth of nations refers to economic and social variables, it does not properly envisage a transition path toward a new socio-economic system, but only an economic growth process. In fact, in *The Nature and Causes of the Wealth of Nations* the focus is on the realization of an increasing amount of economic activities by a course, starting when the use of a disposable agricultural surplus (according to human behavioural principles) triggers both the creation of new physical resources (like capital accumulation) and the introduction of institutional organizations (the market first of all), and later continuing with the increase of manufacturing and of foreign trade faster than agriculture (Smith 1776: IV.9.39), thanks to the division of labour and state support. There was no awareness that manufacturing could overtake commerce or that waged labour would overtake self-employed labour, and no understanding of the irreversible changes that technological progress would have in production and in everyday life. After all, this consciousness couldn't exist, because those phenomena appeared historically soon after, so making evident the dismantling of the old socio-economic system.[6]

On the contrary, the achievement both of manufacture and of waged labour, and the spread all over the economy of the distinctive mode of production they entailed represent an evolving stage of mankind according to Marx, who devoted his work to the analysis of this epoch-making transformation, giving rise to a new socio-economic system: capitalism. The change began when the feudal system abolished serfdom, creating both the waged worker (the worker separated from his means of subsistence and so owning exclusively his labour power) and the capitalist (the owner of money, keen on increasing his capital), as well as the markets of the means of production (labour and capital) among those of all other commodities.

> With this polarization of the market for commodities, the fundamental conditions of capitalist production are given. The capitalist system presupposes the complete separation of the labourers from all property in the means by which they can realize their labour. As soon as capitalist production is once on its own legs, it not only maintains this separation, but reproduces it on a continually extending scale. The process, therefore, that clears the way for the capitalist system, can be none other than the process which takes away from the labourer the possession of his means of production; a process that transforms, on the one hand, the social means of subsistence and of production into capital, on the other, the immediate producers into wage labourers. The so-called primitive accumulation, therefore, is nothing else than the historical process of divorcing the producer from the means of production. It appears as primitive, because it forms the prehistoric stage of capital and of the mode of production corresponding with it […] The industrial capitalists, these new potentates, had on their part not only to displace the guild masters of handicrafts, but also the feudal lords, the possessors of the sources of wealth. In this respect, their conquest of social power appears as the fruit of a victorious struggle both against feudal lordship and its revolting prerogatives, and against the guilds and the fetters they

laid on the free development of production and the free exploitation of
man by man.

(Marx 1867: vol. 1, part VIII, Chapter 26)

The mechanism of productive growth, that enlarges the accumulation of
capital through profit and in this way reproduces capitalism, is the result
of two different (but connected) features characterizing manufacturing:
the division of labour and the machinery, whose development contributes
to change both economic and social conditions as industrialization goes on
(Marx 1867: vol. 1, part IV, Chapters 14 and 15). Thus it is the spread of
the industrial production that transforms the traditional socio-economic
organization into capitalism, that is, into a system different from all the
previous ones not only in respect to the structure and to the amount of
output, but also relative to all the other social activities the men perform.
However, what triggers the transformation path toward capitalism, giving
rise both to economic growth and to social change? In the British
experience, according to Marx, this trigger was represented by the forced
enclosure of open fields practised by a new class of owners (keen to
counterbalance economically the power of the king)[7] to enable their
exploitation: on the one hand, the origin of the waged labourers and of the
capitalists, and on the other hand the accumulation of capital are both due
to this separation of peasants from their means of production. As to all
these aspects, Marx's explanation for the transition to capitalism clears
the path for the introduction of a new socio-economic system and the
elements characterizing it, but, moreover, the embedded social revolution
transforming human life.

The twofold change that occurred in socio-political and economic life,
resulting from the application of the technological process to agricultural
and industrial productions, is considered by Polany as an important feature
of the transition toward the capitalist economy and of the evolution of this
socio-economic system experienced by British and Western civilizations in
the last two centuries. This thesis is detailed in different points stating:

'[that at] the heart of the Industrial Revolution of the eighteenth
century there was an almost miraculous improvement in the tools of
production, which was accompanied by a catastrophic dislocation of
the lives of the common people' (that this 'satanic mill' that ground
men in masses represented) an avalanche of social dislocation,
surpassing by far that of the enclosure period, came down upon
England; that this catastrophe was the accompaniment of a vast
movement of economic improvement; that an entirely new institutional
mechanism was starting to act on Western society; that its dangers,
which cut to the quick when they first appeared, were never really
overcome; and that the history of nineteenth century civilization
consisted largely in attempts to protect society against the ravages of

such a mechanism. The Industrial Revolution was merely the beginning of a revolution as extreme and radical as ever inflamed the minds of sectarians, but the new creed was utterly materialistic and believed that all human problems could be resolved given an unlimited amount of material commodities.

(Polany 1944: Chapter 3)

Thus, according to Polany, the role of the state was fundamental for the advent of and for the stabilization of the new socio-economic system, because the emergence of new classes (some leading transformation, some others bearing its consequences) required the implementation of new institutions supporting development by the politics and by the state, like new laws protecting both the new interests and the declining ones, enabling the spread of new habits and new lifestyles, introducing new productive routines.

Summing up, there are four aspects that characterize the development shared by Smith, Marx and Polany: the nature of process (and thus the time-span) of the transformation that involved both the economies and the societies of their times; the creation and the diffusion of new social classes and of new labour conditions; the building and the spread of new institutions (codes, routines and economic behaviours) reflecting both the needs of the evolving reality and the socio-historical environment; and state support to this transformation. To these elements is due, in turn, the implementation of a change in the structure and in the dimension of the economy, as well as of the other social fields, leading to a transition towards a new socio-economic system (according to Marx and Polany): capitalism.

Capitalism and economic development: the 'first comers' experience

The preceding analysis of the transition path towards capitalism reveals the awareness of scholars that the emergence of the new economic system had been a part of a more general change in the socio-political conditions, that this process was shaped by specific historic events and that it was supported by state policies. The quoted authors' agreement on this conclusions (reached mainly by exploring the British experience during the eighteenth and the nineteenth centuries) extends also to the features differentiating the new socio-economic system from the previous ones. The first shared aspect of the capitalism is a new condition of mankind, as the working and social lives of humans changed once and for all as they were freed from a lot of constraints posed by nature. The spread of technological progress and the improved material conditions represent the second trait of capitalism according to the authors examined. The third trait is a systemic atmosphere of fast-growing links among subjects, goods and organizations, producing continuous change through competition and adaptation and requiring an incessant institutional support to arrange and manage economic activities. All these aspects were previously unknown or their appearance in the past showed a very low intensity so a new systemic result could not materialize.

A novelty and a point of no return for mankind, from a socio-economic and ontological perspective, were waged-earner status[8] (forcing man to sell his energies and skills to survive and avoid the threat of unemployment) and the entrepreneurial position (involving the responsibility of organizing efficiently resources and people to provide goods and services safe from the risk of losing his own assets). In fact, waged labour, generally accompanied by an increasing technical division of labour (fostering the need for a continuous updating of worker capabilities), by the increase of working time, and by the urbanization of most production activities, on one hand required the rearrangement of everyday life and of the course of existence, and on the other hand caused the disruption of the social structure based both on the extended family and on the clan (increasingly deprived of their role of units of production). In addition to this social change, the improvement of the material conditions triggered the demographic transition that lengthened life spans, increased population and unbalanced the socio-economic relations between young and old people. As to the new social figure of the entrepreneur, the increasing competition among producers (due to the technological opportunities, to the extension of the markets and to the customer preferences) pushed the birth of the firm, a productive unit facing more complex and uneasy processes of decision-making, of business organization and of production coordination. The incessant need for balance, competition and adaptation in economic activities was for man a new environment of the economic life that simply was not present in pre-capitalist economies.

In the short run it was the new technological aspects that made the emerging new socio-economic system evident: in fact, they removed the distinctive constraints of human nature and of the natural environment, such as those regarding the amount of mechanic energy at one's disposal for production, the possibility of performing productive operations quickly and precisely, the availability of materials that do not exist in nature, and the fast displacement of people, goods and information. The Watt steam engine represented a momentous invention allowing man to produce mechanic energy by heat, thus avoiding the constraints the natural resources, such as water and wind, presented in the matter of amount and regularity of production. The technological progress experienced later in production and distribution of the energy (because of the discovery of new fuels like coal, oil, gas, and nuclear and because of the results of electromagnetism) on one hand developed the application of this power to the manufacture and spread the factories far from the energy sources, and on the other provided electricity for all kinds of production and consumption. Thanks to a greater quantity of energy, to its flexibility, and to the economic advantage of applied research, technological progress could provide new methods of production (increasingly intensive in capital and labour skills), new goods (sometimes made of stuff created on purpose), and new services that changed material life. In the end, as the production of these goods and services increased creating enlarged demand, a system of fast transport of goods, people and information was required to support a larger market and a more abundant production. Networks of communication (roads, railways, courses, electromagnetic waves) reduced distances by connecting places and people, thanks to vehicles that could provide transportation of goods and people (cars, trucks, trains, planes, ships), or of information (telephones, television, computers). Given the dynamic nature and the increasing complexity of technological progress, the technological maturity that enables a self-sustained growth moved ahead, according to Rostow (Rostow 1991: xvi-xvii), setting the point of no return higher and higher for 'latecomer' countries that approached their own development in the presence of others that were already developed.

Socio-economic and technological aspects both contributed to the creation of a new environment (for human activities in general but for economic activities in particular), characterized by a decreasing number of constraints from natural rhythms and forces and by an increasing amount of social relations and material ties, due to the dependence on other human beings and on goods. This environment, which exhibits a fast growing systemic complexity, represents an additional feature of capitalism assigning to the economic subject the role of social agent interacting with other social agents[9] (by using capabilities of competing and of adapting) and conforming their behaviour to an assorted set of economic rules necessary for the system to work. These institutions refer to the mechanics and dynamics of the economic system (Gregory and Stuart 2004: 19) and:

1 to the arrangements of the decision-making mechanism;
2 to the mechanisms coordinating the economic activities and subjects;
3 to the rules governing the disposal of productive resources;
4 to the systems of economic incentives;
5 to the procedures governing the public choices.[10]

Each one of these rules concerns a topical moment in economic life, by establishing first who can implement the different economic activities and how; second, by showing the way the actions of different economic subjects are coordinated in order to facilitate the working of the system; third, by making evident rules to govern the access to the use of resources; fourth, creating a set of rewards and punishments connected to the implementation of an economic activity, and fifth by underling how the state interferes in the economic activity in order to foster the aims that bring advantages to all the members of the community. The inspection of every single mechanism in the two environments of pre-industrial and capitalist systems highlights the differences concerning who can implement an economic initiative (and which measure acts as planned), which are the ways allowing members to coordinate their actions with those of the other economic subjects, what they can handle and how much they are granted with protection in doing the economic activity, what they earn by implementing it and how much the state interferes in their projects.

As a result of these three structural features the economies that introduced capitalism first ('first comers') showed in the course of time socio-economic systems where:

> property is predominantly in private hands [...] and allocation of goods, services, and factors of production (land, labour, and capital) is made mainly through market mechanism – with capitalists responding to profit signals, workers to wage incentives, and consumers to prices. In the second place, these economies are highly capitalized – their stocks of physical capital, education and knowledge are large relative to their income flow and huge compared with pre-capitalist societies; the growth of these capital stocks is a major causal element explaining the distinctive character of their performance.
>
> The most striking characteristic of capitalist performance has been a sustained upward thrust in productivity and real income per head, which was achieved by a combination of innovation and accumulation. In this respect, capitalism is very different from earlier social orders whose property and other social institutions were geared to preserve equilibrium and were less able to afford the risk of change.
>
> (Maddison 1991: 5)

As to the long-run dynamic forces that caused the economic development in those countries Maddison provided historical data showing the importance of the different elements participating in the process (Maddison 1991). The change in the cultural atmosphere and the rational approach to science and to technology were, once again, detected as the fundamental factors pushing the awareness both of man's centrality in managing the development process, and of his capability of overcoming the difficulties and the constraints that appeared in his path. This spirit of secular humanism allowed adapting behaviour to the need, not only changing rules and habits, but also providing new instruments and supporting unprecedented experiences in all fields of social life. The emergence of this spirit (and of a lot of specific historic conditions and socio-political needs) was due to the legal protection of the property purchase/sale; to the un-discretionary legal and fiscal systems; to the legal discipline regulating financial activities; to acceptance of legal relaxation of kin and family ties; to the achievement of the centralized state; and to all institutional changes that favoured entrepreneurial and managerial capabilities, certainty, transparency, financial support to economic activities, decentralized responsibility and collective socio-economic protection.

This stress on the institutional change as a basic force in fostering the development process in general and the economic transformation in particular, not only confirms the importance of appropriate institutions as a favourable environment for socio-economic improvements, but opens also the debate on which institutions really caused the 'big push' in the Western countries' experience and on the way new institutions were affected by the old ones and by the historic conditions (see Chapter 3 for the analysis of both problems). As to the first question, according to Maddison, a supported and widespread technical progress (that is the advance in technical knowledge and in productive routines, both decisive engines for the technological progress) can be considered among the most important forces that enabled, inch by inch, the structural change of the economies. In fact, it works deeply inside the economic mechanisms:

> Technical progress is the most essential characteristic of modern growth. Its effects are diffused throughout the growth process in a myriad ways. It augments the quality of natural resources and human capital, and the impact of foreign trade. But investment is the major vehicle in which it is embodied, and their respective roles are closely interactive. There are no doubts of its importance in modern economic growth, or the contrast between its role in capitalist and pre-capitalist development. A major driving force of modern economies is the strong propensity to risk capital on new techniques that hold promise of improved profits, in strong contrast to the defensive wariness of pre-capitalist approach to technology.
> (Maddison 1991: 66-7)

Another long-run dynamic force that influenced the economic development of the 'first comers', analysed by Maddison, is the stock of physical resources: the quantity and the quality of the machine-work characterizing the available endowment of equipment. Its decisive role depends on the fact that it releases the embedded scientific and technical progress during the production process, in compliance with the methods of production. But as these productive techniques are executive procedures to produce goods by means of machine-work, of materials and of labour energies and skills, human capital is the other element affecting the production growth. Thus, both increasing investments (or the growth of physical capital per worker) and increasing levels of human capital (or the quantitative change and the structural transformation of the population, an higher activity rate and a longer life, as well as an improved education, health and information of the labour force) can be considered crucial for economic development, because they raise the productivity of labour, alongside the organizational and managerial progress that makes up entrepreneurship.

To finish this review of the long-running forces that enabled the 'first comers' to introduce capitalism and in addition to the support of the state, to institutional change, to technical progress, to the stock of physical resources and human capital, a reference can be made to natural resources, geographic position and trade (elements already cited by Smith).

The theory of economic development at the time of 'latecomers'

Although capitalism evolved gradually throughout the ages presenting different forms of its basic structure all around the world (Gregory and Stuart 2004: Chapter 2; Screpanti 2001: Chapter 6), the aforementioned constituents and features of capitalism (new conditions for mankind, the spread of technological progress, the improved material conditions, and a systemic environment for economic activities) kept unchanged throughout the last two and a half centuries to show the scenario the economic development promotion (that is the spread of capitalism in a traditional economy) tries to achieve. This continuity and the historical analysis of the starting conditions of the countries that undertook economic development, on the one hand enabled them to repeat the experience of the 'first comers', but on the other hand also opened a debate among scholars and policy-makers about the resources and the best policies that are necessary to succeed. Development economics has disputed these topics during the last seven decades, providing quantitative analysis, theories and recipes that acknowledged the importance of a large amount of the forces listed by Maddison, but generally neglected both the approach of the classics previously reviewed and the setting-out that Schumpeter[11] first gave to this disciplinary investigation.

According to Schumpeter economic development, coming along with (and thanks to) a transformation in the socio-political domain, flourishes through a variety of peculiar activities, like:

1   the introduction of a new good [...] or of a new quality of a good;
2   the introduction of a new method of production;
3   the opening of a new market;
4   the conquest of a new source of supply of raw materials or half-manufactured goods;
5   the carrying out of the new organization of any industry.

(Schumpeter 1955: 66)

These activities can be realized as a result of the presence in society of two levers implementing a virtuous process: the technological progress and the innovative entrepreneur. The first element, as already noted, is a cultural atmosphere and a material context inside which innovations can take place, the second is a particular entrepreneur who is dissatisfied when he merely receives the interest deriving from the ownership of the capital because he is keen to make profits by using his capital as an instrument to introduce the innovations in his firm. Thus, in light of the Schumpeterian theory, economic development is the structural change of a traditional economy (associated with the transition towards the capitalism) that is realized by the intentional creation of an increasing number of economic goods, relations and organizations in a socio-economic environment that is characterized by new subjects, habits and rules (not just an increase in the values of specific economic indices).

Despite this record, the models used to explain economic development up to 1990s ultimately considered the phenomenon to be 'synonymous with rapid, aggregate economic growth' (Todaro and Smith 2012: 110), experienced by a completely autonomous country. Nevertheless, in an attempt to take into account historical replications of the process (which occurred one after another in Western countries) along with the evolutionary changes that the 'first comers' experienced in improving material conditions, Rostow presented 'an economic historian's way of generalizing the sweep of modern history' by a set of stages-of-growth, explaining 'both a theory about economic growth and a more general, if still highly partial, theory about modern history as a whole'(Rostow 1960: 1). According to this reading, and because at the time all the world societies could be classified by means of their economic characteristics within one of the five stages of growth (traditional, going through the preconditions for take-off, take-off, drive to maturity, age of high mass-consumption), economic development appeared as a sequence of steps, each one characterized by specific structural forms of the economy.[12] But the sharp separation of the stages (contradicted by the overlapping in some countries experience), the ambiguity in describing both the productive structural changes and the triggers causing the transition from one stage to the other, the determinism and the linearity of the path, prevented this representation from providing an explanation of the phenomenon that was persuasive and consistent with the contemporary processes of economic development that some societies were experiencing.

It was not only the multifaceted nature of the development that dropped in other contemporary explanations of the phenomenon, but also its process dimension. The Harrod-Domar model, for example, focusing on the income rate of growth (the only representative figure for the economic development, outcome of the increase in the saving/income and in the capital/output ratios) reduced the process to a linear increase of a single variable (Harrod 1939; Domar 1946). Thus the mechanism of the economic development was based simply on an adequate rate of investment, obtained thanks to both domestic profits (even from exports) and to foreign investments, creating an accelerated accumulation of capital and a diffused technical progress in production processes, leaving all environmental conditions (re-investment of profits, ability of attracting foreign investments by the economy, adequate institutions and human capital, etc.) undisputed or uncared for.

If in the Harrod-Domar framework the problem of structural change (a crucial item for economic development according to Schumpeter, which was also implicit in Rostow's stages of growth) was disregarded, it did not have better luck in the models by Lewis and Chenery, which are considered the cornerstones of the homonymous approach. In effect, the Lewis model, based on the principle of the efficient allocation of resources, explains how the transfer of labour from the traditional sector (agriculture) to the modern sector (industry) gives rise to both the absorption of agricultural labour excess by a growing industrial sector and the achievement of the full employment in the economy (Lewis 1954). But this 'two-sectors surplus labour model', except that it presents some relevant problems rising from several assumptions (whose criticisms can be found in Todaro and Smith 2012: 118-120), neither considers changes in income distribution and in consumption pattern that are more favourable to the workers, nor a modification in the capital/output ratio due to the technical progress, both crucial features of the development process.

As well as the theoretical shortcomings, the effectiveness of these explanations was questioned by the 'pattern of development analysis', where applied studies showed that the development processes at work after the Second World War were often affected by internal constraints (resources, population, institutions, government policies and objectives) and by international limitations (access to international capitals, to technology and to trade). Thus for the first time it was acknowledged that the 'developing countries are part of an integrated international system that can promote (as well as hinder) their development' (Todaro and Smith 2012: 121), as they are 'latecomers'. This new environment for the development of traditional societies (introducing in the process new constraints to be taken into account) was considered by the economists who, in an attempt to deepen it and to provide suggestions to manage these new variables, worked out two sets of theories: the 'international dependence models' and the 'market efficiency models'.

The international dependence theories were based on the idea that between developed and developing countries there are unbalanced relations working against the poorer economies and affecting both the development of their international trade and capital movements, and the efficient and effective allocation of internal resources. According to these interpretations such an environment for 'latecomer' countries' economic development can be traced back to their colonial legacies, to a time when the interests of domestic social groups were subordinate to foreign interests, keen to retain their political/economic and cultural power, and to the need of an underdeveloped world for the development of the 'first comers' to continue. In such a framework the chances of succeeding in developing the economies are few, and inequality, poverty and international economic disparities will widen, moving the destination further away. The real cause of these failures is due to the centre-periphery structure of the international relations system, or to a false-paradigm model applied by domestic governments because of a cultural dependence (that is because of the acceptance of mainstream analyses and policies elaborated in the richest countries by economists, advisors and international organizations), or to a dualistic form of capitalist economy (a chronic condition for the existence of capitalist society – Todaro and Smith 2012: 122-6). Although this approach suffers from the ideological contrasts of the Cold War, it points out both the need for an economic development model more realistic to the requirements, to the interests involved, to the policies adopted in the development process, and the urge of a new international economic order (a set of international institutions) that is able to support and spread the process by stopping the prevailing powers.

The international economic organizations, supporting 'market efficiency models', proposed, as a solution for the problems of development, a whole range of market efficiency models and of recipes (privatization, liberalization, deregulation and stabilization of the economies) that channelled the policies and the institutional transfer suggested to developing countries together with the richest economies ('Washington consensus'). This neoclassical counter-revolution brought back to the misapplication of the basic principles of a 'modern economy' (private property, individual interest, market exchange and comparative advantages) some pathologies experienced by developing countries (underdevelopment, poverty, inequality and international disparities), thus portraying the development as the timeless outcome of the correct enforcement of the rules pushing the growth of economic variables. The failed development and the correlated problems resulted as a consequence of the distortions in the allocation of resources, whose responsibility was the state intervention both in government regulation of economic activities and in price control, generating restrictions and untrustworthy conditions for individual economic initiatives, barriers to the integration of the economy in the world markets, rents, little competition and corruption. Although relieved in the different approaches provided ('free-market', 'public-choice' and 'market-friendly' models), such an emphasis on the market efficiency blamed the state for all the failures found in real development processes (Todaro and Smith 2012: 126-31).

As far as 'something of significance can be gleaned from each of four approaches we have described'[13] (Todaro and Smith 2012: 131), the economics of development provided, up to the 1980s, a theoretical framework to explain the phenomenon experienced by the 'latecomers' that was a long way off reality, and thus less suitable than that used by the economists who experienced transformation path of the 'first comers' from a traditional society to capitalism. The shortcomings of this view depended on the fact that it tended 'to embrace a narrow somewhat ethnocentric, utilitarian linear and static economic approach. In particular, it paid relatively little attention to the extent and quality of institutional infrastructure and social capital' (Dunning 2006: 179).

Frontiers of development economics: new development paradigm vs. political economy of growth

In the last two decades the economic environment and the international situation have changed, which in turn has also transformed the setting for the development of the 'latecomers'. Among the main events and phenomena that remodelled capitalism, a particular relevance must be assigned to the information technology revolution, because it has affected both the production activities (thanks to the pervasiveness, to the ability to spawn process and good innovations, and to the complementarities with old technical processes that this 'general purpose technology'[14] presents) and everyday life (through the progress in the systems of information and communication and as a result of new products). And if on one hand, the spread of faster means of transport and communication has greatly reduced the costs to move goods, people and information throughout the world, on the other hand, the creation of new goods and the supply of new services have increased the consumer choice and opened the new markets in lower-income countries. The changed technological framework enabled a new wave of globalization, accelerating the creation of world markets for financial services and for tradable goods (supported by new institutions like the World Trade Organization) and the empowerment of multinational firms. But this technological advance created also a new ideological reconfiguration of beliefs and ways of thinking in societies, together with new forms of relationships among organizations operating in different social fields or at different hierarchical levels, and the awareness of the importance of institutions for the management of economic activities.

A momentous transformation also occurred in international relations. The fall of Berlin Wall in 1989 stopped bipolarization in the world political chessboard, giving rise to one pole power (United States) that had to face political challenges carried out by adverse regimes (like in South America), had to cope with local conflicts or crisis as in Somalia, Caucasus, Iran and had fight long-lasting wars like the First and Second Gulf Campaigns and the war in Afghanistan, and had to compete with new emerging economies like China, India, Brazil. This new state of affairs cannot be considered without also considering the impact it has on a lot of developing countries, especially for those in the MENA region, because in this period, the 'United States dominates the Middle East to an unprecedented extent. In a region historically penetrated by competing Western powers, there are no longer any serious challenges to American hegemony' (Hudson 2005: 284).

The answer economists give to the questions of development problems inside this new framework is twofold: some Nobel Laureates and their followers tried to discuss a new development paradigm (NDP), while the mainstream economy proposed the 'political economy of growth'. The starting point of the NDP is first of all cultural, because it takes into account a wider idea of development (one that is not bound to economics), and the inconsistency between its measure by the per capita gross domestic product (GDP) and by the human development index (HDI). As a result of this conceptual breakthrough:

> Development represents a *transformation* of society, a movement from
> traditional relations, traditional ways of thinking, traditional ways of

dealing with health and education, traditional methods of production, to more 'modern' ways. [...] Change is not an end in itself, but a means to other objectives. [...] Given this definition of development, it is clear that a development strategy must be aimed at facilitating the transformation of society, in identifying the barriers to, as well as potential catalysts for, change.

(Stiglitz 1998: 5)

The acceptance of this definition means to reject the idea that the development is a matter of economics, namely a technical problem (where lower-income countries are identical to developed ones apart from the inefficiencies in resources allocation), that requires the implementation of policies that will increase the capital stock, adjust fiscal imbalances or remove political rents, measures that all lead to working markets and to a better macroeconomic framework. Instead, according to the NDP, similarly to the classic economic theories, development is a 'holistic and multi-faceted, yet contextual, concept that embraces a variety of human needs and objectives, [concerns] with the dynamics of structural societal transformations, [...] emphasizes the importance of institutions, [...], regards means and ends as being interwoven and part of the development process' (Dunning 2006: 183).

On this starting point, the specific arguments of the paradigm had been examined by different scholars. Stiglitz points out the structural dynamics of the process, conceived as a societal transformation needing both the creation of consensus, participation and ownership, as well as the promotion and the implementation of learning processes, of human capabilities and of social capital (Stiglitz 1998). Sen emphasizes that the end of development is the eradication of some of the curses affecting developing countries (poverty, lack of economic opportunities and of human rights, tyranny) by means of pursuing substantive freedoms in political, economic, and social fields, plus guarantees of transparency and of protective security (Sen 1999). And North investigates the increasing importance of institutions for the economic growth (due to the greater complexity of economic relations), calling for appropriate incentive structures and enforcement mechanisms to attain the market efficiency by lowest transaction costs (North 1990). Although North's interest is not primarily in development, his studies are relevant for the topic because not only are they concentrated on a variable hold (the institutions) as central to the process, but they also gave rise to a long debate on the institution-building problem for developing countries (see Chapter 3).

On the opposite side of the economic thought, theoretical advances develop the efficient allocation of a resources paradigm investigating specific economic problems like complementarities and coordination failures in the development process,[15] some distributive distortions affecting the growth, and the explanatory variables affecting growth in a global perspective. In the framework of the so called 'political economy literature' that studies the role of interest group or policy-making institutions in resource allocation and rent distribution, 'the part of that literature that is concerned with economic growth examines the impact of such processes on the incentives of economic agents to invest and to improve productivity in the long run' (Castanheira and Esfahani 2001: 159), or 'compile the most comprehensive assessment in developing and transition countries' (McMahon and Squire 2003).

As the reviewed literature shows, development is a comprehensive process, continuously increasing in complexity as new countries move along its path, so the 'latecomers' experience a phenomenon in a way that is different to that faced by the 'first comers'. Although there are similarities in the process (the transition towards the capitalism), some determinants have changed and the environment is different, both in terms of local socio-institutional conditions and in respect to politico-international situation. As the impact of these elements is unpredictable there is no standardized outcome, as demonstrated by the different forms of capitalism realized in the world.

3 Institutions and development in the Middle East and North Africa

Between economic challenges and stability policies

The need for new institutions to support the development process in the Middle East and North Africa, recurrently emerging as a crucial challenge for the countries of the area, is highlighted both by the economic literature reviewing the determinants of the growth of Arab countries and by the international statistics comparing the economic outcome of world regions. While the first studies argue that well-developed institutions can play a decisive role in promoting the economic growth by market efficiency (Okeahalam 2005), by trade openness and by FDI flows (Daniele and Marani 2006; World Bank 2006), the empirical works providing growth accounting reveal that the quality of institutions is responsible for the lowest productivity performance shown by the economies of the region (Makdisi, Fattah and Limam 2007). In addition, the index value of the International Country Risk Guide (ICRG), which appraises the institutional capacity, the reputation and the governance of an economy by four indicators (i.e. government's reputation for securing contracts, the risk of expropriation, the rule of law and the bureaucratic quality) ranked the MENA region in 1995 (Knack and Keefer 1995) and again in 2000 below the world average. These results started an intense debate in the past decade that raised many questions, such as why didn't the MENA region update its institutions in order to promote the transition to the capitalism? Are these motivations temporary or are they embedded in the social habits of the people living in the Middle East and North Africa? Finding answers to these questions initiated a deep inquiry into the historical and theoretical relations between the developmental process and economic institution building, both aspects highlighting the general terms of the problem and drawing attention to the regional distinctiveness.

Although the causal relation between economic institutions and development has been empirically submitted to trials and disputes (Glaeser, La Porta, Lopez-De-Silanes and Shleifer 2004), nevertheless, the importance of these institutions in promoting development stands as a significant issue in economic research. There is widespread consensus among economists on two matters of this causal relation (Nelson and Sampat 2000). On one hand, it is agreed that institutions support technological advances, the formation of physical and human capital and the efficient allocation of resources; on the other hand, it is agreed that economic institutions shape the behaviour of economic actors, defining both the way the activities of each social field (private, economic, political) have to be ruled out and the interactions necessary to undertake them inside the society. Formal and informal rules (as well as their enforcement) thus affect the economic activity creating the incentives and wealth-maximizing opportunities that push individuals and organizations to operate.

Special attention to the institutional building process and to the role played by its specific, decisive components (habits, beliefs and social organizations) had been paid by historians in the recurrent debate on the rise of capitalist institutions in Western economies, which began in the early twentieth century (Weber 1930, German edition 1905; Tawny 1926) and continued recently (Ogilvie 2007; Mokyr 2008). These scholars put forward evidence showing that new economic institutions have emerged thanks to the contribution of social activities (political, religious, professional, etc.), the transformation of old practices (commercial traditions), the influence of new convictions (e.g. the Protestant doctrine) and the introduction of new entities (modern state). In particular, considering the last element, they have observed that, in contexts where the relationships between state and society are weak and variable, institutional change is more problematic than in contexts where these relationships are predictable.

Such evidence asks the economists for a deep investigation that, considering the theoretical implication of institutions imagined as 'behavioural rules embedded in social activities', goes beyond the traditional economic concept, so as to present a complete, consistent theoretical framework capable of explaining how new institutions emerge from the society, how old ones are replaced and how institutions organize themselves in a coordinated structure of different domains. In this framework, a lot of problems regarding the institution-building process for the development of the MENA region can be questioned, among them, for example, the failed emergence of capitalist institutions in Muslim society: since many economic institutions deeply-rooted in capitalism have not appeared in countries characterized by such a culture, the debate on this indisputable fact is topical, giving answers to questions concerning the inappropriateness of MENA institutions. All these issues will be developed in this chapter in order to support the idea that the institution change in the MENA region had been conditioned in recent centuries not by the values of Muslim societies, but by the ineffectiveness of the state in coping with social and economic needs, a situation that causes an endless conflict of authority between state and society.

Institutions for development: lessons from economic and historic studies

In recent decades, the problems related to the institutions in the development process have been considered by different professionals. On one hand, the consultants of the international economic organizations promoted the institutional change of lower-income countries asking for loans to foster the development by the imposition of 'virtuous practices' (in the form of 'governance-related conditionalities'), which have been generally unsuccessful.[1] On the other hand, the results of the empirical works carried out by the researchers supporting the New Institutional Economics were criticized by other scholars because the institutions proposed as necessary for development contrasted with those found out by the historians. Nevertheless, the problem of institutions for development stood – and still stands – as a central topic of the debate among both economists and policy-makers. Thus this problem must be dealt with properly before going beyond the main scientific outcomes obtained in the different fields of research.

As for economists, there is an abundant literature devoted to empirical works and based on cross-country data that aims to answer questions about the causality relation between institutions and economic growth, the way institutions affect economic activity and the type of institutional arrangement that fosters long-term growth. The theoretical starting points of the analysis are, on one hand, the explicit assumption that the guarantee of property rights, the market, and the rule of law are the institutions introduced by 'first comers' to implement their development process, and on the other hand, the belief (taken for granted) that the less-developed economies represent the infant stage of developed ones. The methodology applied in these works is based on econometric tests, and the problem of institutional quality measurability is solved thanks to the data provided by risk-rating or credit-rating agencies, enabling economists to compare more- and less-developed economies in specific time frames. Finally, the risk of expropriation by the government, the degree of corruption and the quality of bureaucracy (strength of the rule of law) are used as respective proxies for the aforementioned institutions for development.

The general result obtained by this literature, documenting 'large cross-country differences in economic institutions and a strong correlation between these institutions and economic performance' (Acemoglu and Robinson 2008: 2), does not attract the attention of contributors to this debate. Scholars tend to concentrate on the procedural framework of the research rather than on their conclusions which are judged to be shallow because neither 'a range of serious problems with data, methodology, and identification' (Aron 2000: 100) nor the theoretical concept of the institution arising from these devices are considered. As to the first element, the indicators representing institutions are constructed using indices (supplied by organizations like the Political Risk Services 'whose primary purpose is to provide assessments of the various forms of political risks') based on not fully public information and that 'reflect the subjective judgements of analysts at the risk assessment organization' (Pande and Udry 2005: 5 and 7). Moreover, the measurement of institutions generally cannot distinguish the attributes of institutions from the evaluation of their performance, the indicators sometimes present an indirect effect on growth through macroeconomic variables (as, for example, human capital or investment) and the studies 'frequently do not test the sensitivity of their results to different model specifications, data outliers, measurement errors, reverse causality between regressors and growth, and bias' (Aron 2000: 100).

Bearing in mind these important criticisms (discussed in Aron 2000; Jütting 2003; Glaeser, La Porta, Lopez-de-Silanes, and Shleifer 2004; Pande and Udry 2005), the results of this research approach can be summarized as follows:

> Exploring the causal link between institutions and economic growth has proved extremely difficult. Despite creative and insightful efforts, the existing research strategy does not establish this link, due to both conceptual problems with the measurement of institutions and the limitations of econometric techniques. In particular, the existing research does not show that political institutions rather than human capital have a causal effect on economic growth. Indeed, much evidence points to the primacy of human capital for both growth and democratization.
>
> (Glaeser, La Porta, Lopez-de-Silanes, and Shleifer 2004; 296-7)

Regarding the concept of the institution, cross-country literature shares expressly – or not – that which is proposed by the 'efficiency approach'. This approach starts from the idea that institutions emerge from the voluntary behaviour of agents (who strive to cope with their social life) and that these institutions become social rules because they are the best way to carry out a task both in terms of using resources and obtaining results. In fact they are based on two principles (the return maximizing rule and the transaction/information cost minimizing guideline) providing both wealth in a specific context and benefits to the entire society in terms of output.[2] Scholars supporting this explanatory model (bringing us back to the traditional neoclassical paradigm) tested it by reviewing the pre-industrial Europe and North Africa economic history in search of organizations and connected rules which governed economic activities for a long time. Such institutions, considered to be efficient as they offered solutions to different transaction problems, were serfdom, village communes and craft guilds (Ogilvie 2007). As the community's reputation was the main law enforcement mechanism (Greif, 2003), the persistence of serfdom over time is explained by its capability to regulate relations between peasants (labour force) and lords (class ensuring protection and justice) (North and Thomas 1973). The centuries-long survival of trade corporations and of community system organization, instead, was due to the fact that they were alternative markets for insurance, military protection and capital collection in the absence of state regulations (Hickson and Thompson 1991). Also, early commercial institutions (such as the Maghribi traders' coalition) operated for a long time because they were able to reach an efficient level of both coordination and trade through a system of intermediaries or agents performing long-distance business and handling merchants affairs and capital. According to the efficiency approach, state formation offered all of the old efficient economic institutions the chance for survival, but only to the ones that were able both to adapt their structure and routines to that of a capitalist economy, and to submit to (and benefit from) the rule of law: thanks to the protection of private property and to the support to the market that the state institution-building process provided, the profit maximizing and the transaction/information cost minimizing basic principles could enter the economic activities, which were well-organized by the commitment and the law enforcement.

This explanation for the emergence of new institutions, fitting effectiveness with an efficiency principle based on a rational choice and focusing mainly on contracts and cooperation among agents, has not considered some important problems that could create conflicts about disposable resources. New institutions, in fact, are not always created out of cooperational choice. Instead, they are frequently the result of conflict arising from the distributive problems that emerge when groups disagree about the relative pay-off, information asymmetries and different interests and powers, as well as economic externalities and distortions of markets (for example, those related to labour in the case of forbidding non-member participation), which eventually lead to the disequilibria of the existent institutional set. In these cases, the problem of contracts commitment and enforcement can be disentangled, if the coercive power (the state) is not simply an observer but a third party and a delegated impartial enforcer that has the legitimacy and the credibility to solve conflicting interests. The development path of modern Europe gives examples of this kind. In the wake of the late nineteenth century, the efforts of workers' movements to restore their position in the labour market (modified by the industrial revolution) led to the emergence of welfare state institutions. The social and insurance programmes promoted by the state (which stood side by side with the previous voluntary and friendly societies' aid) in the attempt to create legitimate coordination between employers and employees in different industries, and to decrease the social and political costs associated with the unequal distribution of power, gave rise to laws restoring the balance of powers.[3] Also, the emergence of constitutional rules in some early modern European countries (such as the Netherlands and England) gave rise to economic institutions, such as property rights and financial markets that impacted the distribution of resources and economic opportunities, and also overseas trade (Korpi 2001).

Moreover, institutional building and changing processes, as dynamic changes, sometimes result from the simultaneous interaction of a set of agents in different fields (for example, economic and political domains), shaping the adaptation and creation of institutions. If market efficiency results from two mechanisms (namely competition and learning), the competitive pressure among subjects could determine the replacement of existing rules by new and more efficient ones (for example, a payment deferment) or the emergence of a new form of organization (the credit market allowed by laws), as a correcting mechanism pushed by the process of learning. This process of corrective adaptation can be more difficult to achieve in the political field since, unlike economic actors, political actors lack property rights and the competition that fosters efficiency in market institutions is absent in political domains. In addition, political uncertainty and social adaptation increase the costs of changing the existing political asset (Person 2000). Thus, the complementary or conflicting implementation of behaviours by a set of agents belonging to different connected domains (like economy and polity) don't always result in a contemporaneous co-evolution or in a hierarchical order of actions, but rather in a dynamic interplay (as the one between the state and the civil society).

Returning to the cross-country approach to institutions, although it failed to provide final, indisputable answers about the relationship that economic institutions have with development, it called for a deeper investigation of the concept in order to explain both the causality between political regimes and the quality of economic institutions (beyond the simple syllogism based on the sequence democracy, private property and development), and the mechanisms governing the institution building process and the absorption of social values. In addition, the debate gave rise to the need of providing 'a broad view of institutions while at the same time extending the remit of these institutions away from purely economic outcomes toward broader socio-economic development outcomes' (Casson, Della Giusta and Kambhampati 2010: 138) and toward procedural (rather than theoretical) behaviours, as requested by the policy-makers (Chang 2007b).

Some of these problems were known from historic analysis of the contribution of informal institutions (in particular the influence of shared community values like culture and beliefs) to the development of the 'first comers'. Starting with the work of Weber on the role of the Protestant Reformation and of the Calvinist doctrine in the wake of capitalism in Western Europe (Weber 1930), the cultural approach to the institutional analysis has tried to explain the different trajectories followed by societies in their peculiar institutional foundations (even in the presence of similar technology). As it does for values, beliefs and preferences shared by societies, culture too can both influence the equilibrium of the existent institutional arrangement and alter this arrangement when different sets of beliefs coexist in a specific social field (Greif 2003). What is more, not only religious beliefs (such as Weber's view of Protestantism and its emphasis on hard work and savings) are taken into account, but also some operational ways of conducing economic activities are considered, together with different political systems (democracy vs. authoritarian regimes). In his work on the institutional origin of the industrial revolution, for example, Mokyr emphasizes how the transformation that took place in the eighteenth century in Britain (leading to the industrial revolution) was not entirely a result of actions promoted by efficient institutions (property right system, credit markets, patent system and apprenticeship): a strong contribution was provided by the pre-existing culture of 'politeness' (respect of contract, based on a self-enforcing mechanism such as reputation). The gentry, and the figure of the 'gentleman', became a positive model of reliance that gave signals to (and favoured the imitation by) the middle class, thus creating the cooperative environment that helped the commercialization and modernization of the economy. This particular ideology also helped the political system to develop adaptive efficiency, making Britain a unique environment for the industrial revolution to take place (Mokyr 2008). The analysis of the role played by the civic society (or civic culture) represents another step in our understanding of the relationship between culture and institutional development. As a form of social capital that encourages social integration, civic society would help economic growth through political liability (Putnam, Leonardi and Nanetti, 1993). To sum up, the cultural approach, inspecting all these variables, provides on one hand, an explanation of the emergence of institutions in specific social contexts and, on the other hand, an account for their self-sustaining character and slow-changing nature. Their endogeneity (where socio-political and economic institutions are embedded in mental models and social beliefs) explains their tendency to persist and to assume peculiar features in different socio-political contexts.

Towards a comprehensive concept of 'institution'

Despite the recognized impact of institutions on socio-economic behaviour and the convergence on the need for a deep theoretical inspection (among historians and economists), the notion of 'institution' still remains ambiguous and sometimes trivial. No attention, in fact, is paid to the difference between the 'function' of an institution (that is, the task it might carry out: examples of such tasks in the development process are the promotion of the capital accumulation, the diffusion of self coordinating mechanism for the economic activities, the establishment of the rule of law, the human capital formation, etc.) and the 'form' of an institution (that is, the set of rules or of organizations in place to pursue an aim, like the property right laws, the market system, the justice courts system, the educational system, respectively) (Chang 2007b). The indexes of the institutional quality, for example, mix up indicators of institutional functions (the risk of expropriation removal meaning that the capital accumulation or the promotion of investments are sought, the government reputation of contracts whose degree measures the will to support the expansion of the exchange in the economy, etc.) with others capturing the institutional forms (the absence of state ownership conceived as a real protection of private ownership, the degree of corruption in government that enables the market forces to perform properly), sometimes favouring the second to the first ones or vice versa (Aron 2000). However, the theoretical studies and the international economic organization practices, preferring a specific model of the economic mechanism, usually refer to the form of institutions (privatization of economic activities, openness of the economy, deregulation). Either way there is no awareness of the fact that each function can be executed by different forms of institutions and that the effectiveness of a functional task does not overlap the efficiency of the institutional form used to perform it.

Neither the difference between the 'institution building process' (the setting up of forms of institutions by choosing models and means to be implemented) and the 'institutional process' (the actual working of institutions) have been explored, it has been taken for granted that, once introduced, an institution necessarily produces standard effects. The trade-off between 'imitation' and 'innovation' in changing institutions is thus ignored, as well as the environmental problems of the new institutions (i.e. its legitimacy and its sustainability in the context of the socio-cultural and economic inheritance of the former system). The lack of reference on these topics in the recent economic literature, or the insufficient attention to the arguments presented above, is due on one hand, to a limited and static concept of institutions (imagined merely as a constraints to channel human being's behaviour) and on the other hand it is also due to the 'structural adjustment programmes' suggested by the International Economic Organization (spreading the idea of a single form of institution for similar purposes, both in developed and in developing economies, as well as in recovering ones).

The need for a deep analysis of economic institutions, one that would fill the knowledge gap, has emerged in these remarks and in the debates discussed in the previous paragraph. Such an analysis would need to start from the nature of social rules, an aspect emphasized in recent studies. This feature is a cornerstone of Aoki's definition, stating that economic institutions are 'self-sustaining salient patterns of social interactions, as represented by meaningful rules that every agent knows and that are incorporated as agents' shared beliefs about how the game is played and to be played' (Aoki 2007: 6). Other scholars, investigating institutional rules, argue that they are 'purposeful' in the sense that 'institutions can (and do) serve multiple functions' (Chang 2007a: 5), that they have a logical structure and that they are 'constitutive', because they create an institutional fact assigning a special status that allows 'a person or object to perform functions that it could not perform solely in virtue of its physical structure' (Searle 2005: 22). Moreover, institutions are two-sided entities that hold, besides the previous substantial character, a 'mental representation': people's attitudes and beliefs are constitutive and complementary characteristics that enable institutions to exist, to be codified, transmitted and replicated. Finally, as formal rules represent legal dispositions and informal ones represent social conventions, both the state and the society are entitled to create them.

If institutions can be regarded as behavioural rules organizing the interactive capacity of subjects in a specific social domain (a defined field of activity), the outcome they produce could be imagined as a 'match', that is, as a purposeful process conducted following a settled scheme (fixed in each historic period, but changing over time). The 'players' of this game (human beings and organizations) try to reach their 'aims' by 'game rules' that is by choosing activities among 'allowed acts' according to a set of rewards and sanctions scheduled in a 'consequence function'. So the algorithm that must be applied by any player of a game (whatever the domain) gets through three different steps (Aoki 2007):

1 The 'game form', that is the operating instructions for the game, including the set of players, the aims, the consistent actions with their rewards and sanctions and the game rules.
2 The 'state of game', namely the placing and the arrangement of all successful game schemes, representing the relevant features of the ways the play is repeatedly performed.
3 The 'plan of actions', i.e. representing the strategic arrangement of actions, which is implemented by the players (characterized by limited rationality) in line with the state of the game and with the beliefs about the behaviour of other subjects.

Each stage of the game, defining a specific level of feasibility (abstract, applied and planned, respectively), embeds different kinds of constraints to social actions in every domain: the game rules present which actions are allowed and which are forbidden, the game schemes reveal the different schedules of allowed actions that are successful, and the agent's plan of action shows the schedule of strategic behaviours believed as the best practice at the moment. Given that the social game is a three-layer process and that each level presents social constraints, a further analysis is required to explain:

1 the kind of social constraint (among abstract, applied and planned rules) representing institutions;
2 the hierarchical relations of domains and the relative position of economic institutions;
3 the process of institutional change.

Economic analysis provides two different solutions to each one among these problems, giving us two different approaches to economic institutions.

According to Williamson, an economic institution is represented by the game rules, which are the formal rules (explained in the game form and enforced by the rewards and the sanctions of the consequence function) that emerge from the application of the principles of neoclassical theory to the institutional environment, provided by political, administrative and judicial domains. Thus, the strategic game arrangements overlap with the rules of game (the state of game is nothing but the living form of the consequence function) and economic institutions appear as subordinated to political ones. As to the emergence of economic institutions, Williamson outlines a four-level configuration of domains (each imposing constraints to the level below) resulting in a hierarchical structure:

1   The upper stage is the 'social embeddedness level', where informal norms like customs, habits, believes, traditions, taboos, social conducts, etc., are present in force. They are embedded in social behaviours and connected to religion, culture, ethics and general rules governing the society. They change very slowly and 'have mainly spontaneous origins – which is to say that deliberative choice of a calculative kind is minimally implicated' (Williamson 2000: 597).

2   Below this upper stage is the 'institutional environment level', representing the rules of the game or the formal rules (that are the product both of evolutionary process and design opportunities) like constitutions, laws and property rights. Executive, legislative, judicial and bureaucratic rules are established at this level, and the 'delimitation and enforcement of property rights and of contract laws are important features' (Williamson 2000: 598). These institutions change in the medium period (10-100 years).

3   The third stage is the 'governance institutions level', that contains the institutions creating the order and the governance of the society by sustaining the organizations, by reshaping incentives, and by adapting structures. To provide governance to economic organizations (to create suitable economic institutions) 'transaction cost economics turns its attention – additionally and predominantly – to the ex-post stage of contracts' (Williamson 2000: 599).

4   At the bottom there is the 'optimal institutions level', providing the rules to optimize the economic apparatus using the neoclassical analysis. 'Adjustments to prices and output occur more or less continuously. Agency theory, which emphasizes ex-ante incentives alignments and efficient risk bearing, [...] makes provisions for non neoclassical complications' (Williamson 2000: 600).

The economic institutions appear at the bottom of the pyramidal structure of domains as a rational transaction-costs-saving response to the restraints imposed by socio-political domains so that, depending on laws and on social norms, they are exogenous in respect to the economy. This notion of institution is just a timeless rule without either process of implementation or an explanation of the changing process; as they are channels of homologation, the institution change in a developing economy is fully consistent with a mere institution transfer. In fact, there is widespread consensus in economics on which recipe is suitable to build economic institutions in development conditions: to implement an institutional transfer process, that is, to imitate the formula of 'privatization, market and liberalization' (sometimes connected to 'democracy'). But the above concept of economic institution gives rise to some theoretical and methodological problems. On one hand, it doesn't explain why the political power is entitled to create economic institutions, on the other hand, no information is provided on how the social values are embedded in economic institutions (unless indirectly through the second and the third level).

The second approach to economic institutions (Hayek 1976; Shotter 1981; Dixit 2004; and Aoki 2007) points out that, besides the formal rules that govern the social activities (including both general codes and specific laws), there are informal institutions (like routines) representing their successful use (the game schemes collected in the state of the game) and, therefore, constituting a source of good practices to be imitated to succeed in the subject's plan of action. The three levels of constraints acting in social games don't create a hierarchical pyramid, but represent the stages of an algorithm applying and realizing the formal rules while carrying out the social activities on one side, and fitting them for each game of relevance on the other. Thus institutions are revealed by the state of the game (Aoki 2007: 5), as 'the fundamental concept of institutions ultimately boils down to the idea of recurrent patterns of behaviour-habits, conventions and routines' (Langlois and Robertson 1995: 1).

This approach, defining institutions in a procedural and operational way, provides us with an opportunity to explain both the institutional process and the institutional change process. As to the institutional process, two important features are revealed: path-dependency of steps and learning by doing in performing institutional behaviours; while with regard to institutional change processes, the temporal gap between the introduction, the full application and the effectiveness of a new institution is brought to light. For both, the dynamic nature of the processes is emphasized. Finally, this approach tries to combine the agency view with the structural view[4] in a dynamic framework in which more aspects of institution are treated as endogenous. This is the case of the institutional change process, because:

1   institutional change is endogenous as it implies an equilibrium shift in behavioural beliefs shared by individuals. Changes occur when the development of new skills, or of learning processes drive new successful possibilities and strategies of action that, repeated and coordinated, give rise to another state of the game;

2   a particular institutional set (equilibrium) prevails as an endogenous outcome of agent's interaction. Institutions are thus common knowledge (rules known and embedded in beliefs) regarding the achieved equilibrium path;
3   the endogenous emergence of new institutions is a historical process;
4   values and norms are endogenously shaped by individuals (although they are exogenous to their each), so that different social norms result in different institutional arrangements, and different game forms are possible in a certain domain to carry out the same function.

As to the problem of the relations among institutional domains, a small digression from the subject is needed. Given that social activities represent sets of behaviours achieved by interconnected subjects, they can be grouped into different categories and conceived as 'systems', also of institutional type (being institutions 'recurrent patterns of behaviour-habits').[5] Each system presents the 'duality property', that is, it can simultaneously be a complex entity (because it is composed of subjects and relations) and an element of a higher-level system. Thus the institutional structure represents a kind of 'hyper-structure' (a set of sets characterized by hyper-hierarchy), and each institutional domain is a 'complex adaptive system'[6] embedded inside the diffused knowledge. This applies also to economic institutions governing social activities (Potts 2000: 68-70), whether they are completely included inside the economic domain or carried out between economy and other domains. In fact, social activities presenting economic interests are those that are performed:

• by private subjects or organizations acting in economic domain;
• by private subjects/organizations acting economically in connection with public and administrative domains;
• by private subjects or organizations (acting in social domains) whose habits and norms have economic relevance (family and religious fields of activity).

In this framework,

> [...] institutions arising in different domains may not be hierarchically aligned in such a way that social norms precede a political institutions, while decisions made in the context of a political institutions determine the game forms in economic and organizational domain. Rather, institutions may arise encompassing different domains, and/or institutions in different domains may co-evolve through complementary relationships, leading a complex structure of over-all institutional arrangement.
> (Aoki 2007:14)

As the endogenous approach underlines, institutional change is a result of an interrelated process implying the destabilization of shared beliefs, the emergence of competitive behaviour among agents and a complementary change in different domains. In fact, although the arising institutions present a higher degree of effectiveness (if compared with previous ones) in coping with the current problems, changes in individual choices are not enough to spur on their emergence. The new institutional set comes into conflict with the old one and it will prevail only thanks to the co-evolution of institutions in other connected domains. The history of continental Europe shows examples of this kind, as in the case of a professional set of instructions (the 'lex mercatoria': a set of ethic rules determined by medieval merchants) that became formal rules (commercial codes) enforced by the state when the bourgeoisie gained control of the government in the second half of the nineteenth century. In this respect, the question on the possibility of states to be entitled to promote a change of institutions when the polity does not present co-evolution in respect to the economy or to the society arises. Given the interplay of formal and informal institutions in shaping the overall institutional quality, changes in the formal structure do not always result in adaptation of the informal one (North 1990, 1993). The reason is that informal institutions, especially in developing countries where they represent a stable and alternative market to cope with state inefficiencies, are highly context specific: they are, in fact, a social phenomenon that relies on peculiar norms and interpersonal networks (Leukert 2005).

The problem of capitalist institutions' failed emergence in MENA

The theoretical framework presented above, which is supported by the results of historic and economic research, points out that institution building is a process of transition – from an old set of formal and informal rules to a new set of rules – pushed by social needs and new routines and/or pulled by state policies and legal norms, that is hampered by the old institutional set (generally triggering permanent conflicts) and where there must be co-evolution among the different domains of social activities in order to succeed in the development process. In addition, while disproving the fact that any single cultural variable (such as religion, traditions, practices) or social organization (such as hereditary rules, credit system, bookkeeping) can, by itself, stimulate the emergence of new economic institutions, this approach reveals that cultural variables can contribute to their self-sustaining character and their slow-changing nature, and that social organizations can contribute to specific institutional forms which are shaped to perform basic functions in the economic transition process from a traditional to a capitalist socio-economic system.

When applied to the MENA region, in order to explain the reasons behind the institutional deficit preventing the area from developing (see World Bank, *MENA Economic Developments and Prospects*, from 2005 to 2011), such methodological framework shows which problems, among those that have been raised in the debate on the topic, can be properly discussed. The adaptability of Islam to capitalism, although examined in that context by a part of the literature on this subject, is an irrelevant issue, as it is related to the endorsement by Islam of basic capitalist principles (such as a decentralized mechanism for the coordination of economic activities, waged labour, a free initiative in production, private disposal of natural resources for production, financial markets, research for profit, etc.). So this issue must be questioned in terms of the compatibility between Islamic economic doctrine and capitalist standards with regards to the nature and the aims of an economic system,[7] and not by reviewing the adoption of some capitalist institutional forms by regional countries. However, the reasons why the Muslim societies (followed by the new MENA states) failed to transform the institutional forms of their traditional economies (where rules and economic organizations dominated) when capitalism first began to spread across the world, must be scrutinized in order to account for the impact of the Muslim societies on the transformation of economic institutions, and for the incidental asymmetric co-evolution of the domains of economy, society and state.

As to the failed transformation of traditional Muslim institutions, some scholars (Kuran 2003 and Pryor 2007) believe that is the consequence of the unintentional interaction of Muslim classical society (rather than Islam belief) with economic objectives (efficiency and equity), resulting in an institutional trap impeding modernization in MENA countries. Among the rules responsible for this institutional stalemate there are as follows:

1   The law of inheritance, which favoured the fragmentation of wealth by splitting two thirds of the testamentary estates among an extended kinship and leaving only one third to the will of the individual, thus inhibiting capital accumulation and keeping commercial enterprises small.
2   The 'one-by-one oriented contract law' that, referring only to human beings and generally establishing unlimited liability, ignores impersonal subjects like corporations. Although it provides rules that support the joint ownership of property, and although it is based on the same rules and motivations of the Western medieval institution 'commenda' (efficient allocation of risks and expected returns), this partnership (*mudāraba*) did not always result in modern corporation. In the nineteenth century, rather, it evolved in familiar trade ventures, because the demise of one of its members and the lacking of legal personality create the advantage to keep partnerships small.
3   Legal pluralism (i.e. the possibility of choosing the court to be judged in commercial disputes), that resulted in legal privileges supporting the non-Muslim merchants, notably the Western ones.
4   Arbitrary (un-codified) taxation and the weak property rights that were the consequence of the policies for providing public finance by the

Ottoman Empire (discussed in Chapter 1). Both the 'sell at auction tax-system' and the fiscal policies introduced in the framework of the defensive developmentalism produced an unpredictable and erratic taxation, while the land and property right reforms discouraged the acceptance of belongings, as they were established to provide public revenues rather than to protect the availability of resources to undertake entrepreneurial activities.[8]

By considering some organizational forms of traditional Muslim countries' economies which could not be transformed in a 'capitalist' way, two elements have received attention. The first is the *waqf*, a proper Islamic trust foundation, which emerged as a charitable institution a century after the rise of Islam and later transformed into a means of overcoming the insecure property rights (especially for landowners) owing to opportunistic taxation of Muslim officials. The *waqf* system was thus not only an entity that provided public goods, but it was also a safeguard institution that aimed to control wealth and to reduce the risk of expropriation of assets, as it was considered to be sacred. What is more, as it aimed to supply public and semi-public goods, the *waqf* also functioned as a pre-modern state organization (a culturally-based organization) for the provision of social services. However, with the growing complexity of the business environment, the *waqf* did not adapt its rules of operation, or reallocate resources or provide new urban services. Soon new organizations evolved for these purposes, and were partly financed by the dismantling of the *waqf* system.

The second mechanism of the traditional Muslim economy that did not evolve in a capitalist way is the system to pool financial resources for commercial missions. This was not a distinct entity like the *waqf*, but a system of procedures and options connected to the contract of *mudāraba*. The 'commercial partnership established under the Islamic law typically involved one sedentary investor who financed a trading mission run by a single travelling merchant' (Kuran 2004: 73) and yet this did not lead to the creation of credit markets. Generally, in the debate on this topic this failure is attributed to the persistence of some economic norms rooted in religious belief, like the prohibition of putting interest on a loan (*riba*, common to the other monotheistic religions in the past), of drawing up insurance policies and of taking financial risks; all bans hampering the development of financial markets and thus of investments. But recently, when the MENA and other Asian financial markets offered new chances to those who had capital, these interdicts were crossed, building proper Islamic institutions (Islamic contracts and banking) that operated in accordance with Islamic law and principles (*Sharia*). Although carrying out the same function of conventional banking, these new financial institutions follow a proper operational path in accordance with basic traditional Muslim principles, such as the prohibition of *riba* and the sharing of profits and losses, thus providing a peculiar form of venture capital (Akyol 2007). In addition to the profit/loss sharing, different kinds of contracts, like the mark-up loan, and several types of fixed rate are now offered (yielding 'profit' rather than 'interest', but varying from country to country) which do not differ much from the interest-bearing loans (Pryor 2007).

As the previous analysis shows, contrary to what is claimed, MENA economic institutions evolved whenever the working activities required an adaptation of the rules in force to face new challenges; thus the failed emergence of capitalist institutions in the MENA region must be attributed to the stagnation of the economy. With reference to this topic, the analysis of the MENA region's economic history provides a line of enquiry devoted to answer the question why, after it experienced a period of intensive economic growth in the tenth and eleven centuries, further economic improvements (for example, an increase in the per capita wealth) or innovations connected to the capitalism didn't follow, as expected. Exploring the literature that deals with this problem, Kuran finds a shared belief about the fact that Muslim societies influenced economic performance, even if the opinions about the role of cultural variables were different. There are approaches to this end: the 'economic irrelevance thesis' (stating that economic descent 'was caused [...] by changes in material conditions – changes to which the world view and moralities of Muslims merely adapted'), the 'economic advantage thesis' (claiming that 'Islam's effects on growth could have been consistently positive, yet eventually overwhelmed by other factors') and the 'economic disadvantage thesis' viewing 'Islam as a source of growth-inhibiting attitude' (Kuran 1997: 46-51). Except for the different opinions about the direct influence of Islam on economic performance, what emerges from all the explanations is, once more, a tendency to put the blame on the social culture of Muslim societies (deriving from secular interpretations of Islam to applied social activities) for protecting social stability and equity, thus preventing economic development as well as the transformation of traditional institutions into capitalist ones.

However, regarding the harmful influence that the equity and stability principles that inspire Muslim societies had on the failure of both institutional change and capitalist upsurge, something must be pointed out. That 'Islam came to support the status quo through its legitimation of policies aimed at social stability' (Kuran 1997: 54) was a positive element that supported growth when the economy was flourishing, but a factor that worsened economic conditions in the case of stagnation. In fact, according to Kumar and Matsusaka, the principles of the Muslim society and culture fostered the economic development by implementing the so-called 'village economy', a local economy in which 'village capital takes the form of social networks, kinship, patron-client relations, in-depth knowledge about trading partners, [...] supporting transactions based on repeated play and full information about transacting parties' (Kumar and Matsusaka 2004: 1-2). This economic organization produced both decreasing transaction costs (in a period when transportation and communication costs were high) and externalities (like an increasing social capital, of the village kind) as generations of people followed one another. In addition, the trading pattern mentioned above allowed an efficient and unopposed spread of trade all over the Mediterranean (where Muslim societies were diffused), at least up to the advent of technological progress that provided cheaper transportation and different trade patterns.

The communalist Muslim principles became ineffective when (because of these technical shocks) a new form of economic system emerged as a consequence of these technical shocks. This new system, 'the market economy', was antagonistic and more efficient than the communalist system, so that it quickly replaced the old system all over the Mediterranean. Its strength was secured in a different form of social capital, the 'market capital', which 'takes the form of knowledge about how to use third party enforcement institutions such as courts, auditors, standardized accounting procedures, and commercial laws' (Kumar and Matsusaka 2004: 2) to support trade between strangers. So, at the beginning of the new millennium there were two models of economy and of social culture: on one hand, was 'communalism' under which 'the prevalence of trust usually makes merchants hire one another as their partners or agents', on the other hand, was 'individualism' developed in Europe that 'commonly hire non-merchants' (Kuran 1997: 61). According to Greif, Maghribi traders and Genoese merchants were representative of these two different kinds of cultural beliefs and trading patterns (the former was more conservative, the latter was more proactive and willing to adapt labour organization and legal rules to increasing markets), and also of their respective failing and successful destinies (Greif 1993, 2003, 2012).[9] In fact, as the implementation of market capital was easier in societies characterized by poor social capital and development, 'it was the very success of the Islamic states in the Middle Age that made it difficult for them to modernize, because economic success in pre-industrial times required significant investments in village capital' (Kumar and Matsusaka 2004: 35). In addition, the survival of the two institutional models was supported, not only by internal features, but also by the structure of the political power: a common central authority governing a huge set of village economies (overall in the case of Ottoman empire) on one hand, and on the other hand a group of small autonomous European states who were bound to compete by trading with strangers to continue to exist. Just the presence of this competition pushed Western economies to invest in market capital, whose main features are the capabilities of maintaining relationships with foreigners.

The fact that the failed capitalist development of the MENA region could be attributed to the persistence of a communalist system (considered inconsistent with capitalism), as well as to the social culture of Muslim societies, can be questioned using Putnam's results on the capitalist development of North and South Italy (Putnam, Leonardi and Nanetti 1993). In fact, the development experience of North Italy after the Second

World War is the proof of the consistency of the two different types of social capital in the development process, because:

> Individualism promotes growth not by breaking social ties but, rather, by weakening and diversifying them. [...] Strong ties based on blood bonds sustain cooperation within small groups, whereas weak ties that link biologically unrelated people nourish wider cooperation and sustain greater social complexity. [The last kind of ties were represented in the North by] [c]ivic engagement that is more limited in the South, where cooperation is generally based on strong kinship ties. The difference reflects the legal system's greater effectiveness in the North than in the South where the absence of credible state enforcement [can be found].
>
> (Kuran 1997: 64)

In light of this type of support it can be upheld that it is the imbalance between political and socio-economic domains that prevented capitalist development in the MENA region. In fact, to partially offset the disadvantageous Mediterranean trading relations, the Muslim economies adapted and by exploiting their comparative advantage they made a trade diversion towards less developed economies of Africa and Asia (homogeneous in respect to social institutions, but less developed because of their village's social capital, Kuran 1997: 62), thus reducing the need for institutions in the economic domain to be changed. However, the political authorities of Muslim world, instead of supporting the economy to cope with the new menace, gave, inch by inch, increasing concessions to European traders and used the revenues from these trading rights to continue their policies, ignoring the fact that Arab and Turkish merchants disappeared in Mediterranean markets and their economy became increasingly dismantled. The political abuse of the economy to pursue, unsuccessfully, both social stability and the strengthening of the 'nation-state' in the nineteenth century produced economic decline and colonization, as defensive 'developmentalism' demonstrates. As shown in Chapter 1, European powers were more interested in managing economic activities in the MENA region in a regime of concessions, than in modelling the institutions of host countries in favour of their capitalist interests (with the partial exception of France). Thus the ultimate explanation for the failed development of capitalism and of capitalist institutions in MENA region can be found in the state-society dialectics.

State-society divergence as a starting point

If we move away from the failed evolution of traditional economic structures and institutions of Muslim society, and look instead towards the introduction of the capitalism as a result both of the competitive/conflicting dialectics among different social parties (solved through the establishment of the state as a partial enforcer) and of state policies (as was the case of British property right laws in the eighteenth century – Richardson and Bogart 2008), we see that the institution-building process in the MENA region takes a particular configuration with respect to the experience of modern Europe, simply because of the different roles played by civil society and state, and because of their reciprocal relationships in the Muslim world.

Briefly, it must be pointed out that these differences go back to the concepts of society and state. In the European experience, civil society emerged as 'an intermediary entity, standing between the private sphere and the state', and including the 'organized social life that is voluntary, self-generating, (largely) self-supporting, autonomous from the state, and bound by a legal order or set of shared rules' (Diamond 1994: 5). Within its framework, formal and informal groups (associations, social movements, unions, etc.) act collectively, expressing interests, ideas, passions, and aiming to counterbalance the state power; however, despite this, civil society needs the legal protection of the state to ensure the autonomy and the freedom of all citizens that can be threatened by someone else's behaviour. Thus the state, which was granted its authority by society, representing the national community of all the citizens, rose to protect individuals through the rule of law.

However, the history of Muslim society is different. First, 'civil society in Arabic refers to assembling in cities, in contrast to Bedouin and rural life' (Karajah 2007: 27), thus it represents an upgrading of the cultural processes and lifestyles. In addition, Islam, contrary to primitive Christianity (founded as a religious monastic order and for this reason doomed to conflict with the state when later it widened to influence the entire society of European countries) emerged in Mecca as a civil-society philosophy, protesting against the prevailing state of affairs.

> Although Muslim societies accepted state as a necessity for the realization of Islamic teachings, very early in Islamic history the *ulama*, the merchants and the professionals, found that their interests could be better protected if they formed their society independent of state. As George Makdisi (1981) has argued very convincingly, the lawyers, law schools and legal education started developing in the tenth century as guilds. The events that prompted this development was the coercion of the *Abbasi* state to impose *Mu'tazili* theology and the attacks of *Hanbalis*, *Shi`is* and *Ash'aris* against each other. The legal institution that made guilds possible was that of *waqf*, trust property that was beyond the control of state laws. […] The institution of *waqf* was also supported by the guilds of other trades and professions. […] *Sufi* orders were also organized like civil societies. They also had their *waqf* institutions. These orders were often in the form of *Futuwwa* (chivalry), joined by soldiers who were professionals but were not on the pay role of a government. They practiced as *ghazis* on the frontiers of Islam. […]. It is significant to note that most minorities in Muslim societies

adopted trade as profession, as the guilds provided them a strong civil society [...].

Islamic civil society was based on the principle of the rule of law. *Shari'a*, which in the common understanding covered every aspect of social and economic life, had its origin in divine revelation and thus reassured that protection of interests by law, was a Divine Will. The absence of a church or any organized body having exclusive rights to interpret Divine Will left the interpretation and development of laws to society at large [...]

Islamic law conceives duty to be of two types: *Fard 'ayn*, individual duty, and *Fard kifaya*, societal duty. The former is a duty that Law demands of every individual personally to fulfil; it cannot be delegated to others. *Fard kifaya* is a duty that Law demands of society as a whole to perform.

The society can appoint some persons on its behalf or some individuals can volunteer to perform it. *Imama* (leadership), *Qada* (judgeship), *Ifta* (interpretation of laws) and other such functions are regarded *Fard kifaya*, duties performed by individuals on behalf of the society. Thus Islamic law developed the idea of a social order which could function according to laws even where there was no Islamic state.

(Masud 2010)

For this reason Muslim societies lived almost in harmony with Caliphates till the tenth/eleventh century: the welfare of the state and the worship of the leaders were sacred (because they personified the society), the individual rights were sacrificed for them and the state alleged 'omniscience and the capacity to solve all citizens' problems', positioning itself as the sole protection against foreign dangers. 'Hence, any loyalty to other entities was considered to some degree a betrayal of the state. At the same time, sacrificing family and tribal ties was considered a grave risk' (Karajah 2007: 31), as they were a safeguard against state despotism. Thus the society was at one with the state, which in turn was committed to managing its power over families and tribes: in this framework no space for civil society existed.

Once the political domain stopped its co-evolution with the other social domains and became authoritarian and/or unable to protect communities from the foreign threats, the conflict between society and state increasingly developed on the political field for the entitlement of authority and for the rule of law. During the Ottoman Empire, as the state laws and policies both conflicted with socio-communalist needs and rules and were without authoritativeness, the political domain was increasingly ineffective in shaping social rules, in building new institutions or in keeping the state institutional process alive. When, later, the national states emerged from the colonialism as unknown entities in the history of the region,[10] they received the loyalty of citizens as long as they provided them with protection and welfare. 'Offering anything in return for the society's support for its agenda'

(Karajah 2007: 31-32), on one hand, the state needed to use its greater trustworthiness and its authoritativeness in respect to the social rules, and on the other it gave a chance to the rise of commitment both to tribal groups and to civil society as substitutes at a pinch. As a consequence:

> [state policies] tend also to assume an articulatory form, represented by various degrees and manifestations of 'corporatism'. This stems from the fact that in these societies neither 'philosophical individualism' nor social classes have developed well enough to allow for the emergence of politics as we see it in Western, capitalist societies. As with corporatism in general, Middle Eastern corporatism ranges between a more 'organic', solidaristic and communitarian strand at one end of the spectrum and a more organizational, interest-based and populist/mobilizational strand at the other. Saudi Arabia and other kin-based monarchies in the Gulf are illustrative of the first strand; Egypt and other sometimes radical, populist republics are illustrative of the second.
>
> (Ayubi 1995: 3)

It is interesting to note that in the first case there is a strong society and a weak state, but in the second there is a strong state that embeds the society and assigns the privilege of citizenship to the supporters of prevailing ruler groups (political or military dictatorship). Sometimes, as argued by Platteau, the protection of Muslim social principles and institutions (like religion) have become a strategy for political rulers to get rid of countervailing powers. Many historical examples provide evidence of this fact in the long history of Muslim societies: during the first century of Islam, for instance, there was competition among groups (such as merchants of the cities and Bedouins) who were defending different social organizations, but who were really supporting leadership of certain candidates in the caliphate; the same happened during periods of political vacuum, when religious figureheads became substitutes for a missing central power (*sufi* networks operating as opponents to the Ottoman state, or the *Shi'ism* movement in Iran). The resulting socio-religious/political equilibrium can be an unstable one as rulers can present dual qualities: they are political leaders and guardians of the faith (or of Muslim principles) and confer upon themselves the legitimacy accorded by Islam to preserve power and extend control over rebellious territories (as Tamburlaine did when he invaded the old Mongol territory, or Abdur Rahman in his attempt to establish his authority in Afghanistan in the 1880s, or more recently Ali Bhutto in Pakistan in 1977). The emergence of new institutions as a dialectic between social groups and the state in the Middle East is complicated by this feature, and the costs and risks of reforming institutions is very high because of the ease with which Muslim values can be used and manipulated to support political or social interests, due to the absence of a religious hierarchy that is able to impose an Islamic orthodoxy in *Sunni* countries.

The institutional-building process in the MENA region evolved success-fully, as long as the 'village economy' was effective in managing economic activities, but when it had to face the threat of a striving 'market economy' it failed, because of the inconsistency between the source of its institutional entitlement (the society) and that of market economy institutions (the state). The difficulties that the introduction of the modern state ran into (and still does) in the MENA region prevent co-evolution between economies and political arrangements and the evolution of the traditional (capitalist-consistent) Muslim institutions too.

4 Demographic dynamics and development implications in the Middle East and North Africa

Demographic dynamics represent for the 'latecomers' a shattering phenomenon that affects their development process more intensely compared to the 'first comers', both because of the higher speed of growth of the population and of the greater responsibilities of the state towards the new generations. This particularly applies to a region like the Middle East and North Africa where considerable demographic changes have occurred in the recent decades. After a sharp population increase in the 1960s and 1970s, there was a decline in fertility and birth rates fell, decreasing the speed of the population growth and resulting in a new and potentially more favourable situation with respect to the baby boom. Despite the different demographic transition faced by the regional economies (Tabutin and Schoumaker 2005), mostly dependent on territorial differences, cultural factors, institutional arrangements and peculiarities in political choices of local governments, all Arab countries have experienced, since the 1980s, delays in marriage, a shift to smaller families and an increased number of unmarried men and women. At the same time, the considerable decline in the dependent population (those people under 16 and older than 64 who are sustained by working people aged between 16 and 64) has been accompanied by a significant rise in the working-age population, which has been enlarged by a cohort of young people, who represent both an active economic group in reproductive age (so feeding the market with a supply of new entrants) and human capital endowment for the regional economies.

The analysis of the demographic dynamics of the Middle East and North Africa in an historical perspective lies upon a theoretical framework (the demographic transition process and its different phases), useful for the representation of the different transition models followed by the regional economies. In turn, the different trajectories can find an explanation in the light of the different public policies (family and human capital programmes for example) and of the political choices of local governments. The analysis reveals how the population growth has not been a hindrance to the economic development of the region when national governments have adopted combined policies to reduce fertility and improve human capital, which was the case of many countries in the 1960s and the 1970s. Nowadays, when the young cohorts becoming adults join the labour force, the question is whether or not this temporary condition represents a window of opportunity rather than a break in development.

The relationship between demography and economic development, emphasized by the analysis of population age structure, put the new challenges into focus: the creation of jobs, that is the priority of the MENA governments' agenda to reduce current unemployment rates and reabsorb new entrants in the labour market. Job creation needs to be accompanied by the implementation of appropriate measures in favour of human capital improvement and training, of market regulation, and of standards adoption. This is most urgent in the light of three factors: the rising participation rate (especially of women) in the workforce, a massive wave of young workers entering the labour market and finally intraregional migration movements from labour-abundant regions to the oil-rich countries with low-population growth (which no longer represent a mechanism for achieving demographic balance). Investing in such priorities for the Middle East countries, basically countries of young populations, is of particular concern for strengthening a sustainable development path based on a new social contract, questioned by the revolution in 2011, the so called 'Arab Spring'.

The demographic transition process

The concept of demographic transition is used in demographic and economic literature to describe the process of population change in quantity and structure undergone by all developed countries in their evolution from a pre-industrial economy to a post-industrial society. 'The classic demographic transition starts with mortality decline, followed after a time by reduced fertility, leading to an interval of first increased and then decreased population growth and, finally, population aging' (Lee 2003:170). The representation of this stylized fact, based on demographic data recorded in Western economies, expresses the rate of population growth as resulting from the values both of the birth rate (the number of childbirths per 1,000 people per year) and of the death rate (the number of deaths per 1,000 people per year). Behind the demographic transition the socio-economic development operates, reducing the death rate by the progress of health care and the birth rate by women's decreasing fertility, thus pushing countries from a first phase of high birth and death rates to a final phase in which birth and death rates stabilize to low values.

The process results from the following phases (Figure 4.1):

1   In the first phase, typical of pre-industrial economies, high birth rates balanced with high mortality rates result in low population growth. Pre-capitalistic societies present a complex mechanism of population growth (dependent on the availability of food) that determines the population level through mortality rate (repressive brake) and fertility

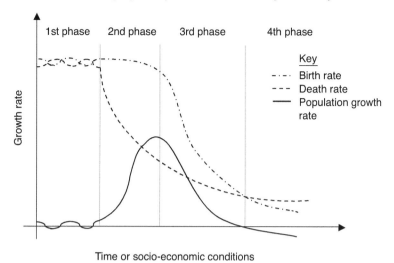

Figure 4.1 The demographic transition process

Source: Authors' elaboration in accordance with Lee 2003.

rate (preventive brake). The increase in land productivity ensures higher family income, thus facilitating rising fertility rates and population size. The surge in demand for food and the resulting increase in relative price in the cities damages the poorest people, and impacts deeply on mortality rates. Natural disasters (such as drought and famine) together with poor health conditions (diseases, epidemic and infection that in particular kill off the young population), which counterbalance the rise in fertility, help to curb the rate of population growth.

2   In the second phase, thanks to the increase in agricultural productivity and to the improvement in public health sanitation, a real 'population boom' occurs, as a significant reduction in mortality and still high birth rates, lead developing economies of the industrializing and urbanizing countries to a greater life expectancy and to an increasing young population. This is mainly due to a decline in mortality that is not evenly distributed across the population (the sharp decline occurs mostly in infant mortality) and to the existence of young cohorts that drive down the average age. In this phase, the birth rate remains high due to a certain inertia in family planning. Implementing effective family planning is not, in fact, a process that can occur overnight: the use of contraceptives, the improvement of women's education and the establishment of sensitizing programmes (causing changes in child mortality rates and increasing chances of survival for children), and the perception of amelioration of social and economic status deriving from having fewer children are all processes that need time in order to influence fertility choice of parents, and eventually encourage the shift from large to smaller families.

3   In the third phase, where industrializing economies approach maturity, changes in fertility decisions, increasing female literacy and participation in the labour market as well as the shifting value of children (moving away from being merely a presence that provides support for families or being carers for old parents and becoming people whose education is worthy of investment) lower the total fertility rates (or TFR: the average number of children per woman over her lifetime) so that the birth rate comes closer to the death rate and there is a subsequent stabilization of the population growth.

4   Most post-industrial countries experience a fourth phase characterized by the reduction of the TFR below the replacement level (2.1 children per woman) thus contributing to a decrease not only in the birth rate but also in the total population, when the birth rate value is under the death rate (which is, in turn, further reduced by an higher life span).

Although the phases of the demographic transition represent a sequence of stages experienced both by the more developed countries and the less developed ones, there are a lot of differences in the processes that these countries undergo. An obvious difference is when the transition began, but the most important differences are in the features of each stage, namely the speed of the rate of population change. The more developed countries presented a lower rate of population growth during their second phase and a lower rate of population reduction in the third, in comparison to the less developed countries. The European population, for example, grew at a rate that oscillated between 0.5 and 1.5 per cent up to 1950 and later declined by one per cent annually reaching a growth rate very near to 0 in the 1990s. However, for the less developed countries, the population growth rate started at about one per cent per year and reached peak of 2.5 per cent by the mid-1960s before rapidly falling (Lee 2003).[1] These different trends are mainly due to the fertility transition that occurred first in Europe between 1870 and 1930 (when the TFR shifted from six to seven childbirths per woman to three) and then again in the second half of the nineteenth century (when in 20 to 30 years the replacement value was reached). The first moment of this transition was run out quickly in the less developed countries during the 25 years between 1965 and 1990. So, while in the 1990s many countries of the 'Western bloc', having completed the demographic transition experienced, on average, a lower population growth and moved to low rates of natural increase,[2] many developing economies still experienced a high population growth because the birth rate remained high.

In addition to the aforementioned reasons, applied research shows that a number of other factors deriving from economic policies (such as improvements in health care, pension systems, the level of education, as well as the lengthening of time women spend in education before their entry into the labour market) boost the decline in TFR. Among these reasons, a major aspect that influences the timing of the demographic transition is investment in education, especially in rural areas or in contexts where children perform an economic (informal or familiar) activity such as land cultivation or retail activities in family-owned shops. This shift from work to education tends to keep their productivity down during childhood (thus limiting the chances of a successive baby boom). What is more, with urbanization taking place, children are likely to be less economically productive when the return on investment in education is higher, and acquired skills are better paid in the labour market. This process, in turn, gives higher returns to families who invest in children's education, rather than to families that use children in production/labour activities. As for women, when they have the opportunity to acquire some form of education or to enter the labour market (due to having fewer children and hence more time) they delay marriage, and have children later (Birdsall, Kelley and Sinding 2001). In countries where the adverse effects of overcrowding are more evident, birth rates, along with behavioural factors (including choices regarding fertility), are controlled by the state through strategies of birth control, such as the 'one-child policy' (officially planned by the Chinese government) or monetary incentives to have fewer children (a policy in India).

The demographic transition involves not only an absolute increase in population, but also a change in its structure. The prevalence of young people in the second phase leads to a higher incidence of older people in the third, which has implications for public expenditure: the increasing importance of the younger age group relative to the older one augments the need for investment in childcare and education. In addition, as the young cohort begins to enter the labour market, governments need to create jobs at exponential rates. In the third and fourth phases of the demographic transition, the aging of the population is accompanied by the need for increased pension contributions (on salaries of active workers) and additional taxes (on labour income) to maintain an unchanged standard in the provision of social services.

Population dynamics and demographic transition models in the MENA region

From the Second World War the population of the Middle East and North Africa has grown very rapidly, faster than all regions in the world, with the except of Sub-Saharan Africa. The total population of the MENA,[3] which was 100 million in the 1950s, doubled in 20 years and reached 300 million at the beginning of the 1990s. In 2010, according to the *UNCTAD Handbook of Statistics*, the population of the region had risen to around 446 million, and it is projected to climb to more than 600 million by 2050 (UNCTAD, 2009). The demographic weight of MENA countries varies considerably: countries such as Bahrain, Qatar, Oman and Kuwait have a relatively small population, but other countries like Egypt, Iran and Turkey have the largest populations, accounting alone for 54 per cent of the total regional population in 2010 (Table 4.1).

Despite these impressive figures, the MENA region's average annual population growth rate (increasing from 2.4 in the 1950s to three per cent in the 1980s) has slowed in the last decades (decreasing to an average 1.8 per cent at the end of the 1990s, and it is projected to further decrease to an annual growth rate of one per cent in 2030 (see Figure 4.2 for the average population growth rates over 50 years). At aggregate level, population change can be attributed to the rapid growth of the biggest countries in the area: the Egyptian population grew from 21.5 million in the 1950s to 44.4 million in the 1980s, reaching more than 70 million at the beginning of the twenty-first century. By 2010 the population of Egypt was around 81 million and is estimated to reach 130 million in 2050. As for the other big country of the region (that is Turkey) its population grew from 21.5 million in the 1950s to the 46 million in the 1980s and reached 64.5 million at the beginning of the twenty-first century. In 2010 the population of Turkey was 73 million.

Table 4.1 MENA population by country (in thousands)

Countries	2010	2050
Arab world		
Algeria	35,468	49,610
Bahrain	1,262	1,277
Egypt	81,121	129,533
Iraq	31,672	63,994
Jordan	6,187	10,240
Kuwait	2,737	5,240
Lebanon	4,228	5,033
Libya	6,355	9,818
Morocco	31,951	42,582
Oman	2,782	4,877
Qatar	1,759	2,316
Saudi Arabia	27,448	43,658
Syria	20,411	36,910
Tunisia	10,481	12,710
United Arab Emirates	7,512	8,253
West Bank and Gaza Strip	4,039	10,264
Yemen	24,053	–
Other MENA countries		
Iran	73,974	96,975
Israel	7,418	10,649
Turkey	72,752	97,388
Total	**453,610**	**641,427**

Source: Authors' elaboration of data from *UNCTAD Handbook of Statistics* 2012 and 2009.

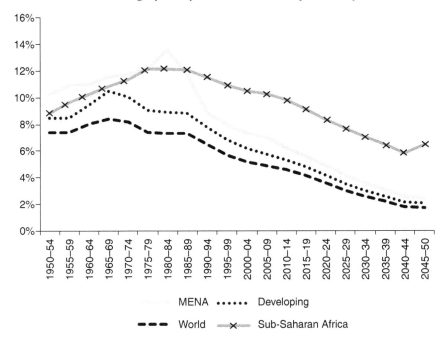

Figure 4.2 Population growth rates (1950–2050)

Source: Authors' elaboration of *UNCTAD, Handbook of Statistics*, 2009.

Note: 5 years' average; last interval 6 years' average.

From a sub-regional perspective, if we consider the economies leading to the sub-groups in which the region is conventionally divided, namely into Maghreb (Morocco, Algeria, Tunisia, and Libya), Arab Mashreq (Egypt, Jordan, West Bank and Gaza, Lebanon, Syria, and Iraq) and the Gulf Cooperation Council (GCC) (Saudi Arabia, Kuwait, Bahrain, Qatar, UAE, and Oman) we see how the Maghreb and the Mashreq groups showed similar increasing demographic rates at least until the end of the 1980s, when Maghreb countries started growing at a slower and more regular rate. The Maghreb population, at 22 million in the 1950s, reached 50 million in the early 1980s and grew to around 85 million in 2010. It is estimated to reach 100 million by 2025. But Mashreq countries, which had a population of nearly 34 million in 1950, grew to 74 million at the beginning of the 1980s, peaking at almost 150 million in 2010. It is estimated to reach 198 million in 2025. As for the GCC, the population grew from 4 million in the 1950s to 7.8 in the 1970s before it tripled in the 1980s (reaching 13 million), experiencing rates of growth from 2.3 to 4.5 per cent each year. The rate of population growth dropped to under two per cent in 15 years at the beginning of the 1990s (and the GCC accounted for 23 million people), going up to three per cent by the end of the 1990s and falling again to two per cent in the following 20 years: so in 2010 it had reached 45 million. It is estimated to grow to 50 million in 2025 (Figure 4.3).

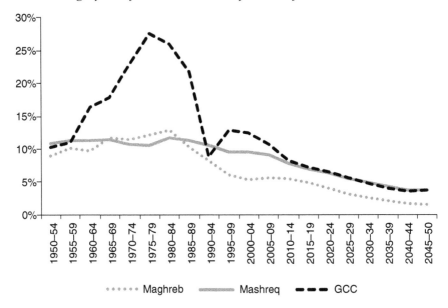

Figure 4.3 Population growth rates by regional sub-groups (1950–2050)

Source: Authors' elaboration of UNCTAD, *Handbook of Statistics*, 2009.

Note: 5 years' average; last interval 6 years' average.

From the 1950s on,[4] the demographic transition of the MENA region can be roughly described through the three following periods (Figure 4.4):

1   1950–1985: characterized by decreasing birth rates and declining death rates, mainly due to a reduction in infant mortality. High fertility rates still create pressure of rapid population growth. Baby boom occurs, leading to increase of population cohort aged 0-14 and 65 and above, which is economically inactive. This population is referred to as dependent population.

2   1985–2010: characterized by a new and more favourable situation with respect to the baby boom of the 1960s and the 1970s. The decline in fertility of the late 1980s and subsequent falling birth rates are the cause of the decreased population growth rate during the twenty-first century.

3   2010 and beyond: characterized by a reduction in population growth rates and a progressive increase in the dependent population. In the actual phase the shift from both high death and fertility rates to low rates is still accompanied by a high rate of growth of the labour force.

In addition to these considerations we notice that, at country level, demographic transition seems not to be perfectly synchronized, with some countries (Turkey, Lebanon, Tunisia, Gulf States and Israel) experiencing a sustained demographic transition (that is a persistent decline in fertility and

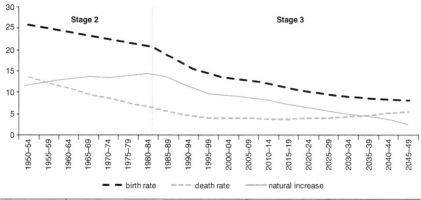

Stage	Stage 2	Stage 3
Birth rate	Falling but still high	Falling
Death rate	Falling	Low
Natural increase	Increasing	Decreasing
Reasons for changes in birth rates	Improvements in medical care, sanitation and diet. Family planning programmes, investment in human capital and women's education, increase in women's participation to labour market. Late marriage. Policy of birth control (population policy).	
Reasons for changes in death rates	Improvements in medical care, sanitation, water supply and health status. Reliable food supply and implementation of measures to counteract famine and disease. Health policy implementation.	

Figure 4.4 Main phases of demographic transition in MENA

Source: Authors' elaboration on *UNCTAD, Handbook of Statistics*, 2009.

Note: 5 years' average; last interval 6 years' average.

mortality) and others (Egypt, Iran, Morocco and Yemen) undergoing a delayed demographic transition (a later decline in fertility and mortality rates) (Figure 4.5).

According to Taboutin and Schoumaker (Taboutin and Schoumaker 2005: 521) five demographic transition models can be identified in the MENA region, using different criteria for taxonomy: Palestine and Yemen, with a very high population growth rate and very rapid growth, represent the 'traditional model' (early marriage and high fertility); Egypt and Iraq, with still high birth rates and population growth above two per cent, belong to 'early but slow and hesitant model'; Morocco, Algeria, Libya, Oman and Jordan represent a 'classical model' of on-going transition (progressive and irreversible decline in birth rates) with steadily declining birth rates in the past two decades, and population growth rates of about two per cent; Iran represents a 'late and very rapid model' with impressive fertility decline in the 1990s and the slowest growth in the region, alongside Lebanon (1.3 per cent each year). The Gulf States (Bahrain, UAE, Kuwait and Qatar) and other countries to a different extent (Turkey, Tunisia, Lebanon and Israel) represent the 'very advanced model' with very low birth rates and annual population growth rates above one per cent.

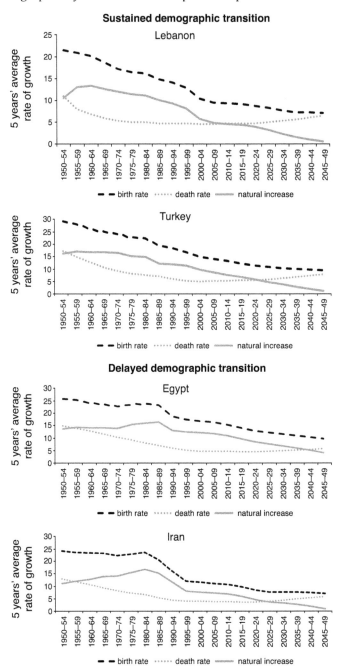

Figure 4.5 Demographic transition in selected MENA countries

Source: Authors' elaboration of UNCTAD, *Handbook of Statistics*, 2009.

Note: 5 years' average; last interval 6 years' average.

The case of Israel deserves further consideration, as its demography is characterized by imbalanced growth between the ethnic/religious groups, with strong implications for the political system and representation. The rate of population growth, at 1.6 per cent in the 2006 (see Figure 4.6 for the demographic dynamics of Israel in the period under consideration), is mainly due to the natural increase of the Arab population, but is also partly due to migration. This is in spite of the introduction of immigration and citizenship laws that were designed to encourage the immigration of Jews and their families, and the more recent debate on the adoption of immigration policies capable to boost export industry by bringing quality human capital to Israel. Since the establishment of the state of Israel more than three million people have immigrated and about one third have emigrated. Those who remain are the young and more educated people and they are also the taxpayers and the workforce.

The situation is such that

> in the future we are likely to encounter in Israel a relatively weak population, composed of a group of relatively young Jews with an affinity for religion, with many children and poor, groups of adults, and also elderly people in need of support and an Arab population with many children.
>
> (Bystrof and Soffer 2008: 55)

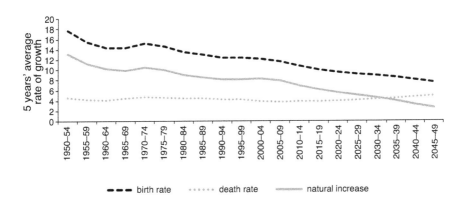

Figure 4.6 Demographic transition of Israel

Source: Authors' elaboration of *UNCTAD, Handbook of Statistics*, 2009.

Note: 5 years' average; last interval 6 years' average.

Did demographic policies matter?

The main reasons for the different demographic transition models can be attributed, together with territorial (percentage of urban vs. rural population) and cultural factors, to peculiar institutional arrangements and to the political choices of local governments, that is, to a series of key policies implemented by the regional states that influenced the ability of countries to exploit the demographic dividend. Among such policies can be reviewed:

1   Health policies: improvements in medical care and sanitation, programmes to prevent epidemics and encourage the use of antibiotics, educational programmes directed to the general public that attempt to safeguard the health care of the community, ad hoc programs for children and women health.

2   Family programmes: aiming to reduce fertility, mainly implemented through education initiatives that target women and mothers. The main scope has been to sensitize women to methods of birth control (use of contraceptives) and childbearing, and to encourage new forms of behaviour that will eventually lead to a new perception of family (shift to a desired size of family and wanted children).

3   Human capital programmes: investment in education and better schooling, policies aimed at increasing the participation rate of women in education and reducing abandonment of education at second level, fostering continued education and creating a better educated labour force.

Under the pressure of the rapid population growth of the 1960s and the 1970s and due to the costs of the high-dependency, representing a burden on the state, MENA governments adopted policies to reduce fertility. The direct effect of the implementation of such health policies was the decline in mortality, the slowdown of fertility rate and the change in population structure (size and age distribution). The lower fertility rate improved the health of both children and mothers, resulting in a virtuous cycle when having fewer children gave women more opportunities, increased their training and labour market participation. In trying to investigate the main forces behind population change, demographers and economists have, in fact, underlined how there is a complex interaction between human capital improvement and fertility: lower fertility increases spending for children's education and eventually encourages the shift from large to nuclear families. When women start families later and have fewer children they are more likely to invest more in their own education and in entering the labour market. Increased investment in human capital and in women's education in turn can be instrumental in changing fertility decisions and behaviour and in lowering population growth (Schultz 1994, Becker 1960). The delay in the time of marriage and of first births on one hand, increases the awareness of the risks of having children too early and, on the other hand, lowers mortality of children through better knowledge of childbearing. Finally, decreasing child mortality, the adoption of contraceptives and improvements in wealth may be instrumental in the shift from large to nuclear/smaller families.

Policy change, such as the increase in compulsory schooling is, in this case, helpful in the improvement of women's participation in the educational system and in the reduction of the age of marriage and of first births. It is relevant to note, however, how complex the link between education and demographic change is, as the only direct effect of increasing women's education remains in delaying the time of marriage and the entrance into reproductive years, and hence in reducing fertility rates. In Turkey, for instance, we have seen how schooling and marriage are incompatible, and the effect that increased schooling had on marriage and fertility when compulsory schooling is completed (Dayıoğlu, Kırdar and Koç 2009). At the beginning of the period 1997-1998 the age for compulsory schooling was raised in Turkey from five to eight years, so that children who were 11 years old and younger in 1997 were expected to remain in school for an additional three years. As a result of the policy, at age 17, three years after the end of compulsory schooling, the predicted proportion of married women went down from 15 to 10 per cent, and the proportion of women who gave birth decreased from 4.2 to 3.5 per cent. In 2006, the implementation of a new education policy extended high school education in Turkey from three to four years. The debate on compulsory schooling' policies considered the possible effects of such measures on delayed marriage, on reduced fertility and on improved health outcomes of children and mothers. In particular, the extension of compulsory schooling until age 18 could make a large difference in marriage and in early fertility patterns, suggesting, in the Turkish case, how marriage and early fertility would drop significantly from ages 15 to 18.

In Tunisia, however, reduction in fertility was mainly due to the evolution of the mean age of marriage (19.5 years in 1956, 22.6 in 1997, 24.2 in 1984 and 24.5 in 1995), which took place both in rural and in urban areas. The Family Planning Programme of Tunisia that was adopted in the 1960s, involving public services, non-government organizations (NGOs) and religious authorities, is often cited as a successful case. Although the political drive to control fertility started at independence, it was only with this national family planning programme that the country achieved a general knowledge of contraception: the contraceptive prevalence rate rose from around 30 per cent in 1978 to more than 60 per cent in the 1990s.

On the other hand, in countries like Egypt (but also Morocco and Yemen), the delayed demographic transition was mainly due to the persistence of practices related to culture and tradition (such as early marriage, a high rate of teenage childbearing and short intervals between births) which are more diffused in rural areas. What is more, family planning and demographic policies were implemented quite late: in fact, concern about the high population growth was first expressed by the Egyptian government in the early 1950s, but it was ten years before a national family planning programme was established to reduce fertility. It wasn't until the 1980s the National Population Council was founded to coordinate family planning and policies aimed at increasing women's participation in education and the labour market and to foster cooperation with civil societies' association in the programme. Despite the delay, such initiatives yielded some positive results: contraceptive use in Egypt doubled in 15 years, from 24 per cent in 1980 to 48 per cent in 1995 and family planning methods and sources became universal among women (UNECA 2001).

In this discussion, Iran deserves attention as it throws doubt on a direct relationship between changes in population policy and fertility behaviour. In the decade following 1979 Iran witnessed a steep surge in population growth, but there was a noticeable reversal of this trend in the 1990s, mainly due to the significant changes that occurred in the fertility behaviour of Iranian women. It is true that a deceleration of the growth momentum in the 1980s is common to almost all MENA countries (excepting Israel and UAE) and even to countries with the highest growth rates (GCC, Syria, Jordan and Libya), but Iran stands out for it is characterized, contrary to the regional and international experience, by a counter-cyclical fertility surge: Iran experienced a baby boom during a period of serious economic contraction and this occurred mostly during (not after) a period of revolution.[5] This evidence seems to suggest that neither war nor family planning policies provide adequate explanations for the genesis of the baby boom and bust in Iran, as the slowdown was in force before vigorous family planning programmes were reintroduced in the late 1980s and early 1990s. This suggests that it was Iran's demographic structure that shaped the transition, despite the ideological, social and institutional changes that occurred at the time of the revolution (Hakimian 2001: 8).

In addition to the main forces that influence the demographic patterns of these economies (the 'structural components' such as age and gender composition, and the 'behavioural components' such as marital status and fertility decisions), the territorial conditions, such as the presence of a diffused rural area (this is the case of Egypt, Morocco and Yemen), have in some cases slowed down the demographic transition process of disadvantaged areas. Territorial conditions, in fact, may impact human capital accumulation by affecting adult literacy rates (and women's participation rates), which tend to be lower in areas distant from the city where the access to education is more difficult.

Since the mid-1970s all Arab countries have experienced delays in marriage, a larger percentage of nuclear families and an increased number of unmarried men and women. According to the UN definition, marriage patterns can be classified in three main categories (Rashad and Osman 2001: 20):

1   the 'Western European' pattern (brought over in North America and Oceania), based on late marriage and high permanent celibacy;

2   the 'non-European countries' pattern of early and universal marriage, typical of the developing countries;
3   the 'eastern European' pattern, with a later marriage timing than the developing countries and high marriage prevalence.

In recent decades important changes have occurred in characteristics of marriage in Arab countries, which still remains a legal and social turning point for the status attainment: many countries have abandoned universal marriage for the Western European pattern. Egypt, Oman and Yemen are still in a stage of early and universal marriage, countries such as Tunisia, Morocco, Syria and Saudi Arabia are at an intermediate stage of late and universal marriage, while countries such as Lebanon and Jordan have moved to a late and non-universal pattern. Although the forces that influence changes in marriage patterns are not uniform in all countries (as in deeply based in culture and social norms), the role of education in delaying marriage is very clear. In countries such as Algeria and Yemen, for instance, the chances of an uneducated woman being married young (age 20-24) are around three times the chances of an educated woman; in other countries, such as Egypt, delayed marriage is notable but only after secondary education is achieved (Dayıoğlu, Kırdar and Koç 2009).

Dependency ratio, demographic gift, and development in the MENA region

Economic studies on population and demographic change have traditionally focused on population growth, often neglecting a critical dimension of change: the evolution in the age structure of population (Bloom, Canning and Sevilla 2002). As the population can be grouped in the 'working force' (those aged 15-65) and in the 'dependent population' (the young of 0-14 and the elderly of 65 and over), a change in the balance between the two groups may have important economic and social implications. When the labour force increases and the dependency ratio (defined as the proportion of the dependent population on the productive population) declines, the economy undergoes a unique opportunity: savings and labour increase, and more resources are freed for investments. At the same time, the costs of pensions, sanitation and education (aimed both at the elderly dependent population and at the young independent population) decrease (in percentage of the GDP) and more resources can be driven to productive sectors. Thus policies that take advantage of this opportunity can be implemented, since in developing countries the provision of services such as sanitation and education is mostly provided by the public sector and mainly financed through government expenditure. Privatization of the provision of such services is still scarce and alternatives to public financing (i.e. private insurance systems) is a small market. This window of opportunity (referred to in the literature as 'demographic gift': a chance occurring when the young cohort becomes adult and joins the labour force) thus calls for the capacity of a country to exploit this favourable and temporary condition.

The turning of the demographic gift in economic growth depends on many conditions (Nassar 2007):

1   The adjustment of the social welfare system, that is, the ability of local governments to implement measures to cope with an aging population and with low dependency ratios and to reallocate the public expenditure towards health, social protection and housing in order to improve the quality of life (especially of the young) and to empower women and their participation in society.
2   The implementation of labour market policies, in order to support employment and the lifetime education of the labour force. Among these, the investments in the economic sectors more able to absorb the entrance of the youth into the labour market and in the more productive sectors (such as the private sector and the newly emerging ones, based on technology and on high skill) can be listed. Initiatives to promote labour market flexibility through developing training programmes, also need to be taken into account.

The increased supply of labour, resulting from the demographic dividend, calls for policies aimed at favouring economic sectors' absorptive capacity, or at improving the productive employment of workers by promoting managerial and administrative skills. Migration policies that favour intra- and international mobility of labour (when investments are not sufficient to allocate the growing number of working-age people) are also of central importance, as migration may act as a balancing mechanism between supply and demand of labour across national borders (Shakoori 2005). The MENA region is experiencing this unique demographic opportunity, based on the decreased dependency ratio and the increase of the young and active population group. This young cohort represents a new wave of workers entering the labour market (and so raising pressure on jobs) and also human capital endowments of different types (and skilled too) for economies. But this particular composition of the population (that will be pointed out by using 'population pyramids') is not perennial, hence why it constitutes an opportunity.

Population pyramids, highlighting the composition of a country's population according to sex and age rising from 0 to 100 for both males and females, measure age groups on the vertical axes (by 5 year age intervals) and the total number (or percentage) of people being members of each cohort is measured on the horizontal axis. Figure 4.7 gives three pictures of the age structure of the Middle East and North Africa region in three different moments, starting in 1950. In this year the MENA region had a population of around 100 million, and this population was very youthful. The concave side of the distribution shows an expanding phase of population: in fact, the wide base indicates high birth rates, which are highlighted by the

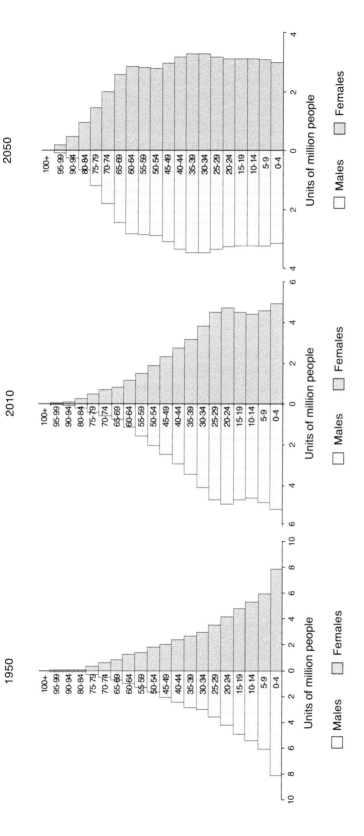

Figure 4.7 MENA population by age and sex (%)

Source: Authors' elaboration of UNCTAD, *Handbook of Statistics*, 2009.

large bars of the youngest age groups; the narrow top indicates a high death rate. We can see that children under 15 years old constituted almost 50 per cent of the total population, so that the region had to support a very high youth dependency ratio.[6] Such distribution, in favour of young groups, has particular implication on future population growth; such as youths that reach adulthood will contribute to a successive baby boom. In 2010 the regional population, at more than 400 million, is still very young, but the age composition is more biased towards the labour force population, leading to a decline in the dependency ratio. The dependent young population (0-14) accounts for about 20 per cent of the total population, which is biased in favour of the working force group. The youth labour force alone (15-39) represents more than 30 per cent of the total population. The 2050 distribution shows a stationary population pyramid, since the base of the pyramid is as wide as the reproductive age groups, indicating an almost stable population. Such a shape, similar to that of countries with a high standard of living, shows low birth rates and an increase in the quality of life and in longevity, thus it is mainly an outcome of the impact of structural and behavioural factors (successful family planning, improvement in medical care and nutrition and change in attitude towards fertility).

An historical analysis of the demographic pattern of the MENA region in terms of age composition of its population reveals how the change that occurred in the past has broken down the traditional demographic balance (caused by high fertility rates, coupled with high mortality rates) leading to an imbalance in the age structure of population. Recently, as Figure 4.8 shows, Arab countries have experienced a considerable increase in the

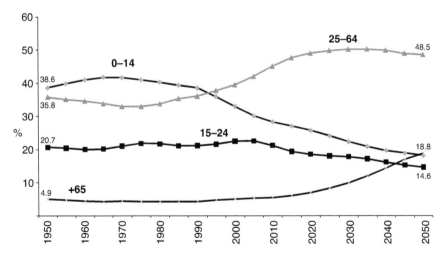

Figure 4.8 Population age structure in Arab countries (1950–2050)

Source: Authors' elaboration of UN, *World Population Prospects*, 2010.

number of people in the working age groups (25-64) passing from the 35.8 per cent of the 1980s to 45.1 per cent in 2010 (UN 2011). The working age population is projected to reach almost half of the total population (48.5 per cent) by 2050. However, the slow decline in the transition group from childhood to adulthood (15-24), reaching the value of 21.1 in 2010, has been accompanied, since the mid-1990s, by a rapid decrease in the dependent population. In fact, the dependent young population (0-14) decreased from the 38.6 per cent in 1980 to reach 28.3 per cent in 2010, and it is projected to reach 18.8 per cent of the total population in 2050; the elderly group (above 65), which almost remained stable till the 1990s, has slightly increased (5.5 per cent in 2010) and will reach 20 per cent of the total population in 2050.

Thus the window of opportunity for Arab countries, which in the last few decades has opened up thanks to the overall decline in the dependency ratio, eventually turning the demographic change into social and economic development, calls the national governments to focus their interest on the working age group (Shakoori 2005), as this cluster has a central implication for the future development of the Arab region for several reasons:

- it sustains the population momentum[7] as it is a group in the reproductive age;
- it creates imbalances between demand and supply in the labour market, as it is an economically active group which feeds the market with supply of new entrants;
- it could contribute to population growth and further demand for higher education, when family choice of the working group is towards early marriage and high fertility.

The economic challenge of a growing young population

In the literature on the debate about the effects of the demographic transition on economic growth, three approaches are ascribed:

1. The 'pessimistic' view: in this approach, based on Malthus' writings (Malthus 1798), in the presence of slow technological progress and fixed resources for growing food, population growth results in relatively scarce resources and a diet below subsistence level. The rapid growth of the population also has a negative impact on personal wealth and living standards: as more people demand capital goods (such as housing and infrastructure) governments move investments towards the supply of such goods, rather than to more productive sectors.

2. The 'optimistic' view: in the medium-long term, population growth, in presence of technological progress, can fuel economic development (Kuznets 1967 and Simon 1981). In agriculture, for instance, new techniques and the possibility to cultivate new lands present a solution

to the problem of scarce resources, simultaneously enabling the exploitation of new sources of energy. Human capital and capital accumulation that accompanies the increasing population can boost demand with multiplier effects on economic growth and welfare.

3 The 'neutralist' view: these theories, born in the 1980s (Bloom and Freeman 1986) and mainly based on the results provided by empirical studies, highlight an ambiguous or absent correlation between population and economic growth. Such results do not validate the direct effects of rising population on countries' saving, per capita GDP and scarcity of natural resources.

These approaches put little emphasis on two key variables that greatly influence the impact population growth has on economic development, which are of central relevance for the Arab region: one is the age structure of population, the other is the institutional setting and the political measures implemented by national governments to face the changing composition of the population and the demographic dividend. The vast economic literature on these issues focuses on many variables linked to the demographic growth of the Middle East and North African countries: the increasing demand for housing (due to the rapid urbanization in the 1970s and the rising number of young adults in the labour force), the demand for migration, the scarcity of water and resources and the saving-consumption nexus.

Not neglecting the urgency of such issues, in this concluding section the implication that the on-going demographic transition has on the labour market and on the government measures in support of the changes in motion will be examined, as they are central for the future generation who are the most important to the population: the young workforce.

In the early 1970s the rapid demographic surge of the population was not perceived as a bearer of problems to economic growth because of disequilibria in labour markets, as it was accompanied by the rapid expansion of the oil countries, which followed the boost of the oil prices. The GCC countries, undergoing an intense phase of reconstruction, also started to import foreign labour from other neighbouring countries of the MENA region, especially from labour-abundant economies such as Egypt, Jordan, Lebanon, Syria and Yemen: intraregional migration worked as a compensation mechanism for the rapid expansion of the population. However, external resource imbalances between countries that were oil-rich and those countries that had no oil was in part replaced by the huge inflows of remittances, with the volume of worker remittances strictly depending on oil prices. In fact, for the MENA region it has been estimated that any increase of revenue by the Organization of Petroleum Exporting Countries (OPEC) cartel equal to one billion dollars was accompanied by an increase in remittances in the region of 39 million dollars (Shihata and Sherbiny 1985).

In the mid-1980, everything changed suddenly when the oil bust stopped the rapid growth of the regional economy. Even the political changes of the countries where people migrated from or of their end destination had an effect on migration and on the inflow of remittances: the Iran-Iraqi war stimulated demand for foreign labour coming from Egypt and Jordan to fill the vacancies left by Iraqis who were drafted into the army, resulting in an increase in the volume of remittances. However, the conflicts in the Gulf that followed the Iraqi invasion of Kuwait resulted in the exodus of labour from the Arab Gulf and in a significant decline in remittances. From the 1980s different economies of the Middle East and North Africa (especially the Maghreb and Egypt) have implemented structural reforms to support private investment and growth in the export sector, also in the hopes of reducing the dependency from external sources of financing (i.e. remittances). And yet, the fact that the decentralization process was unable to distribute decision-making power to the private sector serves as an example of the limitations of this top-down approach to local development. Industrialization programmes had, in fact, limited spill-over effects on the economy as a whole, as programmes were mainly directed by the public rather than by the private and were linked to nationalist objectives rather than financial ones. The rising level of unemployment of the 1980s, together with the decreasing opportunities for emigration, raised concerns for economists for the rapid demographic growth of the MENA countries.

One of the main apprehensions in coping with this problem is related to the rise of unemployment and the capability of MENA countries to absorb new entrants into their labour market: by 2000, economies had to absorb 30 million entrants into the labour market and by 2025 they will have to absorb another 160 million (Williamson and Yousef 2002). In fact, the population dividend of the Arab region has led to a huge increase in the Arab working-age population, and to the rise in participation rates. Changes in the population structure and in fertility decisions have also increased the number of women entering the labour market, providing the region with the major challenge of creating jobs. Despite the good results in employment creation in the past decade, unemployment rates are still high across the region: the last available real data from the International Labour Organization indicates adult unemployment rates[8] of 11.56 per cent for Turkey, around 10 per cent in Tunisia, 8.6 in Jordan, 7.2 in Morocco and 4.3 in Egypt (Table 4.2). For the young generation the situation is much worse: youth unemployment rates for both sexes range from 14.7 per cent in Israel to 30.7 per cent in Tunisia, 27 per cent in Jordan and around 25 and 23 per cent for Egypt and Iran respectively. Gender differentials are common: in countries such as Egypt, Jordan and Syria, female unemployment rates are twice as high as male unemployment rates. Even in Kuwait and the UAE, who have the lowest values in adult unemployment, youth unemployment rates are much higher.

In the Arab countries, in order to reduce current unemployment rates and reabsorb new entrants in the labour market, employment levels should grow faster than the working age population. If we also consider the rising participation rate, the projections for the period 2000–2015 suggest that

Table 4.2 Unemployment rates for selected MENA countries

Countries	Years (last available)	Total adult unemployment rate (%)	Youth Unemployment rate (%)		
			Total	Male	Female
Egypt	2007	4.30	24.80	17.16	47.89
Iran	2008	7.11	23.01	20.21	33.95
Israel	2009	6.63	14.72	15.67	13.88
Jordan	2009	8.59	26.98	22.60	45.89
Kuwait	2005	0.73	11.32	11.83	10.01
Lebanon	2007	6.07	22.12	22.26	21.54
Morocco	2009	7.28	21.88	22.77	19.37
Saudi Arabia	2008	2.65	28.24	23.64	45.81
Syria	2007	4.85	19.09	13.11	49.07
Tunisia	2005	10.22	30.68	31.35	29.32
Turkey	2009	11.56	25.28	25.40	25.05
United Arab E.	2008	2.76	12.10	7.88	21.77

Source: Authors' elaboration of ILO, *Key Indicators of the Labour Market*, 2009.

employment, in selected Arab countries, has to rise by more than four per cent annually. Thus, Algeria requires the strongest acceleration (five per cent) and the target for Egypt, Morocco and Tunisia is lower (3.6).

Employment growth requirements are much higher in the MENA region than other regions that experience fast job creation, such as East Asia, the Caribbean and Latin America (Dhonte, Bhattacharya and Yousef 2000).

Together with the need for the creation of new employment opportunities, the regional population structure influences the provision of basic services (health, education, food, infrastructures, housing). At present, given the prevalence of the young age group and, among them, of new entrants into the labour force, the system of social protection and public expenditure should be more channelled towards policies in favour of the younger and more vulnerable groups (i.e. provision of education and health services) while at the same time driving and reallocating the resources invested in the supply of services to the older population (i.e. pension schemes and insurance system). In the 1980s, when the region entered a period of rapid growth, mainly based on the increase in the price of oil in 1972, the dominant role of the state was followed by the implementation of formal social protection schemes and public expenditure (in health, education and pension schemes) together with food subsidies that represented consistent and stable measures to reduce people's vulnerability (Tzannagos 2000). With the economic reversal of the 1990s the formal social protection system became more unstable; less money was devoted to the provision of basic services and, with the increase of risk and vulnerability for the population, informal networks and parental ties strengthened their role in the alternative welfare system. In the case of education, for instance, it is worth acknowledging how most MENA countries allocated a large share of government budget to education. When the last available data (2008) is compared with the data from the mid-1980s, it shows how public expenditure on education has generally decreased, as is also the case for Egypt, Israel, Qatar, Saudi Arabia and Syria. But in other countries such as Iran, Tunisia and Turkey, the same comparison reveals an increase in the public expenditure for the provision of education (Table 4.3). Despite the fact that the present composition of the regional population is in favour of the younger people, the available data shows an average relative stability in public investment in education in the last decade. The almost-stable expenditure has not been followed by economic returns because of the inefficient use of the invested resources, the low participation of the private sector in the provisions of public services, and because of legal and regulatory complexities. While MENA governments' public expenditure has become unsustainable, the reliance on out of pocket spending is very low.

In the mid-1970s demographic growth was channelled by effective policies, leading to the deceleration of the growth momentum of the 1980s in almost all MENA countries. Such policies were more effective when local governments achieved a slowing growth rate of the population through a combination of direct measures (family programmes and health policies) and indirect measures (investment in human capital). In the expanding phase of the late 1990s, the decline in mortality and the slowdown of fertility led to the change in population structure not being managed through the implementation of new strategies (i.e. training measures, sets of new standards in the labour market) and thus questioning the sustainability of development strategies in the presence of an age distribution in favour of the young active groups.

Table 4.3 Public expenditure on education as a percentage of total government expenditure

Countries	1975	1980	1985	2000	2005	2006	2007	2008
Egypt	5.01	4.25	5.62	–	4.79	4.00	3.68	3.76
Iran	3.13	–	3.77	4.38	4.72	5.06	5.49	4.79
Israel	7.12	8.77	9.13	6.55	6.16	6.17	6.36	–
Lebanon	–	–	–	2.00	2.64	2.77	2.59	2.05
Morocco	5.21	5.89	5.94	5.76	5.87	5.50	–	5.71
Oman	1.30	1.85	3.57	3.14	3.54	4.02	–	–
Qatar	1.15	2.53	4.12	–	3.28	–	–	–
Saudi Arabia	2.30	4.33	7.13	5.94	5.65	6.23	6.42	5.71
Syria	3.95	4.58	6.08	–	–	5.33	4.85	–
Tunisia	5.03	5.24	5.54	6.85	7.19	7.15	7.19	–
Turkey	–	–	1.79	2.59	–	2.86	–	–
United Arab E.	0.88	1.33	1.75	1.98	1.32	1.14	0.95	0.90

Source: Authors' elaboration of UN (2012) *UNESCO Institute for Statistics Data centre.*

The present situation, as recently highlighted by the 'Arab Spring' revolution that spread from Tunisia, Morocco, Egypt and Algeria to the Maghreb and the GCC countries (i.e. Bahrain, Yemen and Syria), is, in fact, an expression of the economic and political discontent of the Arab population, and of the young in particular, that put into question the sustainability of the development strategies adopted by the regional economy and the solidity of the social contract. As we have seen, policies implemented by the MENA countries to sustain growth in the face of the recent demographic dynamics, have been mainly based on the involvement of the public sector. However, a growing informal social safety net has emerged in the form of NGOs and civil society's organizations, which are more and more involved in the socio-political and economic life of the Middle East countries and in the provision of social services. The state managed the supply of social services to citizens for 50 years, from the end of the Second World War until the 1990s: since then, driving forces such as changing economic conditions and in particular the changing demography of the region, have faced the existent social contract calling for the ability of institutions to adapt to the changing needs of the population. In particular, the dissatisfaction of young people makes evident that state policies are unable to find a solution to the wastefulness of human capital, due to the fact that a large percentage of unemployed persons have second and tertiary education: according to the *World Development Indicators* of the World Bank, unemployment levels peaked before 2008 being between 50 and 75 per cent in GCC countries and in Iran and Israel, while in Maghreb this fluctuated between 33 per cent in Algeria and 50 per cent in Tunisia; only Turkey and Syria were around 40 per cent.

5 The performance of MENA economies between internal conditions and external shocks

That the MENA economic performance during the post-colonial period presents lights and shadows is a recurring assessment in the literature. In fact, although some scholars emphasize that, at the beginning of the twenty-first century, the international comparison among the world's developing areas places the region in an acceptable position between East Asia and Sub-Saharan Africa (together with South Asia and Latin America – see Noland and Pack 2007: 1), some others point out that ultimately the region failed in narrowing the income gap with industrial countries (Nunnenkamp 2004: 2). In addition, while most of the research recognizes that during the first two decades of the period MENA economies showed high rates of growth (Yousef 2004: 91), an increasing number argue that they presented 'a weak economic performance over the past 20 years, despite their favourable geo-strategic location and a high density of national and international structural adjustment efforts' (Brach 2009: 1). Researchers have provided a long list of explanations for this fluctuating performance. It has also been stressed that economic outcomes have been affected by demographic problems, globalization challenges and political instability (Noland and Pack 2007); the role of exogenous shocks and institutional deficiencies (Nunnenkamp 2004), of technological gaps and of privatization and trade liberalization failures (Brach 2009) have been emphasized; the inadequate political systems, wars and conflicts (Yousef 2004) and 'bad economic policies, such as excessive government interventions, large public sectors, restrictive trade policies, inefficient mass subsidies, and badly managed fiscal policies' have also been referred to (Esfahani 2009: 161).

Although the deepening of such explanatory items gives an understanding of the outcomes of regional economies during the last half century, further investigation is needed for a more accurate appraisal of development process carried out. In fact, ensuing the methodological approach presented in previous chapters, the performance of MENA countries must be analysed in the light of several factors: the regional endowment of physical and natural resources (geographic position and raw materials), the international relations environment in which the development process took place, the stock of capitals (physical, human, and social ones), institutional and technological improvements and state support to the path towards capitalism. Following this approach it will thus be possible to identify the regional 'exceptionalism'[1] and to properly recognize the reasons why the reverse was triggered in MENA economic performance at the beginning of the 1980s, the main determinants of the failed recovery during the following two decades and the regional economies that performed better. In addition, as the economic performance of a lower income country cannot be bound only to the achievement of particular values for some macro and microeconomic variables but it must cope with specific development issues (poverty, inequality and welfare), thus the outcome of MENA economies in respect to these challenges needs to be treated too. All these issues will be developed in two chapters: in this chapter the environmental issues and economic trends will be deepened, and in Chapter 6 on economic policies, the 'social contract' and the welfare structure of MENA countries will be analysed.

The geographic and political environment of MENA development presents a relevant complexity, not only because the local endowment of natural resources, like oil, affected both regional economies and the world ones, but also, because this peculiarity shaped political stability of the countries in the area and international relations. Thus oil shocks, conflicts and authoritarian regimes became intertwined, creating an unfavourable atmosphere for the development or one that heavily prevented it. Given that the MENA countries comprise a set of 20 economies different by dimensions and potentialities (although homogeneous in respect to economic history and institutions), the impact of environmental and demographic variables (both creating shocks) has been dissimilar. So, the clustering of regional states according to both parameters (population and oil production) is needed to highlight the economic cycles, their determinants and the structural evolution of the economies.

MENA development and the endowment of geographic and natural resources: The role of oil

In recent decades, geographers and economists reverted to analysis of the relationship between geographic environment and economic growth, trying to expand some analytical instruments of the traditional spatial economy like the agglomeration principle, transport cost, industrial location, urbanization, city expansion, regional convergence (Henderson, Shalizi and Venables 2001) or seeking inspiration from comparative econometric studies of world geographic regions (Gallup, Sachs and Mellinger 1999). The main results of these works, confirming some intuitions by Adam Smith, show that a country endowed with coastal regions or rivers with densely populated towns can implement trade and approach development thanks to low transport costs, large markets and technological improvements induced by previous conditions. But some other studies, although acknowledging that the long-term economic development of world zones is positively affected by these elements, and negatively by particular geographic constraints (like landlocked territories or diseases – Sachs and Warner 1997), maintain that institutions are 'the fundamental cause of long-run growth' (Acemoglu, Johnson and Robinson 2005).

As to the development process of MENA countries, the geographic environment of the region presents disadvantages and opportunities, well managed by the people living in its territory in the past when it produced a long lasting prosperity for centuries. In fact, the coexistence of fertile planes and aquatic spaces (the Mediterranean, the Black and Red seas, the Persian Gulf, the Atlantic and Indian Oceans, rivers like the Nile, the Euphrates and the Tigris), side by side with arid deserts and sometimes with unfavourable climate, pushed forward both the expansion of long-distance trade and of commercial and manufacturing towns, and the implementation of some socio-religious principles (poverty alleviation and wealth redistribution for example), all elements that enabled economic upgrading (Michalopoulos, Naghavi and Prarolo 2010). Yet, in relation to the current transition towards capitalism, scholars ask themselves if geography still matters, and, if this is the case, what is its role in development?

This topic was discussed, before the aforementioned approaches and even before the Smith's intuitions, by Ibn Khaldûn in his work *Al Muqaddimah*, an introduction to social history that appeared in 1377. This Tunisian scholar, a medieval forerunner to some modern economists (Weiss 1995), explains why certain countries are more developed than others by making reference both to geographic factors and institutional settings. Ibn Khaldûn first 'insists on the influence of the climate on the development of civilization'. He reaches the conclusion that temperate zones offers better conditions than areas with 'extreme conditions' for the development of techniques and thus of production. A second element that he believes to support development is 'an institutionalist flavour' (Parent and Zouache 2008: 2). Despite these antecedents, the literature on growth determinants in the region is rather poor, so that the impact of geographic features on the MENA development will be appraised using available (and more general) studies on the issue. From this point of view, the region appears to have several advantageous geographic features (e.g. coasts, rivers, populous towns and so on) counterweighing the detrimental features. However, as they are barely connected by transport networks, positive developmental externalities cannot be exploited.

Natural resources can also be considered geographic site endowment whose exploitation can implement and support the development process, as both the experience of 'first comers' and the 'latecomers' shows. Nevertheless, the recent literature has mainly pointed out the risks for the growth of the economy arising from an intensive use of natural resources (Thorvaldur and Zoega 2001). A long list of economic distortions has been put in evidence in cross-country analysis. First of all, the crowding-out of other kinds of capitals, second the reduction of foreign direct investments due to the exchange rate volatility (caused by the price fluctuations of that resource). In particular, when legality is lacking and property rights are vague, entrepreneurs engaged in natural resource industries can become rent seeking, fostering corruption (damaging the social capital) and distorting the allocation of investment (such as those devoted to the education) in favour of their activity, thus influencing public expenditure for human capital creation. They can also inhibit the formation of a financial market (and thus discourage saving), if their rents are a high percentage of the GDP. All these effects can slow the economic growth, not changing the fact that natural resources trigger the process.

As to the relation between natural resources and development, MENA economies confirm this stylized, virtuous fact,[2] having enjoyed the economic benefits of the oil industry both directly (by the revenue from the exports) and indirectly (by the remittances that migrant workers sent to their non-oil MENA origin countries). The region counted on its main subsoil product (oil) greatly, both because deposits of such energy resources are spread across its territory (14 of the 20 states included in it are oil producers)[3] and because their exploits were thought to strengthen the area both economically and politically, as the structure of oil industry grants the economic and political leverage to whoever is controlling the choke point. The upstream phases of this production are the research for oil fields (exploration) and the equipment of well drilling (development), and the downstream stages are the arrangement of pipelines, railroads and tankers to move the crude oil (transportation) towards the plants transforming it (refining) into products like gasoline and fuel (marketing). Thus the strategic actor of this industry is the one who owns the right to extract the oil. But it was the willpower of the oil-MENA countries to grab this right and use it best as they could that triggered a conflicting economic reshuffle and destabilized political rearrangement of the international relations in the area. To understand the 'political economy of oil' in Middle East and North Africa a short description of the evolution of oil industry control in the region is necessary.

Up to 1950s, the oil industry in Middle East presented a general structure that was equally spread all over the region. From the beginning of the century, all the states where oil fields were discovered granted European operating companies (joint ventures between the largest British oil producers like the Royal Dutch Shell or the Anglo-Persian Oil Company-BP and the most important US ones) concessions to extract the oil in return for royalties. These concessions, sponsored by the European powers in charge of Protectorates or of Mandates in the region, were given only to one company (generally an English one) in each country, presented a fixed structure for the partnership (the 50 per cent of the joint venture shares was owned by the contracting company and the remaining by the other partners in equal parts) and acknowledged the veto power for each company to explore or open new drilling wells in the old Ottoman Empire. As a consequence of this 'one company-one country' pattern of concessions it was not only the case that the state owner of oil fields could not determine the national production, but also that the oil supply was decided by a set of companies ('the seven sisters'[4]) in a regime of non-competition.

This structure of the oil industry and the connected market regime were crushed in 1950s and 1960s when Middle Eastern states nationalized the oil production taking possession of the choke point. The process started in 1953 when Iran made the oil production public and took over the concession holder BP, creating the National Iranian Oil Company (a consortium whose participants were also US oil companies), and when state-owned companies like the French CFP (Compagnie Française du Pétrole, now Total) and the Italian ENI (Ente Nazionale Idrocarburi) entered the international oil sector. Inch by inch Middle Eastern oil countries become more independent from Western oil companies in managing production, supported also by the OPEC (Organization of the Petroleum Exporting Countries) that, starting from 1960, coordinated the market policy of the members. Between the 1950s and 1970s, this gradual reversal in the oil industry leverage gave rise to the attempt to use oil as a political instrument to manage international relations, in particular, to restrain Israeli military expansion by putting an embargo on oil exports towards the countries supporting it during the wars with Arabs in 1956, 1967 and 1973. The 'oil weapon' didn't achieve the desired political aim because of the partial realization of the embargo decisions and because non-Arab OPEC members wanted to expand their production in the presence of a supply deficit. In addition the disagreement appeared among Arab governments: all of them 'opposed Israel, but the cost of attacking Israel with the oil weapon fell almost entirely on Arab oil exporters. This asymmetry made non-oil exporters much more enthusiastic about applying the oil weapon than oil exporters.' (Tétreault 2008: 262).

In spite of this, the control of oil production shifted from oil companies to the governments of Middle East states, completely changing the value added-chain of the industry and the market regime. In fact, when the international oil companies controlled production, the industry was vertically integrated and the 'majors' set both the final price of oil products and those of intermediate goods in order to prevent market gluts and enjoy high profits. They succeeded in doing so by ascribing on one hand the most costly phase of the sector to production (and thereby showing high prices for crude oil) and on the other, by ascribing the less profitable phase to the refining and the marketing carried on in their home countries (thus paying lower taxes). Once Middle East state governments gained control of the sector by state oil companies, the sector segmented into more phases, whose profitability depended on the crude oil price determined by the producers. The upstream phases became for the old 'majors' the most onerous in terms of financial capital requirement and the most uncertain because of the delayed returns, production turned out to be the most profitable stage and the downstream segments (where the international oil companies take refuge to work in) became the most competitive and the least profitable, just as they were pressed between fixed crude oil prices and a fluctuating demand. These changes in the industry separated the crude oil market from the final oil product markets, with important structural effects in both. In the first one, higher crude oil prices caused huge profits for MENA producers, which attracted investments in the research for new oil fields outside the region to enable the entry of new non-OPEC producers and to escape from the 'oil weapon' policy promoted by the OPEC. But higher crude oil prices also increased the cost of the raw material for the refining, and that raised gasoline and fuel prices.

In the course of time such restructurings undermined the crude oil market. In fact, although the oil production of OPEC countries increased up to 1973, reaching a world share of around 50 per cent between 1973 and 1980, it dropped to the 30 per cent in 1985 and regained the 40 per cent only in the 1990s, after the First and Second Gulf Wars. At the same time the world oil production continued to increase up to 1980, because of the enlarged supply of non-OPEC producers that fulfilled the demand of ostracized countries. By 1980, the expanded supply of oil, the reduced demand of fuel and gasoline following the increase of their price and the selling of stockpiles set aside by oil consuming countries to face contingent productive crises, triggered a decline of the oil price that would last 20 years (fluctuating between $40 and $18 per barrel). This drop in price ended at the beginning of the twenty-first century, when the use of futures in trading oil separated the crude oil production from its exchange, pushing its actual price upwards (Figure 5.1).

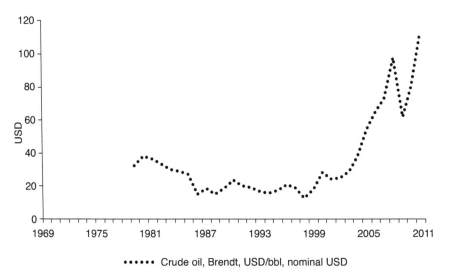

•••••• Crude oil, Brendt, USD/bbl, nominal USD

Figure 5.1 World price crude oil, Brendt, USD/bbl, nominal USD

Source: Global Economic Monitor (GEM) commodities.

Table 5.1 Shares of world crude oil production and world crude reserves for selected MENA countries

Country	Shares of world crude oil production 2011[b]	Shares of world crude oil reserves 2011[a]
Algeria	2.5	9.9
Bahrain	–	–
Egypt	0.8	–
Iran	5.4	10.4
Iraq	3.8	9.5
Kuwait	3.0	6.9
Libya	0.6	3.2
Oman	0.9	–
Qatar	1.4	1.7
Saudi Arabia	12.9	17.9
Syria	0.5	–
Tunisia	–	–
United Arab Emirates	3.7	6.6
Yemen	–	–

Source: Authors' elaboration from a) *OPEC Annual Statistics Bulletin 2012*, and b) *IEA Key World Statistics 2012*.

The evolution of the world oil industry during the last 50 years, where the key players are MENA oil-rich countries and the other Arab states, shows the importance of the resource for the development of the regions' economies, for the management of their international relations and also for the reinforcement of the identities of the new states. In the course of time the oil exporters, in particular, improved their position in all these domains in spite of the fluctuating crude oil market and the failure of the 'oil weapon' policies. In fact, with regard to the economic growth, MENA oil exporters achieved high royalties during the 1970s, when there was a peak in the price of oil, but at the beginning of 1980s the trend detoured for a decade before there was another increase. However, the main reason why MENA oil-rich countries strengthened their role in international relations was that both their significant share of world production (nowadays representing more than one third of the total world production, with the first, fourth and seventh positions held by Saudi Arabia, Iran and United Arab Emirates respectively) and their world reserves (which are more than two thirds of the total world reserves, most of which is held by six of the ten top countries, see Table 5.1). So, the oil mattered and still matters for MENA development.

Political instability as an environmental feature

'Oil and oil-related interests have had, and continue to have, a profound influence on the political economy of the Middle East', although 'oil is not the only relevant explanatory variable' (Luciani 2005: 79). Nevertheless, during the period of Mandates and of Protectorates the discovery of regional oil fields and the interests of British oil companies shaped both the political geography and the international order of the area, as the concerns of a single oil-rich country were reason enough for the existence of more states in the Arab peninsula and for the definition of their boundaries.[5] During the restructuring of the oil industry, when Arab national interests demolished this old geo-economic arrangement, trying to consolidate an Arab international order, the oil policies affected the interstate relations in the region, having a strong impact on both the costs and the conduct of the embargos, and on the ruling of Pan-Arab policy. The two rival fronts were characterized not only in terms of oil endowment, but also with regard to some other institutional and economic features, as they were the 'historically long established, progressive, more developed, but oil-poor Arab states, and the newly formed, traditional, conservative and oil-rich states' (Luciani 2005: 96). The oil interests were related also to the new international order spreading in MENA since the end of 1970s,[6] when 'the region best substantiates global unipolarity [...] with the US as a real rather than a virtual Middle East power after his invasion of Iraq, and its roadmap as a way out of the Palestinian-Israeli impasse' (Korany 2005: 59), and each state placed itself in respect to the new framework of international relations. Egypt sided with the Western powers after the Camp David Accord; Turkey first confronted USSR on behalf of NATO and later tried to find a new identity in the international chessboard of the Middle East as a spokesman of Islamic interests; Saudi Arabia acted as the main producer in the world oil market; oil-poor countries in the Mediterranean aligned themselves to the European Union (and mainly to France, the old colonial power); and the Gulf States increased their political power in the Arab world thanks to their international standing and to the autonomy that oil afforded them.

No matter what the contribution of oil to international and interstate relations in MENA has been, neither two decades of post-colonial Arab order nor the 30 years of a single pole order provided the region with a political environment favourable to development, as the process was carried out in a situation of long-lasting instability. Starting from the 1960s, due to the evolution of the political framework new Arab states and the international relations environment at the time, the region experienced an amount of armed conflicts (see Table 5.2) more sizeable than any other world region. During that time 5.5 per cent of the world's population was resident in the Middle East and North Africa but the armed conflicts in the region were 15 per cent of the total (Elbadawi 2005: Table 4; World Bank 2011a). During the first two decades of development, civil wars of fairly low intensity blew up as a consequence of post independence socio-political arrangements (which was the case in Yemen). This also occurred in interstate wars like the Arab-Israeli conflicts, which exploded in 1967 and 1973 (as was the case in civil wars in the Lebanon and Jordan). However, during the second part of the development period, interstate wars prevailed and more violence

Table 5.2 Years of armed conflicts for groups of selected MENA countries

Country	1960–69		1970–79		1980–89		1990–99	
	Civil Wars	Interstate Wars	Civil Wars	Interstate Wars	Civil Wars	Interstate Wars	Civil Wars	Interstate Wars
Algeria	1	1	–	–	–	–	8	–
Bahrain	–	–	–	–	–	–	–	1
Egypt	9	2	8	2	–	–	–	1
Iraq	–	–	2	1	10	–	7	10
Jordan	1	1	–	1	–	–	–	–
Kuwait	–	–	–	–	–	–	–	2
Lebanon	1	1	9	1	10	1	1	–
Libya	–	–	–	2	–	1	–	1
Morocco	–	4	6	5	10	–	–	1
Oman	–	–	4	–	–	–	–	1
Qatar	–	–	–	–	–	–	–	1
Saudi A.	–	–	1	1	–	–	–	1
Syria	2	1	–	2	3	–	3	–
Tunisia	–	1	–	–	1	–	–	–
U.A.E.	–	–	–	–	–	–	–	1

Source: Authors' elaboration of data from *Elbdawi* 2005.

produced stronger effects on the growth path of important countries. The Iran-Iraq War (1980-88), the Gulf War of 1991 and the Iraqi invasion (2003) were the main conflicts of this phase. Only the group of economies of the Arab peninsula remained (almost) free from armed conflicts (except for a four-year rebellion in Oman and two short interstate conflicts in Libya and Kuwait), all the others experienced more or less devastating military events. It is interesting to record that 'the distribution of conflict years between countries is highly uneven: 65 percent of conflict in MENA since 1960 occurred in Israel, the West Bank and Gaza, Iran, and Iraq. Algeria, Yemen, and Morocco accounted for another 21 percent of conflict years' (World Bank 2011a: 3).

Regarding the impact the fallout of armed conflicts had on MENA development, the damage that should be considered concerns economic, political and health activities. According to the literature disputing the general problem, war, 'especially civil war, is a development issue. Conflict at once is both a consequence of lacking development, and a cause of it. This has the potential of locking countries in a conflict trap' (Gates, Hegre, Nygard, and Strand, 2010: 1), that has long-lasting consequences on the three fields previously mentioned. In particular, in the MENA region the main effects of the conflicts experienced in the past 50 years have been recorded on population health and social conditions, because of high mortality of civilians (in addition to combatants), because of the number of refugees, and because of human rights abuses and fragile socio-political conditions. If, in post-conflict situations, 'economic indicators in the region as a whole tend to recover more quickly than in other parts of the world' (World Bank 2011a: vii), on the contrary political conditions deteriorate by worsening the quality of governance and of institutions, increasing the political repression and supporting authoritarian regimes. Considering the leading position of the state in the economies of the region, the consequences of these conditions are crucial for the economic growth and restructuring.

This vicious circle can briefly be summarized in such a way. Given that the centralized state as an entity is relatively new in Arab countries when compared to the centuries-long presence of a Muslim society in the region, after independence all Arab countries tried to substantiate it as the main subject both of the political life and of the economic activity. In this context, a process of 'social engineering' (Richards and Waterbury 2008: see Chapter 2) was implemented by the states to create political, economic and military élites who could rule public activities, and to compete for the loyalty of citizens with traditional identities with old social authorities (*ulama*, clan, etc.). But the conflicting situation of the 1960s and 1970s pushed the soldiers, sometimes established during a military coups, to the fore. The autocracies they created strengthened in the following conflicting period because

> the most immediate political consequence of armed conflict is that large parts of society become securitized. Policies usually deemed unacceptable by the public can be implemented with reference to the security of the

state. [...] Securitization can lead to political and social exclusion, which in turn is highly destabilizing. Several regimes in the MENA regions have attempted to combine authoritarian rule while maintaining an open and inclusive political strategy. When this inclusive strategy fails, the only way to voice opposition is through riots and violence. Suppressing popular revolts is very costly, and further securitized the political climate. In the end, these half-way attempts at opening up have often led to further suppression or return to armed conflict.

(Gates, Hegre, Nygard, and Strand, 2010: 32)

This vicious circle (supported in some ways by the international order) enabled the majority of autocratic regimes to survive for a long time,[7] to consolidate phenomena like bureaucracy and corruption, to slow or stop the institutional upgrade and to maintain a consistent public budget for military expenses (Table 5.3). All these elements, detrimental to economic activities (especially for private initiatives), are sometimes supported by the new classes created to implement and carry on the development process led by the state. Thus the main way by which the development path of MENA

Table 5.3 Armed forces personnel and military expenditure in MENA countries in 2010

Country	Shares of armed force personnel (% of total labour force) 2010	Military expenditure (% on GDP) 2010
Algeria	2.8	3.5
Bahrain	2.7	3.4
Egypt	3.1	2.0
Iran	2.2	1.9[b]
Iraq	10.6	4.4
Israel	5.8	6.5
Jordan	7.1	5.2
Kuwait	1.7	3.8
Lebanon	5.4	4.2
Libya	3.2[a]	1.2[b]
Morocco	2.2	3.5
Oman	3.9	8.5
Qatar	0.9	2.2[b]
Saudi Arabia	2.8	10.4
Syria	7.4	3.9
Tunisia	1.2	1.3
Turkey	2.3	2.4
United Arab Emirates	1.0	5.4
West Bank and Gaza	6.1	–
Yemen	2.1	4.4[b]

[a] 2009

[b] 2008

Source: Authors' elaboration of data from the World Bank (2011b), *World Development Indicators*.

countries has been affected by armed conflicts is the failed improvement of the environment for economic activities, due to the failed co-evolution of the political domain with respect to the economic one (see Chapter 3).

From boom to bust and recovery: oil cycles and demographic transition

The appraisal of the economic development process of the MENA countries generally starts by comparing this region with the other developing (and sometimes developed) ones. There are a lot of methodological cautions about this practice, due to the structural features characterizing the aggregates, the differences in the number and dimension of the economies included in the regions and the historical and international relations environment in which their development took place (as argued in Chapter 1). Caution should also be exercised when using the benchmark values of capitalist developed countries to evaluate particular phenomena of developing countries (such as their institutional quality), as this is in conflict with the idea of development (a transition path towards capitalism as discussed in Chapter 2). Keeping this in mind, the comparison among developing regions in terms of per capita GDP (Gross Domestic Product), measured both in current USD and in PPP (Purchasing Power Parity), reveals that the MENA region did not move away from the best performers (Figures 5.2a and 5.2b). In fact, during the last 45 years, based on GDP values, the

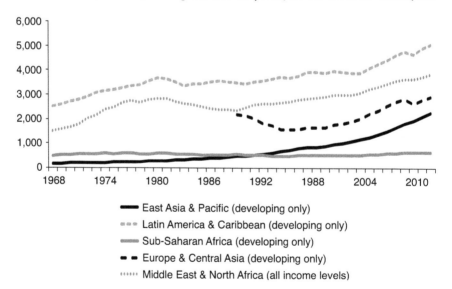

Figure 5.2a GDP per capita (constant 2,000 USD) for selected developing world regions

Source: Authors' elaboration of data from the World Bank (2011b); *World Development Indicators and Global Development Finance.*

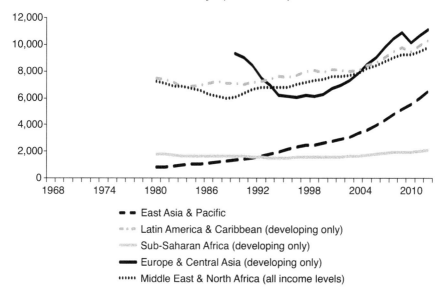

Figure 5.2b GDP per capita, PPP (constant USD 2005).

Source: Authors' elaboration of data from the World Bank (2011b); *World Development Indicators and Global Development Finance.*

MENA region ranked second after Latin America and the Caribbean (but before Europe and Central Asia, East Asia and Pacific, and Sub-Saharan Africa), with a narrowing gap in terms of per capita GDP measured in PPP, from 1980.

The trends of both variables (revealing that only Latin America and MENA had a cyclical development) show also the three phases experienced by the region under consideration: the post-independence boom (which, after two decades, came to an end in 1979-80); a recession phase the following decade (more sharp than that suffered by Latin America and Caribbean countries); and the recovery phase (from 1990 and accelerated after 2001). Finally, it has been confirmed that, during the bust and the recovery, regional economies succeeded in maintaining the same relation between the per capita GDP in terms of PPP and the per capita GDP in current USD (Figure 5.2c).

At first glance these results, which help to place the region alongside the development process experienced by the world economies that are not the fast growing ones (the BRICS for example), represent an aggregate whose components are heterogeneous. In fact, according to the definition shared by the most important international organizations, the MENA region includes a set of Mediterranean and Arabian Peninsula Arab countries (Morocco, Algeria, Tunisia, Libya, Egypt, West Bank and Gaza, Lebanon, Syria, Jordan, Iraq, Saudi Arabia, Kuwait, Bahrain, Qatar, United Arab Emirates, Oman and Yemen) and some non-Arab states: Israel, Turkey and Iran. The

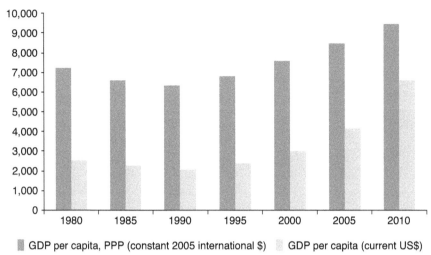

Figure 5.2c MENA countries GDP per capita (PPP constant 2005, international USD and current USD)

Source: Authors' elaboration of data from the World Bank (2011b); *World Development Indicators and Global Development Finance.*

most populous countries (Egypt, Iran and Turkey) contain about a half of total inhabitants of the region, the other six medium-sized countries (Morocco, Algeria, Iraq, Syria, Saudi Arabia and Yemen) share a third of the total inhabitants of the region, and the remaining inhabitants are distributed among 11 small countries (Table 5.4). But, considering the regional economic powers, nearly a fourth of the total GDP is from a non-oil country like Turkey, and another third comes from three oil countries in different proportions (Saudi Arabia, Iran and UAE, respectively): this means that about the 40 per cent of regional population produces more than a half of the GDP, while less than a half is obtained by the other 14 countries, representing the 60 per cent of the total population.

The table shows that as a result of the difference in the contribution of each country to regional population and to income, some unpopulated states have a high GDP per capita, while densely populated states present a low value for the variable. In fact, considering the values in current USD, the unpopulated oil countries were at the top of the placement in 2010 (in order of size: Qatar, Kuwait, United Arab Emirates, Oman, Bahrain and Saudi Arabia) outdistancing by far countries such as Syria, Morocco, Egypt, Iraq and Yemen, which were at the bottom. The complete ranking of MENA economies per capita GDP presents, amid these two groups of countries (the former ranges between 72,000 and 16,000 USD and the latter between 2,900 and 2,500 USD) Turkey, Libya and Lebanon lining up 10,000 USD, and Algeria, Iran, Jordan and Tunisia reaching 45-40 per cent of this value. The poorest country in the region was Yemen, while Israel presented a

Table 5.4 MENA countries population, total GDP (international current USD) and per capita GDP (current and PPP values) in 2010

Country	Population		GDP		Per capita GDP	
	Total	MENA %	US$	MENA %	US$	PPP
Algeria	35,468,208	7.80	161,979,441,019	5.1	4,567	8,395
Bahrain	1,261,835	0.28	22,945,456,867	0.8	18,184	23,690
Egypt	81,121,077	17.86	218,894,280,920	6.9	2,698	6,153
Iran	73,973,630	16.28	331,014,973,186[a]	10.5	4,526[a]	11,479[a]
Iraq	32,030,823	7.05	81,112,411,282	2.7	2,532	3,546
Israel	7,623,600	1.68	217,443,434,073	6.9	28,522	26,525
Jordan	6,047,000	1.33	26,425,379,367	0.9	4,370	5,826
Kuwait	2,736,732	0.68	124,348,317,665	3.9	45,437	50,635
Lebanon	4,227,597	0.93	39,006,223,284	1.3	9,227	14,005
Libya	6,355,112	1.40	62,360,446,571[a]	1.9	9,957[a]	16,854[a]
Morocco	31,951,412	7.03	90,802,867,575	2.9	2,828[a]	4,691
Oman	2,782,435	0.61	57,849,155,213	1.9	20,791	27,257
Qatar	1,758,793	0.39	127,332,413,913	4.2	72,398	77,466
Saudi Arabia	27,448,086	6.04	450,792,000,000	14.2	16,423	22,790
Syria	20,446,609	4.50	59,147,033,452	1.9	2,893	5,262
Tunisia	10,549,100	2.32	44,238,228,308	1.6	4,194	9,443
Turkey	72,752,325	16.01	731,144,392,556	23.1	10,050	15,624
United Arab Emirates	7,511,690	1.65	297,648,476,848	8.4	39,625	47,006
West Bank and Gaza	3,905,364	0.86	–	–	1.123	–
Yemen	24,052,514	5.30	31,042,729,623	0.9	1,291	2,634
Total	453,993,962	100.00	3,175,527,661,722	100.0		

[a] value 2009

Source: Authors' elaboration of data from the World Bank (2011b); *World Development Indicators and Global Development Finance.*

southern European score. Finally, the previous country placement from 2010 was also more or less maintained in terms of purchasing power parity.

To take into account both the endowment of natural resources and of the population (whose importance in affecting growing economies has been highlighted in the previous chapter) and to appraise their influence on the regional development process, it is useful to group MENA countries into three aggregates,[8] modulating these two variables in inverse proportion:

1   the oil-rich labour-importing MENA countries, including Bahrain, Kuwait, Libya, Oman, Qatar, Saudi Arabia, United Arab Emirates;
2   the oil-rich labour-abundant MENA countries, counting Algeria, Iran, Iraq, Syria and Yemen;
3   the oil-poor labour-abundant MENA countries, to which Egypt, Israel, Jordan, Lebanon, Morocco, Tunisia, Turkey belong.

The three groups, or clusters, contribute to the total regional amounts in different proportions. The first one accounts for 11 per cent of the population and 35 per cent of the income recorded, the second group carries weight for about 41 per cent of population and 21 per cent of total GDP, while the third group accounts for 48 per cent of the population, which produces less than a half of total income. The first two groups relied on oil as a trigger for the development, obtaining high oil rents on the GDP (Table 5.5), but experiencing also a high volatility of the income (Elbadawi 2005: 296) because of oil price fluctuations (Figure 5.1).

Table 5.5 Oil rents (% of GDP) for selected MENA countries

Country	1995	2000	2005	2009
Bahrain	15.7	20.6	24.0	16.3
Kuwait	40.6	49.4	58.1	41.2
Libya	26.9	33.8	64.5	42.3
Oman	30.0	42.3	44.0	31.6
Qatar	23.0	30.5	30.0	13.4
Saudi Arabia	31.2	40.3	53.9	44.1
United Arab Emirates	16.1	18.2	22.1	14.8
Algeria	8.9	13.7	21.6	15.6
Iran	21.0	36.3	38.8	23.7
Iraq	–	91.3	–	68.7
Syria	27.2	24.9	24.9	12.6
Yemen	39.3	38.3	39.7	20.0
Egypt	7.5	5.7	10.5	5.3
Tunisia	2.4	3.0	3.6	3.3

[a] value 2009

Source: Authors' elaboration of data from the World Bank (2011b); *World Development Indicators and Global Development Finance.*

That the oil cycle has affected MENA growth is evident from the figures describing the development of current GDP in MENA clustered countries during the last 50 years (see Figures 5.3a, 5.3b, 5.3c). In fact, the first two groups show the same result for the whole region, but with different timings and intensity due to specific features. The oil-rich labour-importing MENA economies, for example, show more intense phases according to the contribution of oil rents to the GDP (see Saudi Arabia and Kuwait), and the fluctuation of oil prices. The same can be said for some oil-rich labour-abundant MENA countries (like Iran and Algeria) that due to domestic circumstances, nevertheless, exhibit a five-year delay in reaching the top-down point (Figure 5.3b). As to the oil-poor labour-abundant MENA countries, they are not harmonized with the regional trends, presenting a constant (but weak) growing trend whose fluctuations depend on home factors (for Turkey see Figure 5.3c).

In spite of everything, oil-rich economies have been affected by oil cycles, the first cluster succeeded in achieving high levels of per capita GDP (Table 5.6), thanks both to the stock of oil and to the low levels of population: thus, a sizable per capita endowment of natural resources (the sectoral structure of the economies being equal) enabled them to obtain a proportional per capital income, as seen in Qatar and Saudi Arabia. This feature was important despite the fact that the rates of population growth in oil-rich

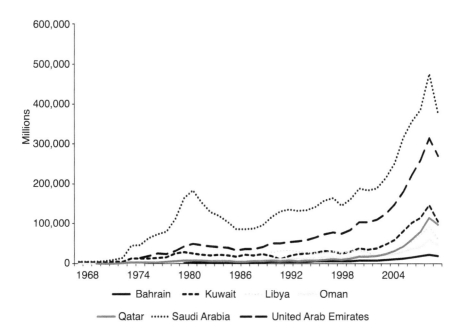

Figure 5.3a Oil rich-labour importing MENA countries GDP (current USD)

Source: Authors' elaboration of data from the World Bank (2011b); *World Development Indicators and Global Development Finance.*

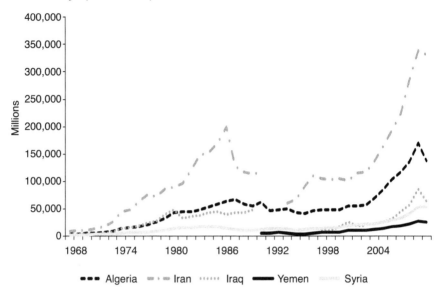

Figure 5.3b Oil-rich labour-abundant MENA countries GDP (current USD)

Source: Authors' elaboration of data from the World Bank (2011b); *World Development Indicators and Global Development Finance.*

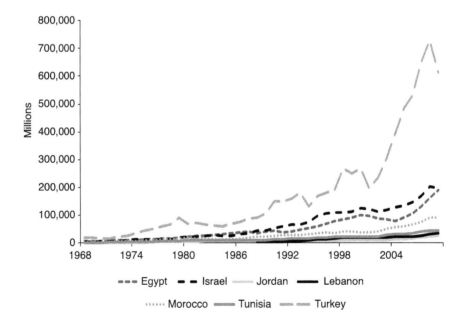

Figure 5.3c Oil-poor labour-abundant MENA countries GDP (current USD)

Source: Authors' elaboration of data from the World Bank (2011b); *World Development Indicators and Global Development Finance.*

labour-importing countries (by far higher than those of other groups during the last 50 years) were not generally overbalanced by a faster GDP boost (as revealed by the GDP rates of growth during the decades). The oil-rich labour-abundant MENA countries, although they presented higher GDP rates of growth in general in all periods relative to the other oil economies, could not achieve the same results in terms of per capita income (they are ranked in the lowest part of the placement) because of their lower per capita endowment of natural resources and the fact that the oil industry was of less importance to their economies. Given that they had no oil, the third group of countries was not directly affected[9] by oil cycles, but by the dynamics of the population. More heterogeneous than the others, this group is a collection of populous countries that experienced per capita GDP rates of growth that were higher than those of population (but not sufficient to balance the cumulative effect of the demographic transition) and that achieved, apart from Israel, medium (Turkey and Lebanon), low (Jordan and Tunisia) and poor (Egypt, Morocco and Yemen) results in terms of per capita GDP.

Table 5.6 Rates of growth of GDP and population for groups of MENA countries

Country	1967–69 GDP	Pop.	1870–79 GDP	Pop.	1980–89 GDP	Pop.	1990–99 GDP	Pop.	2000–09 GDP	Pop.
Bahrain	–	2.5	–	5.1	1.4	3.4	5.4	2.7	6.0	6.3
Kuwait	4.8	8.7	2.3	6.1	0.2	4.7	7.4c	1.6b	5.6	3.5
Libya	–	4.1	–	4.2	–	3.7	–	3.8	4.9	2.0
Oman	57.3	2.9	6.5	4.5	9.7	4.7	4.0	2.3	4.9	1.8
Qatar	–	7.7	–	7.1	–	8.2	–	2.1	12.0d	10.0
Saudi Arabia	–	3.7	14.9	5.1	0.2	5.2	3.1	2.3	3.3	3.1
United Arab E.	–	8.3	14.3a	14.9	1.5	6.1	5.4	5.3	5.3	8.7
Algeria	9.5	2.9	7.2	3.1	2.8	3.0	1.6	2.0	3.6	1.5
Iran	12.0	2.8	6.0	3.1	0.3	3.4	4.6	1.7	5.1	1.3
Iraq	–	3.4	–	3.3	–	2.8	–	2.9	0.8	2.7
Syria	10.3	3.4	8.8	3.4	2.9	3.3	5.6	2.6	4.9	2.5
Yemen	–	1.8	–	2.3	–	4.0	5.5d	4.1	4.2	3.0
Egypt	3.4	2.5	6.9	2.2	5.8	2.3	4.3	1.7	4.9	1.8
Israel	10.9	3.0	5.8	2.8	3.6	1.8	5.6	3.0	3.5	2.0
Jordan	–	6.0	15.0b	3.8	3.4	3.7	4.9	4.2	6.7	2.3
Lebanon	–	2.2	–	1.5	–	0.4	9.6	2.4	4.6	1.3
Morocco	9.4	2.8	5.4	2.5	3.9	2.4	2.8	1.5	4.7	1.1
Tunisia	5.1	2.0	7.2	2.1	3.5	2.4	5.1	1.8	4.6	1.0
Turkey	5.2	2.1	4.7	2.1	4.3	2.2	3.7	1.6	3.8	1.3

a five years   b four years
c seven years   d nine years

Source: Authors' elaboration of data from the World Bank (2011b), *World Development Indicators and Global Development Finance*.

Table 5.7 Per capita GDP in purchasing-power parity (PPP in current international USD)

Country	1980	1990	2000	2010
Bahrain	9,153.2	14,232.9	19,643.3	27,036.5
Kuwait	26,339.0	19,549.9	31,733.7	38,778.4
Libya	13,879.2	9,500.4	9,681.2	14,383.5
Oman	4,731.4	11,981.2	15,485.8	25,458.8
Qatar	51,445.5	53,132.2	54,473.4	88,221.5
Saudi Arabia	16,662.6	14,495.3	17,261.0	22,714.2
United Arab Emirates	33,896.7	32,142.9	39,314.7	46,298.9
Algeria	2,536.9	3,802.3	4,502.7	7,112.0
Iran	3,007.7	4,540.2	6,854.6	12,721.6
Iraq	–	–	–	–
Syria	1,600.3	2,219.2	3,351.1	5,040.5
Yemen	–	1,406.4	2,018.7	2,598.6
Egypt	1,293.9	2,562.7	3,912.1	6,417.3
Israel	7,270.1	13,292.6	21,242.2	29,601.8
Jordan	1,965.7	2,321.9	3,226.0	5,767.2
Lebanon	5,322.4	4,157.5	8,076.7	15,168.4
Morocco	1,147.6	2,036.0	2,667.1	4,794.0
Tunisia	1,889.3	3,177.4	5,272.5	9,454.1
Turkey	2,757.6	5,558.2	7,983.3	13,275.4
West Bank and Gaza Strip	–	–	–	–

[a] value 2009

Source: Authors' elaboration of data from the World Bank (2011b). *World Development Indicators and Global Development Finance.*

The impact of population/oil combination on the MENA growth process can be deduced also from the values of per capita GDP in terms of PPP (Table 5.7), which greatly increased during the last 30 years. In fact, while the first cluster has shown an increase of the values generally lower than two times (excepted Oman and Bahrain), the increases of the last cluster are generally higher than four times (reaching five times for Egypt but remaining at less than three times for Lebanon and Jordan); the oil-rich labour-abundant countries, on the contrary, improved about three times their departure per capita GDP. This suggests that the growth processes of most oil-endowed countries have been less effective than that of the countries experiencing high rates of growth of the population.

Macroeconomic trends and structural change of MENA economies

The clustering criteria (by oil endowment and population size) used to put in evidence two among the three exogenous variables that affect the development process of the MENA region (the first of which are the oil cycle and demographic transition) sustain the cycles that characterized their economies, showing on the one hand the main determinants of the different growth of the groups of countries and, on the other hand giving a concise explanation for both the boom of the first period and for the depression of the 1980s. The third exogenous variable (political instability) can be applied to all the phases; while the low-conflicting intensity still produced a beneficial environment for the economic activities in both the first phase and in the third one, the high-conflicting intensity hindered growth in the second phase.

Such economic phases also emerge in some way at the macroeconomic level. In fact, in MENA economies, inflation and unemployment were severe in the 1980s, especially in countries like Iran, Syria, Egypt, Israel, Morocco, Tunisia and Turkey. To be more precise, rising prices were recorded infrequently in oil-rich labour-importing countries, caused by the Dutch disease affecting non-tradable goods in the expansion phase. However, both inflation and unemployment have frequently influenced the other cluster of oil countries. Excluding the permanent state of war in Iraq during last three decades, Iran presented an increase of prices over 20 per cent in the 1980s and 1990s, with rates dropping to 15 per cent in the first decade of the twenty-first century. Yet, unemployment was the real problem facing these countries during all the periods, and this was particularly acute in recent years when the unemployment rates rose between 10 per cent in Syria to 22.60 per cent in Iraq (Table 5.8). Among the most populous countries in the MENA region Turkey presents permanent, very high inflation, whose rate has never been under 20 per cent (it rose to 23 in the last decade), while Egypt and Israel succeeded in reducing their unemployment rates to below 10 per cent. In the twenty-first century, although in terms of unemployment the performance of this cluster of countries is slightly better than that of oil-rich labour-abundant ones, the rate still fluctuates between 9.65 per cent in Turkey and 14.50 per cent in Tunisia.

The analysis of the aggregate demand of the countries during the last 40 years confirms that investments represent a share that is between one fourth and one fifth of the GDP, with variability in the case of countries like Qatar, Algeria and Iran where investments represent over a 30 per cent share. Household consumption generally presents the highest values among income destinations, yet while in the last cluster they fluctuate between 60 and 75 per cent for the considered period, in oil-rich labour-importing countries they are lower than 20 per cent. The share of the government consumption generally decreased in the last period, remaining at values between 10 and 20 per cent (excluded few exceptions like Saudi Arabia and Israel). As to the external balance only oil countries present positive values, justifying the role of oil and the difficulties of balance of payments of other economies; however, as the negative balance of payments decreased sharply in the period, a slight improvement emerged.

Table 5.8 Rates of inflation (annual % of Consumer Price Variation) and of total unemployment (% of total labour force) for groups of MENA countries

Country	1970–79		1980–89		1990–99		2000–09	
	Infl.	Unempl.	Infl.	Unempl.	Infl.	Unempl.	Infl.	Unempl.
Bahrain	12.6	–	2.3	–	0.8	6.30[a]	1.8	7.15[a]
Kuwait	4.5	–	3.6	–	2.3	0.70	3.5	1.60
Libya	5.1	–	7.8	–	6.7	–	0.1	–
Oman	–	–	–	–	–	–	2.9	–
Qatar	12.6	–	3.8	–	2.8	2.40[a]	5.7	1.95[a]
Saudi Arabia	–	–	0.1	–	1.3	4.30[a]	2.2	5.30
United A. E.	–	–	–	–	–	-1.80[a]	–	4.00[a]
Algeria	8.2	–	9.0	–	18.6	23.50	3.2	18.70
Iran	11.0	–	22.0	14.20[a]	23.8	10.10[a]	15.3	11.25
Iraq	6.9	–	–	–	137.0	–	20.1	22.60
Syria	10.9	–	22.6	4.45[a]	8.1	8.4	4.9	10.10
Yemen	–	–	–	–	25.3	9.90[a]	10.1	15.50
Egypt	7.7	–	17.4	5.80	10.5	9.40	7.5	9.85
Israel	32.5	–	130.0	5.70	12.2	8.70	2.0	9.80
Jordan	10.8	–	7.0	–	5.0	15.8[a]	3.9	14.00
Lebanon	–	–	–	–	–	8.50[a]	–	8.45[a]
Morocco	7.8	–	7.9	15.00[a]	4.4	17.10	1.9	10.80
Tunisia	–	–	7.5	16.10[a]	4.9	15.90[a]	3.2	14.50
Turkey	23.0	–	51.0	9.40	77.1	7.90	23.6	9.65

[a] one year data in the decade or mean for few data.

Source: Authors' elaboration of data from the World Bank (2011b), *World Development Indicators and Global Development Finance.*

Table 5.9 Household consumption (C), investment (I), government consumption (G), and external balance (B) (% of GDP) for MENA countries

Country	1970–79				1980–89				1990–99				2000–09			
	C	I	G	B	C	I	G	B	C	I	G	B	C	I	G	B
Bahrain	28.3	–	–	–	34.2	34.4	20.6	10.8	53.7	18.8	21.7	5.8	39.3	21.6	16.2	22.9
Kuwait	–	13.4	12.3	46.0	45.9	18.9	20.9	14.3	51.2	19.2	38.4	-8.8	37.0	16.6	18.9	27.5
Libya	–	–	–	–	–	–	–	–	58.1	14.0	24.3	3.6	39.9	16.3	14.4	29.4
Oman	21.6	27.7	27.7	23.0	32.6	24.8	27.6	15.0	50.6	16.3	24.3	8.8	37.7	21.6	20.5	20.2
Qatar	–	–	–	–	–	–	–	–	26.4	30.2	31.1	12.3	15.5	33.5	20.3	30.7
Saudi Arabia	24.4	19.6	16.3	39.7	44.7	23.4	28.8	3.1	45.2	20.1	27.3	7.4	32.3	20.3	24.0	23.4
United A. E.	–	–	–	–	–	–	–	–	–	–	–	–	61.2	21.3	7.5	10.0
Algeria	49.4	41.7	15.4	-6.5	51.3	34.0	17.2	-2.5	53.3	28.5	16.6	1.6	36.9	32.2	13.3	17.6
Iran	44.3	24.5	21.8	9.4	65.5	22.9	17.7	-6.1	50.4	34.8	13.7	1.1	47.9	32.1	14.7	5.3
Iraq	–	–	–	–	–	–	–	–	–	–	–	–	–	–	–	–
Syria	66.8	24.9	19.5	-11.2	68.7	23.2	20.5	-12.4	70.4	22.5	12.8	-5.7	62.3	22.6	12.7	2.4
Yemen	–	–	–	–	–	–	–	–	79.0	19.6	16.0	-14.6	69.4	17.9	13.9	-1.2
Egypt	65.1	23.1	23.3	-11.5	68.3	28.7	16.2	-13.2	74.9	20.9	10.9	-6.7	73.2	18.9	11.9	-4.0
Israel	59.2	29.1	37.4	-25.7	59.0	20.7	35.5	-15.2	57.4	24.0	28.3	-9.7	56.1	18.8	25.8	-0.7
Jordan	82.8	35.4	–	–	79.4	29.5	27.3	-36.2	70.4	30.1	23.9	-24.4	82.0	25.1	21.8	-28.9
Lebanon	–	–	–	–	–	–	–	–	106.8	27.9	16.3	-51.0	83.3	24.0	15.4	–
Morocco	69.9	22.6	16.1	-8.6	66.7	24.1	16.6	-7.4	65.2	22.7	17.0	-4.9	58.0	29.9	18.3	-6.2
Tunisia	61.1	26.2	15.3	-2.6	60.8	28.8	16.5	-6.1	61.9	26.1	16.2	-4.2	61.8	24.2	16.7	-2.71
Turkey	75.9	16.8	11.3	-4.0	74.7	19.5	8.9	-3.1	67.7	23.5	11.8	-3.0	70.4	19.1	12.5	-2.00

Source: Authors' elaboration of data from the World Bank (2011b). *World Development Indicators and Global Development Finance.*

Table 5.10 MENA countries value added sectors (% of GDP) and employment (% of total employment) in 2008

Country	Agriculture		Industry		Services		Total
	Value added	Employment	Value added	Employment	Value added	Employment	
Algeria	6.9	20.7[a]	62.1	26.0[a]	31.0	53.1[a]	100
Bahrain	–	0.8[a]	–	15.0[a]	–	84.2[a]	100
Egypt	14.0	31.6	37.5	23.0	48.5	45.4	100
Iran	10.2[d]	21.2	44.5[d]	32.2	45.3[d]	46.6	100
Iraq	–	23.4	–	18.2	–	58.4	100
Israel	–	1.7	–	21.5	–	76.8	100
Jordan	3.4	2.6	30.7	19.3	65.9	78.1	100
Kuwait	–	2.7[b]	–	20.6[b]	–	76.7[b]	100
Lebanon	6.4	–	21.5	–	72.2	–	100
Libya	2.1[d]	–	76.4[d]	–	21.5[d]	–	100
Morocco	15.4	40.9	29.6	21.7	55.0	37.4	100
Oman	1.9[a]	–	55.1[a]	–	43.0[a]	–	100
Qatar	–	2.5[d]	–	51.8[d]	–	45.7[d]	100
Saudi Arabia	2.5	4.3	59.8	19.8	37.7	75.9	100
Syria	17.9[d]	16.8	33.0[d]	30.3	49.1[d]	52.9	100
Tunisia	8.0	–	32.3	–	59.7	–	100
Turkey	9.6	23.7	26.7	26.8	63.7	49.5	100
United Arab Emirates	0.9	4.2	55.5	24.3	43.6	71.5	100
Yemen	7.7	7.9[c]	29.4	–	62.9	–	100

[a] 2004 [b] 2005 [c] 2000 [d] 2007

Source: Authors' elaboration of data from the World Bank (2011b). *World Development Indicators and Global Development Finance*.

As to the structure of the economies, if we consider the value added of each productive sector as a share of total GDP and the portion of employers on the total employment in 2008, Syria, Morocco, Egypt and Iran present the highest scores of value added in agriculture; the greater reliance on that sector is confirmed by the share of employers, higher than the sectoral value added. More than 20 per cent of the population of Morocco, Egypt, Turkey and Iran are peasants and in Morocco and Egypt this figure rise to 40 and 31.6 per cent respectively. As expected, the contribution of industry to the GDP is particularly relevant in countries such as Algeria, Oman and Libya (and significant in all the countries more dependent on oil) but also in Egypt, Jordan, Morocco and Turkey, where shares between 37 and 26 per cent show a certain degree of manufacturing development, a tendency confirmed also by data on the share of industrial employers. Finally, the oil-rich countries, together with Jordan and Israel, have impressive portions of employees in the public sector, with values over 70 per cent in the GCC countries, followed by Turkey (49 per cent), Egypt (45 per cent) and Morocco (37 per cent).

6 'Social contract', human development and welfare in the MENA region

In the MENA region, until the 1980s, the social contract (i.e. the institutional arrangements and the social policies legitimating state-society relations) committed the state to obvious assignments, such as the provision of programmes of education, housing, health care and food subsidies, along with the entitlement of driving the economy. When the state became more vulnerable (in times of crisis and war) and unable to provide social services to citizens, community activism arose, restructuring state-society relations and giving rise to new manifestations of the civil society (Bayat 2000). This was the case in both the economic recession and in the failure of neoliberal policies of some Middle East governments, which pushed civil-society organizations (such as Islamic welfare institutions and non-governmental organizations) – as commonly occurred in other developing countries – to become large providers of welfare programmes, often replacing state governments in many domains of activity. These collective social subjects had, in fact, a remarkable expansion in the 1990s when economic reversal made the formal social protection system more unstable, when the state could not devote as much efforts or money to the provision of basic services (Yousef 2004), and demographic transition, together with the evolution of labour market structures, gave rise to new challenges for the region as the job creation for new generations of young people.

The empowering of these social subjects, matched with a defaulting state, called for a renewal of the social contract between the state and the members of society in order to maintain one of the pillars of Muslim societies (the provision of welfare). In fact, historically, they were based on principles of social justice (where each citizen was entitled to access public services provided by the nation-state), political democracy and economic equality, calling for fairness at all levels (moral, legal, economic and political) to be achieved through the implementation of *falah*, interpreted as individual and collective welfare (Hifazatullah, Badshah, Farooq, Shafiq, Nasir-ud-Din 2011). Thus, in this chapter, the evolution of the socio-economic policy of the region has to be investigated, starting with an overview of the values and the systems of ethics of MENA societies (namely the principles of Muslim communities shaping desirable state-society relationship) to stress the changes that occurred in the MENA regions' social contracts over time. Attention will be paid to public and social services delivery and to the emergence of social activism based on the communitarian spirit, in providing services that are lacking and in promoting growth in critical economic period, thus sustaining social cohesion.

In this chapter, the emergence of the civil society as an organization that provides the welfare system and that shapes the course of the social contract will be assessed, first in the light of the region's performance in terms of poverty and inequality trends and then by moving to a more comprehensive measurement of development, based on the Human Development Index which will make evident the non-income variables such as health and social inclusion. Despite lack of data, the use of different indicators in the empirical literature on this topic can lead to different results: the dynamics of poverty show how economic growth is a sufficient but not a necessary condition for the alleviation of poverty in the MENA region. However, it is true that the region has performed better than other regions; it has been able to maintain the levels of income poverty that are much lower than other developing areas, with changes in poverty mainly attributed to changes in average incomes (growth) and changes in inequality (distribution) (Iqbal, 2006; Lahouel 2007). The impact of other variables (such as public policies and trade openness) on poverty and inequality highlights, despite mixed results, the widespread concern that emerged in the 1990s about the durability of the trend (Adams and Page 2001; World Bank 2002b). Moving to a more comprehensive analysis of human development, the data show how the MENA region has made good progress, although with variability from country to country in improvement in health and access to education due to certain socio-economic and cultural factors, the region has been not able to close gender gap in access to the labour market and economic activities. The historical analysis of the complex poverty-inequality trend and of MENA human development is related to the growth and institutionalization of civil society organizations and of social activism, which is mainly based on the need of poorer countries to meet development goals in presence of weak state.

Muslim society and welfare

The Muslim society is a family-based society, non-racial, casteless and egalitarian that, as such, functions democratically. In fact, together with spiritual democracy, the Quran, in dealing with the organizational principles of social life, establishes three other levels of democracy (Hifazatullah, Badshah, Farooq, Shafiq, Nasir-ud-Din 2011):

1 'social democracy': advocating no discrimination and abolishing all tribal, racial and colour distinction. This means that all people are entitled to social rights and access to public services provided by the nation-state;

2   'political democracy': establishing the basic principles of Quranic social order by abolishing theocracy and the secular views of government that admit any form of tyranny;
3   'economic equality': applying the basic principle of equitable distribution of wealth, that is 'Wealth does not circulate only among your rich' (Quran 59: 7). It follows that highly-skewed inequalities are unfair, as inequalities are permitted in a Muslim society only in proportion to the distribution of skill, initiative, effort, and risk.[1]

Taking Islam as a system of ethics and applying an axiomatic approach to it, as developed by Naqvi in 1994, four main principles to organize social life can be inferred (Sirageldin 2002: 26):

1   unity (*tawḥīd*): the vertical dimension of the ethical system assessing freedom of action with each individual as an integral part of the whole;
2   equilibrium (*al-ʿadl wa'l-iḥsan*): the horizontal dimension of equity stating balance between the needs of the present and future generation;
3   free-will (*ikhtiyār*): individuals are free to follow their own path in social and economic activities, yet potentialities of freedom arise within justice, so individuals are called to exert their freedom within specific social contexts and suiting the needs of changing times;
4   responsibility (*farḍ*): voluntary responsibility, yet society needs to preserve it for the public good; each asset owned by private or public body has a social aspect.

This universal ethical system based on the four axioms implies the management of political domain by policies that should not 'lead to dependency, limit opportunities that develop capabilities for the few, or reduce individual responsibilities for taking action. Policies should enhance motivation to seek knowledge, enhance productivity and transparency in government. They should also enhance intra and intergeneration equity' (Sirageldin 2002: 27). It thus emerges that the Muslim economic organizations tend to be based on the principle of justice at all levels (moral, legal, economic and political) and, as such, to be achieved through the implementation of *falah*: individual and collective welfare. This makes the Muslim society a welfare society, meaning that:

> Side by side with spiritual and moral welfare, the Islamic state is under obligation to give to the economic welfare of the people its due; and, in that respect, the teachings of the Quran are directed through all the channels of economic activity to one goal, namely: the achievement of not only economic justice but of positive economic welfare for every member of the society, so that everyone is enabled to live with honour and dignity. Such a goal is very difficult to achieve, until and unless all the dimensions of human activity are trimmed and fashioned to assist

in that achievement. That is the reason that all human activities in Islamic society are organized in such a manner to achieve that goal [...]. The provision of basic needs to all has to be in the Islamic state fundamentally on the basis of full employment. However, Islam has provided a social welfare tax through *Zakat* for ensuring basic needs to the disabled and un-employed [...]. Islam has also commended generosity in terms of voluntary economic well-doing to those in need, to the utmost of one's capacity and considering one's action as fulfilment of the right of the other person and not merely as ritualistic charity to beggar.

(Hifazatullah, Badshah, Farooq, Shafiq, Nasir-ud-Din 2011: 4)

On this basis the main principles structuring economic activities can be summarized as follows (Taheri 2000):

1   multi-faceted ownership: the acceptance of different forms of ownership as private, public and state ownership;
2   economic freedom within a defined limit: a balance between private ownership (personal interest) and public welfare (social interest), with ownership to be limited for the public welfare;
3   social justice: the rule of two general principles, mutual responsibility and social balance (economic equality). While social justice is, as mentioned, reached through *zakat*, mutual responsibility calls for all members of the society to fulfil the general needs of the society, with the state responsible for the provision of basic needs to its members.

The aforementioned considerations create a desirable relationship between state-society, one that is a social policy completely in line with the Millennium Development goals; developmental (as it promotes economic growth and structural change); democratic (deriving its legitimacy from popular participation and the electoral process); and socially inclusive (providing equitable entitlement for all citizens to participate in social affairs and pursue their life goals (Karshenas and Moghadam 2005).

According to Karshenas and Moghadam, the so-called developed world (as is the case in some European welfare states) adapted some of these principles to proper institutions and organizations that, based on negotiations between parties (unions, employers and the state), were created with the goal of providing specific policies and measures: labour/employment policies, education, social insurance and safety nets. In the case of developing countries, social policies (not generally based on norms of citizenship or worker's rights) followed different trajectories: in authoritarian East and Southeast Asia, for instance, they were bound to the achievement of progress, which in this case was industrialization, and pursued through education and the creation of a competitive labour force. As for the Middle East and North Africa region:

[...] it can be argued that social/welfare policies in the post-colonial era, where they were established, had more to do with nation-building and state-building, and with creating a social base of support for the emerging nation-states or regimes, than with any concept of citizen rights [...]. Nasser's policy of automatic government employment for graduates, as well as land reform in both Egypt and Iran, probably also were motivated by state-building needs. Higher education in the MENA region can be said to have assumed more of a screening role, in allocating scarce formal sector jobs, rather than having the East Asian type developmental functions. Other social policies, such as healthcare, maternity leave, state pensions and permanent employment, were funded in some cases by oil revenues (for example, Iran, Algeria, Iraq), but the beneficiaries of these policies were primarily urban-based and particularly government employees.

(Karshenas and Moghadam 2005: 4)

National identity formation and state building were thus direct goals of different MENA countries (such as Algeria, Egypt, Iran, Morocco, Tunisia and Turkey) during the 1960s and 1970s, and they were to be achieved mainly through the implementation of redistributive policies. While in rentier states such as the GCC, social policy followed a particular path (for instance where human development was not addressed and where education was not compulsory): due to the GCC states' reliance on migration and employment of a non-national labour force, social and economic development was conditioned by the redistributive policies followed by the national government and was reliant on food subsidies and state-sponsored education. Such policies were implemented after the Second World War, when most MENA countries had low levels of development (at least in terms of infant mortality, life expectancy, adult illiteracy), both in absolute and in relative terms (for instance, compared with East Asia). This was due to the political economy initiatives that were followed and to the predominance of people living in rural areas. By the 1990s, following urbanization, the economic condition of the region (mainly resource-driven) changed and so did the demographic structure (see Chapter 4). At that time, the shift in national government policies (such as high spending in health and education) led to a recovery of the region that, if we consider the abovementioned development indicators, has been impressive (Karshenas and Moghadam 2005). Nevertheless, as we have seen in the course of the book (Chapter 3), in recent centuries the achievement of the MENA region had been conditioned not by the values of Muslim societies, but by the ineffectiveness of states in coping with social and economic needs. This causes conflict between state and society, in particular between the development path to be followed and the need to renew the social contract between states and society members accordingly.

The development path and the evolution of the social contract

From the Mandates/Protectorates period to the post independence period, there were many reasons for the state to become the leading actor of the socio-economic life of the MENA region. The nation-building process promoted the state as the provider of society welfare, the role of the armed forces stressed its defensive function against all the foreign threats and the political élites used it to realize their policies en mass. In addition, the trust in oil production, the distribution of oil rents all over the region through migration and the preference of the Western powers for strong states favoured its ruling through the social contracts that, as we have seen, were favourable to the Muslim tradition. But, given that the conditions that were in favour of the state ruling the nation state changed during the development process, how has the socio-economic policy of the region and the social contract stabilized and adapted over time? According to Yousef:

> During the 1940s and the 1950s societies across the MENA region developed social contracts with a distinctively interventionist and redistributive character. These contracts were expressed and institutionalized through explicit commitments from MENA governments, articulated in constitutions, basic laws, and other documents that established the state as an instrument of social transformation, mass political mobilization, and economic redistribution. Although the form and content of these contracts varied, they reflected a widely held understanding of the policies for economic and social development [...]. In some cases, the social contract asserted a commitment to radical populism, with intensive regulation, if not outright expropriation, of private assets and control of organized labor through state corporatist systems of interest representation. In others it reflected a paternalistic rationale for statism, with interventionist policies directed in support of emergent private sectors.
>
> (Yousef 2004: 6)

To summarize, the peculiar features of the social contract that remained in place till the 1970s were:

1   the choice of the state as a central planner of social priorities and of economic activities, promoter of agrarian reforms, of industrialization and of nationalization of private and foreign economic activities;
2   the adoption of import substitution policies to protect the new domestic industry from international competition;
3   the choice of the state as welfare and social services provider;
4   a preference for redistribution and equity in economic and social policy;
5   a vision of the political arena as an expression of the unity of the nation rather than an aggregating of different and contrasting views.

On these pillars many countries (Algeria, Egypt, Iraq, Syria, and to a lesser degree, Jordan, Morocco, Yemen, and Tunisia) built up their socio-economic policies and internal factors shaped their redistributive character.[2] Following the sustained economic growth of the period 1960-1985 (based on migration-remittances and oil revenues), the contraction of the mid-1980s (due to the reduced demand for migrant labour and reliance on remittances flows, declining productivity and a more competitive international environment), put the social contract under strain. The MENA region thus embarked on a structural reform programme (embracing health, education, labour market and public services provision), which followed international institutions, such as the World Bank, who proposed a different paradigm of development to MENA countries, mainly seen as a process of modernization to be achieved through three interrelated routes (World Bank 2005):

1   move from closed to open economies to improve firm competitiveness and to benefit from international best practice and foreign technology;
2   a shift from the public sector towards private-sector led economies to enhance employment opportunities and efficiency;
3   a transition from resource dependence to more diversified economies aimed at reduce dependency from volatile source of growth in order to preserve social expenditure and fiscal stability.

Despite the positive macroeconomic achievement of such reforms, the measures implemented were not capable of renewing the existing structures and, in addition, highlighted some of the limits of the top-down approach to local development. The economic reversal of the 1990s made the formal social protection system more unstable as less money was devoted to the provision of basic services. In the case of education, as we have seen, despite the fact that most MENA countries have allocated a large share of government budget to schooling, the comparison between the last available data (2008) and the data from the mid-1980s shows how public expenditure on education has generally decreased, as is the case of Egypt, Israel, Qatar, Saudi Arabia and Syria. In fact, as we have seen in the course of this book, considerable changes have occurred in the last decade: in the demography of the region (with a considerable decline in the dependent population and a significant rise of the working age population, especially of young people); in the labour market (with the rising participation rate of women, in particular, and a massive wave of young people entering the labour market); and in intraregional migration flows (no longer representing a mechanism for achieving demographic balance). Attempts by local governments to adapt their institutional settings to such changes by reallocating public expenditure, reviewing pension schemes and providing incentives to young people, by dismantling patrimonial structures in society and developing political participation – have ultimately failed. Rigidities in labour market (an overcrowded public sector and private sector growing slowly) and the fact that human capital does not contribute much to growth and productivity (despite considerable results in the provision of education, in the reduction of the gender gap, in the improvement of supply and variety of education) means that the region experiences high unemployment, especially among young people and thus puts the social contract under pressure. The need to renew the social contract has forced the civil society to call for good governance, improve social protection and actively participate in the decision-making process. The events of the 'Arab Spring' have clearly put this call in perspective with the ambitious reform launched by regional government in social and political arenas (such as Morocco, Tunisia and Egypt) also including transparency and accountability programmes (e.g. the 2013 Moroccan plan).

Growth, inequality and poverty alleviation in the MENA region

The relationship between poverty, inequality and growth is complex: if it is generally agreed that economic growth has a positive impact on (absolute) poverty, it is not necessarily true that GDP growth results in a more equal income distribution (less inequality). This complex relationship is explained by Bourguignon in his image of the 'Poverty-Growth-Inequality Triangle' based on the definition of:

a 'poverty' (measured by the absolute poverty headcount index): the proportion of the population below a particular 'poverty line' (e.g. $1 a day), derived from household survey data;

b 'inequality' (or 'distribution'): disparities in relative income across the whole population, i.e. disparities in income after normalizing all observations by the population mean so as to make them independent of the scale of incomes;

c 'growth': the percentage change in mean welfare levels (e.g. income or consumption) in the household survey.

This complex interaction can be explained as follows:

> A change in the distribution of income can be decomposed into two effects. First, there is the effect of a proportional change in all incomes that leaves the distribution of relative income unchanged, i.e. a *growth* effect. Second, there is the effect of a change in the distribution of relative incomes which, by definition, is independent of the mean, i.e. a *distributional* effect. So, if poverty is a function of the growth in mean income and changes in the distribution of relative income, both growth and inequality changes play a major role in generating changes in poverty. The impact of these phenomena will depend on the initial level of income and inequality, with distributional changes of income in the population affecting poverty reduction.
>
> (Bourguignon 2004: 3)

If the dynamics of poverty shows how economic growth is a sufficient but not necessary condition for poverty alleviation, other conditions must be taken into account as the peculiar features that shape human development in the region. In the case of the MENA region (Salehi-Isfahani 2010: 5-6):

- Demographic factors: considerable demographic changes have occurred in recent decades, with the decreased speed of population growth resulting in a new and potentially more favourable situation (with respect to the baby boom of the 1960s and the 1970s) and a significant rise of the working age population (see Chapter 4).
- Labour market imbalances: the region shows segmentation between public sector, government and the private sector jobs. The misallocation of labour across sectors and structural imbalances between demand for and supply of skills, is evident in unemployment rates, which are concentrated among the most educated people and tied to skill shortage at the industrial level (see Chapter 7).
- An educational crisis: high investment in schooling has been characterized by low productivity of education. Despite education leading to important achievements (provision of schooling, reduction of the gender gap, improvement of supply and variety of education at secondary and tertiary levels), and regardless of the outcomes of such investments or the positive outcomes of the reform process, empirical studies show how human capital does not contribute much to growth and productivity (see Chapter 7).

As for poverty, empirical evidence shows how the MENA region has performed better than the others, how it has been able to decrease the poverty trend in the past three decades (being either measured in $1.25 or in $2 level) and how it will have a slowly decreasing rate in the long run (Figure 6.1).

This applies also when using an indicator of depth of poverty as the poverty gap,[3] showing a considerable decline in the period 1980-2008, as it drops from 1.87 per cent in 1981 to 0.60 in 2008 (Table 6.1).

In fact, the available data show how poverty has markedly reduced, passing from 30 per cent to 23.4 per cent in the 1990s, before stabilizing at 20-25 per cent (measured at $2 line) in the next decade, reaching lower percentages in the mid-2000 (17.4 per cent in 2005) (Figure 6.2). Poverty estimates are here derived both in headcount rates at $1.25 and $2 constant PPP dollars per person per day to underline how the jump in poverty rates between $1 and $2 lines suggest a high degree of country vulnerability (World Bank 2006).

Country-specific poverty trends show, despite variability of performance, a decrease in absolute poverty levels in all the considered countries (Egypt, Iran, Morocco, Tunisia and Jordan) and a long-term convergence of this

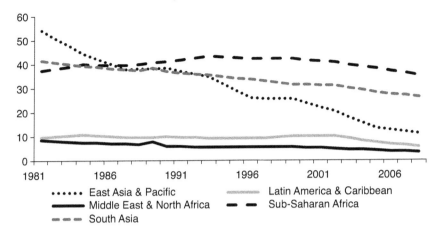

Figure 6.1 Comparative trends in regional poverty at $2 a day (PPP) (% of population)

Source: Authors' elaboration of The World Bank (2011), *Poverty and Inequality database*.

Table 6.1 Incidence of poverty in selected world regions

Region	Poverty headcount (%)			Poverty gap index		
	1981	1990	2008	1981	1990	2008
East Asia and Pacific	77.18	56.24	14.34	34.86	19.07	3.41
Europe and Central Asia	1.91	1.91	0.47	0.50	0.55	0.15
Latin America and the Carib.	11.89	12.24	6.47	4.36	5.38	3.26
Middle East and North Africa	9.56	5.75	2.70	1.87	1.08	0.60
South Asia	61.14	53.81	35.97	20.46	16.13	8.63
Sub-Saharan Africa	51.45	56.53	47.51	21.80	25.36	20.62
Total	52.16	43.05	22.43	21.36	14.83	6.85

Source: Authors' elaboration of the World Bank (2011), *Poverty and Inequality database*.

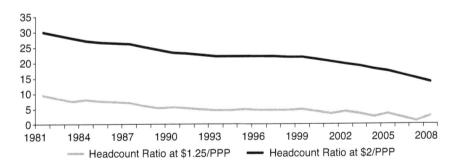

Figure 6.2 MENA poverty trend, 1981–2008

Source: Authors' elaboration of the World Bank (2011), *Poverty and Inequality database*.

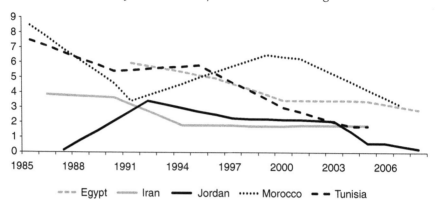

Figure 6.3 MENA country-specific poverty trends (at $2/PPP)

Source: Authors' elaboration of the World Bank (2011), *Poverty and Inequality database.*

trend: while Jordan has achieved the lowest poverty rate, Morocco shows the slowest dynamics in poverty reduction (Figure 6.3).

How changes in poverty may be attributed to changes in average incomes (growth) and in inequality (distribution) (Iqbal, 2006: 9) emerges from the information available. In fact, if we look at inequality in the MENA region, where the evidence is mostly based on data on consumption expenditure collected from household surveys, the region seems to display more equality than any of the other developing countries: the average Gini coefficient for the MENA region (2000-2007) is 38.20, compared to 43.56 for middle-income countries and 36.23 for the high-income group (Salehi-Isfahani 2010: 31). In their calculation of social welfare in the MENA region, Bibi and Nabli also point out how the region, compared to the rest of the world, can be placed in a moderate or middle range of inequality: the 1990s Gini index value for the region, 36.8 points, is lower than that of Latin America (48.9) and Sub Saharan Africa (45.9), similar to East Asia (38.9), and higher than Europe and Central Asia (34.5) and South Asia (32.7).

Furthermore, over the period for which the Gini index is computed (1970-1990 period), income inequality is relatively stable over time (Bibi, Nabli 2010: 37-38). Nevertheless, the inequality trend shows that there is country variability: in Egypt and Jordan, for example, the rates of inequality are lower, and in other countries, among which are Tunisia, Morocco and Iran, the rates of inequality are higher. All countries stay in the range between 30 and 50 per cent of the Gini index: Egypt is stable on values close to 30 for the whole 1990-2008 period; Jordan shows more fluctuation in inequality but this trend has been decreasing since the beginning of the 1990s; Iran, with Gini of 47 in 1968 and 42 in 2000, has the highest rates of inequality, followed by Tunisia and Morocco (average Gini of 41 and 40 for the whole period) (Figure 6.4a), but lower rates with respect to other developing countries, such as Brazil and Mexico (Figure 6.4b).

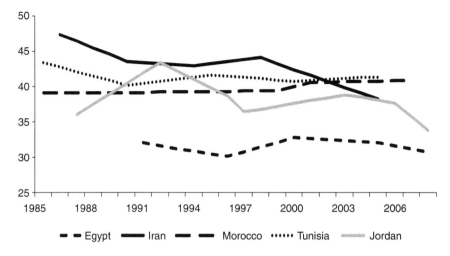

Figure 6.4a Gini index in MENA countries (percentage).

Source: Authors' elaboration of the World Bank (2011), *Poverty and Inequality database.*

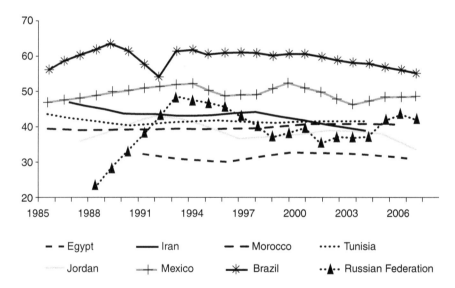

Figure 6.4b Gini index in MENA and in other developing countries (percentage).

Source: Authors' elaboration of the World Bank (2011), *Poverty and Inequality database.*

When interpreting these data, it has to be underlined that inequality of income is not necessarily correlated with inequality in other dimensions of human development (such as education and health, for example) and that, as is the case of the MENA region, there can be a more equal distribution when income is publicly provided (Salehi-Isfahani 2010: 31). In addition, the empirical literature that investigates the relationship between growth and inequality and the role of the latter in determining poverty reduction, found that, in general, growth has been the main source of poverty reduction in MENA. This is the case of Morocco, for instance, where Abdelkhalek found that failed growth was the main explanation for the increase in poverty between 1990 and 1999 in both rural and urban areas (Abdelkhalek 2005); in the case of Tunisia the same results were found for the poverty headcount reduction in the period 1980-2000 (Lahouel 2007).

Turning to the impact of other variables on poverty and inequality, such as public policies, trade and openness, social expenditure and investment in human capital, results are mixed. In fact, removal of trade protection, especially in agriculture, has been beneficial in reducing inequality in Tunisia, but in Morocco a negative effect or no effect at all was found. The World Bank studies suggest that public expenditure on education as a whole has favoured the poorest households and the level of education is important: public expenditure on basic education has been in favour of the poor, while those in university and vocational training have been biased towards the rich (World Bank 2002b). The impact of consumer subsidies on inequality, largely investigated in the literature, show how they have, since the 1980s when they became extensive in the MENA region, a significant impact in reducing inequality working as a pro-poor safety net (Bibi and Nabli 2010: 65-78). According to Adams and Page, the main reasons behind this achievement are in the redistributive measures and policies that continued to be implemented and addressed towards the poor, during the cycle of rapid growth (1970-85) linked to changes in oil prices (Adams and Page 2001: 3-4) and during the period of reduced income growth (1985-2000).

Nevertheless, despite the positive achievement of the region in poverty reduction, widespread concern emerged in the 1990s over the durability of the trend. This concern was raised from at least three sources:

1   The slowdown in economic growth (oil-driven) since the mid-1980s leading to per capita incomes [that were] virtually stagnant in a number of countries, and to major macroeconomic shocks in others.
2   The fiscal retrenchments required of the public sector in many of MENA developing economies limiting employment and public sector wage growth, as well as direct transfers to households and traditional mechanisms of support to the poor.
3   The shift from a state-led, inward-oriented model of economic development to one more dependent on external markets and the private sector producing a public debate over perceived increasing income inequality.

(Adams and Page 2001: 2)

Although the scarce access to household survey data makes it difficult to explain why Middle Eastern countries have different poverty outcomes,[4] and despite the many ways by which growth may impact on poverty, income and welfare distribution,[5] many explanations that have been offered to explain the unique situation of the MENA region, have relied on international migration and remittances and on the role of the public sector in employment creation (Adam and Page: 2003). Since the 1970s the economic growth of the Gulf implemented a huge south-to-south movement of workers from the Maghreb, spurred on by high demand and highly paid jobs. The huge migration flows of the 1970s and 1980s, mitigated during the 1990s by a policy to prevent nationalization and the gradual increase of the Asian presence in the Gulf countries and by the wavering oil prices, were linked to a substantial amount of remittances sent back home by the migrants. Estimates from Page show how, for the period between 1985 and 1999, the mean value for the remittance variable (official remittances as a share of country GDP) is higher in the MENA region (and South Asia) when compared to East Asia, Europe and Central Asia, Latin America and the Caribbean and Sub-Saharan Africa (Page 2007: 843). In a previous work, Adams and Page find that:

> [...] while international remittances may reduce poverty in the developing world as a whole (for the countries represented in the sample)[6] remittances definitively reduce poverty in the MENA region. The results for the MENA interactive variable suggest that, on average, a 10 per cent increase in the share of remittances in GDP will reduce the poverty headcount by 5.7 per cent and the poverty gap measure by 6.8 per cent.
>
> (Adams and Page 2003: 6)

Other explanations for the lower level of poverty in the MENA from an international perspective, are in the labour market structure and in the dominant role of the government in job provision: the public sector, the demand for which increases as more guarantees of insurances and wages are given, still has a dominant role in terms of employment creation in most countries (from 10 per cent in Morocco to 93 per cent in Kuwait and 70 per cent in the GCC), with higher percentages compared with international standards. What is more, since the 1940s the governments of the MENA region have consolidated a strong safety net system based on the subsidizing of a range of consumer goods (basic food stuffs, water and energy), accounting for the low poverty headcount during economic stagnation. Yet, with the lack of micro data as the main limit to the empirical testing, these results suggest how remittances from abroad and public sector employment reduced absolute poverty across the population, but left overall inequality unchanged (Page and Van Gelder 2002).

In spite of a moderate inequality level in 2000, the trend has been on the increase since the 1990s, underlying a change in the political economy of the region: from the redistributive social contract of the post-independence period (resulting in 20 years of increasing growth), equity and poverty reduction, to the structural adjustment policies of the mid-1980s. This was pointed out by Ali:

The Arab region, as an income group, was the only one in which subsidies and social transfer as a ratio of total expenditure declined from 21 per cent in the 1990s to 18 per cent in the 1997, before recovering to 23.8 per cent in 2005. The evidence also shows that the region did not have an excessive ratio compared to other income groups. With the exception of Kuwait and Morocco, all other countries experienced a decline in ratio of subsidies and current transfer to total expenditure. Compared to other country groupings, the Arab countries did not have a significantly higher average ratio in 1990 and they recorded the lowest average ratio in 1997 and 2005. The Arab countries also seem to have abandoned their commitment to equity in terms of employment in the state sector.

(Ali 2009: 16)

The evidence shows that the increase of unemployment rates in the region since the 1970s, under the rising pressure on the labour market, was due to the enlarged total labour force participation rates and to the increase of women's participation in economic activities. The present path of development thus questions the emergence of new social actors providing an alternative welfare system or one that is complementary to the state, as well as society-based solutions for wealth distribution and poverty reduction.

Human development in MENA

Since development is a complex and multidimensional phenomenon, income and consumption measures allow only a partial understanding of poverty and inequality dynamics; other items have to be considered in the analysis, such as health, knowledge, economic provisioning and social inclusion. An important step in broadening the measurement of human progress, from economic growth to human development, has been made with a change in the meaning of the concept to take into account the measurement of capabilities, such as personal freedom and human rights. The Human Development Report project redefined the term in the 1990s as follows:

> Human development is the process of enlarging people's choices – not just choices among different detergents, television channels or car models but the choices that are created by expanding human capabilities and functionings – what people do and can do in their lives. At all levels of development a few capabilities are essential for human development, without which many choices in life would not be available. These capabilities are to lead long and healthy lives, to be knowledgeable and to have access to the resources needed for a decent standard of living – and these are reflected in the human development index. But many additional choices are valued by people. These include political, social, economic and cultural freedom, a sense of community, opportunities

for being creative and productive, and self-respect and human rights. Yet human development is more than just achieving these capabilities; it is also the process of pursuing them in a way that is equitable, participatory, productive and sustainable [...]. Getting income is one of the options people would like to have. It is important but not an all-important option. Human development includes the expansion of income and wealth, but it includes many other valued and valuable things as well.

(Streeten, 1999: 16-7)

In the light of this new concept meaning and taking into account the challenges facing the MENA region during recent decades, how have their economies performed in terms of human development compared to other countries? From Table 6.2 it emerges that, although beginning in the 1980s with a low Human Development Index (HDI) (0.44 points, a value[7] lower than the other developing world areas, except for South Asia and Sub-Saharan Africa) the MENA region was able to improve fast, reaching a medium index value (0.64) in 2011. According to Salehi-Isfahani's calculation, in the period from 1990-2007 the HDI of the MENA region increased twice as fast as its index of GDP per capita, faster than all the other regions (Salehi-Isfahani 2010: 12). Some MENA countries succeeded better than others in achieving higher levels of human development: according to 2011 data, Israel and oil countries (UAE, Qatar, Bahrain and Libya) have the highest HDI (average 0.8), followed by Turkey, Tunisia, Jordan and Algeria (0.69). In the medium range Egypt with a HDI of (0.64), followed by Syria (0.63) and Morocco (0.58). Yemen, with a HDI of 0.46, stays in the lowest rank.

As for health, the region has made good progress, despite country variability, averaging a life expectancy of 70.5, which is higher than other developing regions such as South Asia and Sub-Saharan Africa and closer to Europe and Central Asia (71.3). Data on education, which is a relevant component of human development, show how at primary level, universal education has been achieved in almost all countries; enrolment rates are very high also at secondary level, with percentages higher than 90 per cent in GCC countries, Tunisia and Algeria and lower in Morocco (55.8 per cent) and Egypt (67.2 per cent). Tertiary education shows the highest variability, with highest enrolment in Israel (62.5 per cent), Libya (55.7 per cent) and Lebanon (52.5 per cent), followed by Jordan (40.7 per cent). Concerning the relationship between educational level and employment (see Chapter 7) in the MENA countries unemployment can be inversely related to the level of education: in fact, in most countries unemployment rates tend to increase with the level of education achieved (Billeh 2002). In the case of Morocco, Algeria, Palestine, and the UAE to a latter extent, unemployment rates are higher for people with tertiary education; in Tunisia, Turkey, Israel and Iran graduates are better off but unemployment trends remain significant both at secondary and tertiary levels of education all over the region (see Figure 7.3).

Table 6.2 Human Development Index trends in MENA (1980-2011)

HDI rank		Human Development Index (HDI) Value							HDI rank Change [a]		Average annual HDI growth (%)		
		1980	1990	2000	2005	2009	2010	2011	2006–2011	2010–2011	1980–2011	1990–2011	2000–2011
VERY HIGH HUMAN DEVELOPMENT													
17	Israel	0.763	0.802	0.856	0.874	0.884	0.886	0.888	-1	0	0.49	0.49	0.34
30	United Arab Emirates	0.629	0.690	0.753	0.807	0.841	0.845	0.846	3	0	0.96	0.97	1.06
42	Bahrain	0.651	0.721	0.773	0.795	0.805	0.805	0.806	-3	0	0.69	0.54	0.38
HIGH HUMAN DEVELOPMENT													
56	Saudi Arabia	0.651	0.693	0.726	0.746	0.763	0.767	0.770	0	2	0.55	0.50	0.55
64	Libya	–	–	–	0.741	0.763	0.770	0.760	-5	-10	–	–	–
71	Lebanon	–	–	–	0.711	0.733	0.737	0.739	3	-1	–	–	–
88	Iran	0.437	0.534	0.636	0.671	0.703	0.707	0.707	3	-1	1.57	1.35	0.97
89	Oman	–	–	–	0.694	0.703	0.704	0.705	2	0	–	–	–
92	Turkey	0.463	0.558	0.634	0.671	0.690	0.696	0.699	2	3	1.34	1.08	0.90
94	Tunisia	0.450	0.542	0.630	0.667	0.692	0.698	0.698	3	-1	1.43	1.21	0.94
MEDIUM HUMAN DEVELOPMENT													
95	Jordan	0.541	0.591	0.646	0.673	0.694	0.697	0.698	1	-1	0.83	0.80	0.70
96	Algeria	0.454	0.551	0.624	0.667	0.691	0.696	0.698	2	0	1.40	1.13	1.03
113	Egypt	0.406	0.497	0.585	0.611	0.638	0.644	0.644	2	-1	1.50	1.24	0.88
114	Palestine	–	–	–	–	–	0.640	0.641	–	0	–	–	–
119	Syria	0.497	0.548	0.583	0.621	0.630	0.631	0.632	-6	-1	0.78	0.68	0.73
130	Morocco	0.364	0.435	0.507	0.552	0.575	0.579	0.582	0	0	1.52	1.39	1.26
132	Iraq	–	–	–	0.552	0.565	0.567	0.573	-1	0	–	–	–

HDI rank	Human Development Index (HDI) Value							HDI rank Change [a]		Average annual HDI growth (%)		
	1980	1990	2000	2005	2009	2010	2011	2006–2011	2010–2011	1980–2011	1990–2011	2000–2011
LOW HUMAN DEVELOPMENT												
154 Yemen	–	–	0.374	0.422	0.452	0.460	0.462	4	0	–	–	1.93
HDI GROUPINGS												
Very high human develop.	0.766	0.810	0.858	0.876	0.885	0.888	0.889	–	–	0.48	0.44	0.33
High human development	0.614	0.648	0.687	0.716	0.734	0.739	0.741	–	–	0.61	0.64	0.70
Medium human develop.	0.420	0.480	0.548	0.587	0.618	0.625	0.630	–	–	1.31	1.30	1.28
Low human development	0.316	0.347	0.383	0.422	0.448	0.453	0.456	–	–	1.19	1.31	1.59
REGIONS												
Arab States	0.444	0.516	0.578	0.609	0.634	0.639	0.641	–	–	1.19	1.04	0.94
East Asia and the Pacific	0.428	0.498	0.581	0.622	0.658	0.666	0.671	–	–	1.46	1.43	1.31
Europe and Central Asia	0.644	0.680	0.695	0.728	0.744	0.748	0.751	–	–	0.50	0.47	0.71
Latin America and the Carib	0.582	0.624	0.680	0.703	0.722	0.728	0.731	–	–	0.73	0.76	0.66
South Asia	0.356	0.418	0.468	0.510	0.538	0.545	0.548	–	–	1.40	1.31	1.45
Sub-Saharan Africa	0.365	0.383	0.401	0.431	0.456	0.460	0.463	–	–	0.77	0.90	1.31
Least developed countries	0.288	0.320	0.363	0.401	0.431	0.435	0.439	–	–	1.37	1.51	1.73
World	0.558	0.594	0.634	0.660	0.676	0.679	0.682	–	–	0.65	0.66	0.66

[a] A positive value indicates an improvement in rank

Source: UNDP database, HDR 2011.

Table 6.3 Human Development Index and its components in MENA

	HDI Value	Life expectancy at birth	GNI per capita (constant 2005 PPP$)	Adult literacy rates	Education Gross enrolment ratio (%)		
HDI rank	2011	2011		2005–10[b]	Primary 2001–10[b]	Secondary 2001–10[b]	Tertiary 2001–10[b]
VERY HIGH HUMAN DEVELOPMENT							
17 Israel	0.888	81.6	25,849	–	111.1	89.1	62.5
30 United Arab Em.	0.846	76.5	59,993	90.0	105.4	95.2	30.4
37 Qatar	0.831	78.4	107,721	94.7	105.9	85.2	10.2
42 Bahrain	0.806	75.1	28,169	91.4	106.6	96.4	51.2
HIGH HUMAN DEVELOPMENT							
56 Saudi Arabia	0.770	73.9	23,274	86.1	98.9	96.8	32.8
63 Kuwait	0.760	74.6	47,926	93.9	94.8	89.9	18.9
64 Libya	0.760	74.8	12,637	88.9	110.3	93.5	55.7
71 Lebanon	0.739	72.6	13,076	89.6	103.2	82.1	52.5
88 Iran	0.707	73.0	10,164	85.0	102.8	83.1	36.5
89 Oman	0.705	73.0	22,841	86.6	83.9	91.3	26.4
92 Turkey	0.699	74.0	12,246	90.8	99.3	82.0	38.4
94 Tunisia	0.698	74.5	7,281	77.6	108.2	90.2	34.4
MEDIUM HUMAN DEVELOPMENT							
95 Jordan	0.698	73.4	5,300	92.2	96.8	88.2	40.7
96 Algeria	0.698	73.1	7,658	72.6	107.7	96.5	30.6
113 Egypt	0.644	73.2	5,269	66.4	101.1	67.2	28.5
114 Palestine	0.641	72.8	2,656	94.6	78.9	87.1	45.7
119 Syria	0.632	75.9	4,243	84.2	122.2	74.7	–
130 Morocco	0.582	72.2	4,196	56.1	107.4	55.8	12.9
132 Iraq	0.573	69.0	3,177	78.1	102.5	51.5	15.5

HDI rank	HDI Value 2011	Life expectancy at birth 2011	GNI per capita (constant 2005 PPP$)	Adult literacy rates 2005–10[b]	Education Gross enrolment ratio (%)		
					Primary 2001–10[b]	Secondary 2001–10[b]	Tertiary 2001–10[b]
LOW HUMAN DEVELOPMENT							
154 Yemen	0.462	65.5	2,213	62.4	85.4	45.7	10.2
HDI GROUPINGS							
Very high human develop.	0.889	80.0	33,352	–	102.7	99.7	72.9
High human development	0.741	73.1	11,579	93.2	110.3	90.4	49.3
Medium human develop.	0.630	69.7	5,276	81.9	113.3	69.7	20.5
Low human development	0.456	58.7	1,585	59.8	96.5	35.0	6.2
REGIONS							
Arab States	0.641	70.5	8,554	72.9	95.0	66.5	25.8
East Asia and the Pacific	0.671	72.4	6,466	93.5	112.3	76.9	24.9
Europe and Central Asia	0.751	71.3	12,004	98.0	98.5	90.7	57.1
Latin America and the Car.	0.731	74.4	10,119	91.0	116.8	90.7	42.7
South Asia	0.548	65.9	3,435	62.8	109.8	55.9	13.1
Sub-Saharan Africa	0.463	54.4	1,966	61.6	100.2	35.3	5.9
Least developed countries	0.439	59.1	1,327	59.2	99.6	35.6	5.7
World	0.682	69.8	10,082	80.9	106.9	68.4	27.6

[b] Data refer to the most recent year available during the period specified.

Source: UNDP database, HDR 2011.

Finally, if we look at MENA performance in terms of gender gap, the gender inequality index of Arab states stays in the medium range, with a value of 0.56 in 2011, higher that all the other developing regions, except for South Asia and Sub-Saharan Africa (Table 6.4). The gender gap in access to education has been generally closed in Israel and GCC countries, where there is a higher percentage of the female population that have secondary degrees; as in Israel (78.9 versus 77.2) and Kuwait (52.2 and 43.9). Countries such as Turkey, Tunisia, Algeria, Morocco and Iraq still face huge differences in access to education according to gender. But women's access to the labour market shows higher inequality; the gender inequality index shows how, despite various factors – delaying the time of marriage, and of first births; changes in marriage-related decisions that are driven by public policies (such as family planning programmes and human capital programmes like compulsory schooling); the clear role that education plays in delaying marriage (see Chapter 4); culture and social norms and territorial conditions (access to market in rural areas) –women's participation in the labour market is still restricted. Nevertheless, in the course of the MENA development path, women's participation rates in economic activities have increased, with a more marked increase in countries such as the GCC, Iran, Libya, Tunisia, Jordan and Lebanon (see Figure 7.5.b), on the one hand enhancing status but on the other hand augmenting pressure on the local labour market and on the region's capability to create jobs and productive employment.

From social activism to a new welfare state

Since the rise of the Arab Empire in the seventh century, the concept of the Caliphate, which is based on belief as a unifying element, has become common in the Arab world. It is thus pan-Islamism rather than the nation-state that shapes the sense of community belonging. The concept of the nation-state is, in fact, Eurocentric, as it has been developed in the West since the dawn of modern history, but it was relatively new to the Middle East until the First World War.[8] When the creation of the Arab League in 1945, followed by Nasserism, failed to realize the aspirations of the citizens of the newly independent states to create a supranational entity, the idea of the nation-state was born. After independence, in fact, significant changes occurred in policy objectives and in the theoretical orientation of national governments, particularly the belief that the state could implement appropriate measures to eliminate poverty and embark on a sustainable development path. A state-centric vision followed, until the local governments proved to be too inadequate to achieve developmental goals, due to corruption of the bureaucratic-administrative system and repressive and authoritarian regimes. However, the top-down structural policies of the 1980s, instructed by the international community to overcome these failures, ignored the role of the civil society and the trade unions in promoting local development. In response to these failures, many civil-society organizations

Table 6.4 Gender Inequality Index and related indicators in MENA

HDI rank		Gender Inequality Index		Population with at least secondary education (% ages 25 and ≥)		Labour force participation rate (%)		Fertility	
		Rank	Value	Female	Male	Female	Male	Total fertility rate	Adolescent fertility rate
		2011	2011	2010	2010	2009	2009	2011	2011
VERY HIGH HUMAN DEVELOPMENT									
17	Israel	22	0.145	78.9	77.2	51.9	62.5	2.9	14.0
30	United Arab Emirates	38	0.234	76.9	77.3	41.9	92.1	1.7	26.7
42	Bahrain	44	0.288	74.4	80.4	32.4	85.0	2.4	14.9
HIGH HUMAN DEVELOPMENT									
56	Saudi Arabia	135	0.646	50.3	57.9	21.2	79.8	2.6	11.6
63	Kuwait	37	0.229	52.2	43.9	45.4	82.5	2.3	13.8
64	Libya	51	0.314	55.6	44.0	24.7	78.9	2.4	3.2
71	Lebanon	76	0.440	32.4	33.3	22.3	71.5	1.8	16.2
88	Iran	92	0.485	39.0	57.2	31.9	73.0	1.6	29.5
89	Oman	49	0.309	26.7	28.1	25.4	76.9	2.2	9.2
92	Turkey	77	0.443	27.1	46.7	24.0	69.6	2.0	39.2
94	Tunisia	45	0.293	33.5	48.0	25.6	70.6	1.9	5.7
MEDIUM HUMAN DEVELOPMENT									
95	Jordan	83	0.456	57.1	74.2	23.3	73.9	2.9	26.5
96	Algeria	71	0.412	36.3	49.3	37.2	79.6	2.1	7.3
113	Egypt	–	–	43.4	59.3	22.4	75.3	2.6	46.6
119	Syria	86	0.474	24.7	24.1	21.1	79.5	2.8	42.8
130	Morocco	104	0.510	20.1	36.3	26.2	80.1	2.2	15.1
132	Iraq	117	0.579	22.0	42.7	13.8	68.9	4.5	98.0

HDI rank	Gender Inequality Index Rank 2011	Value 2011	Population with at least secondary education (% ages 25 and ≥) Female 2010	Male 2010	Labour force participation rate (%) Female 2009	Male 2009	Fertility Total fertility rate 2011	Adolescent fertility rate 2011
LOW HUMAN DEVELOPMENT								
154 Yemen	146	0.769	7.6	24.4	19.9	73.5	4.9	78.8
HDI GROUPINGS								
Very high human development	–	0.224	82.0	84.6	52.8	69.8	1.8	23.8
High human development	–	0.409	61.0	64.6	47.8	75.0	1.9	51.6
Medium human development	–	0.475	41.2	57.7	51.1	80.0	2.1	50.1
Least developed countries	–	0.594	16.8	27.4	64.4	84.0	4.1	106.1
Low human development	–	0.606	18.7	32.4	54.6	82.7	4.2	98.2
REGIONS								
Arab States	–	0.563	32.9	46.2	26.0	77.1	3.1	44.4
East Asia and the Pacific	–	–	48.1	61.3	64.2	80.3	1.8	19.8
Europe and Central Asia	–	0.311	78.0	83.3	49.7	67.8	1.7	28.0
Latin America and the Caribbean	–	0.445	50.5	52.2	51.7	79.9	2.2	73.7
South Asia	–	0.601	27.3	49.2	34.6	81.2	2.6	77.4
Sub-Saharan Africa	–	0.610	22.2	34.9	62.9	81.2	4.8	119.7
World	–	0.492	50.8	61.7	51.5	78.0	2.4	58.1

Source: UNDP database, HDR 2011

and NGOs intervened to address the shortcomings of the states, as meso-institutions between national governments and citizens. Despite the fact that the concept of the nation-state had permeated the culture and the political system of the Arab countries since independence, with the increasing delegation of functions to the state (as in the domains of law and welfare), the community has remained the predominant force in influencing individual choices and political preferences, affecting, or even dominating, the whole political system (Clark 2004). In the course of MENA history, community activism has often taken shape in mass collective actions when the state has become more vulnerable (as in time of crisis and war), and when it has been unable to provide social services to citizens: this happened in Iran where, following the 1979 revolution, apartment councils were established by people taking advantage of the collapse of policy control for occupying vacant houses. The same behaviour appeared in the case of displaced persons in Beirut during the civil war (where thousands of people who were engaged in collective occupation of vacant homes moved in the city suburbs to build illegal settlements). Other examples can be the shantytown construction in Turkish cities during the collective land occupation by rural migrants, or the emergence of popular organizations for women, youth and neighbourhoods to provide health in Palestine during the *intifada* (Bayat 2000).

If the early nineteenth century's civil society associations were mainly religious (as was the case of the pious foundation *awqaf*, of Ottoman tradition, based on voluntary beneficence) (Isin 2008), it was followed by secular welfare and charitable associations in the twentieth century. This is the case of NGOs (whose impressive figures range, for instance, from 14,500 registered ones in Egypt to 5000 in Tunisia in 1999) that, according to the rationale behind their activities, can be divided in four groups (Bayat 2000: 19-20):

1   religiously-motivated associations: organized by mosques and Islamic figures, or churches and Christian networks;
2   classical welfare associations: run mostly by upper-class families, with some developmental functions, such as income generation, training and community upgrading;
3   professional NGOs: managed largely by upper-middle-class professionals and by development experts who are driven by training and humanistic urge or by private interests;
4   state-sponsored NGOs: focusing on welfare and development, they target disadvantaged groups as an extension of the state fields of human rights, women's issues, welfare, culture, business and development.

Their spectacular growth and institutionalization, as addressed by Bayat, was mainly based on the need of poorer countries (Egypt, Jordan and Tunisia) to fill the state's inability or unwillingness of facing the challenges of social development, which followed the introduction of neoliberal policies of the 1980s and the support from external funding both encouraging the establishment of NGOs and influencing their activities.

The spread of NGOs and the evolution of the economic structure towards a growing secularization, along with the progressive failure of traditional religious institutions and of the state in meeting the demand for social services, in the 1980s and the 1990s led to the diffusion of another type of organization of civil society, namely the Islamic welfare associations. Considered by some economists as an association trying to gain control over the masses through religion or aiming for the spread of Islamic ideology against civil society institution empowerment (Zubaida 2001), they are, rather, contributing in the Arab region to develop and strengthen horizontal links between agents operating in similar socio-economic domains (Clark 2004).

The first kind of association is based on the manifestation of Islamic activist movements that became known to the international community in 1981 with the assassination of Egyptian President Anwar Sadat, but which have their origin in the creation of the Muslim Brotherhood movement in 1928. These movements can be seen as: a reaction to the growing intrusion of the state in the religious sphere; an attempt to determine the role of religion in the society; an alternative to the secular state institution to promote a different development path, based on the society. In reality, many Islamic welfare organizations are, as in Egypt, Yemen and Jordan, middle class organizations whose main function is to provide jobs for middle class professionals and protect their political status; or to provide social welfare (such as political organizations with controversial identity as Hezbollah and Hamas). Excluded from the formal state apparatus, they have evolved within their societies with a vision of welfare rooted in human ethics and social justice. Such organizations are complementary to state provision of social services, with religious welfare NGOs, as in the case of Lebanon and Iran, sub-contracted by the state to offer social welfare services (Jawad 2011).

In conclusion, civil-society organizations, both based on religious and secular values, have been more than an attempt to cope with the inability of the state to execute its functions, or than a mere challenge to the secular state. They represent a society-based organization that is an alternative to the state: a social class pressing for greater political representation. By creating the modus operandi of economic activities that meet social needs and by carrying on pro-poor programmes that support more vulnerable groups of population (when the formal social protection system has become unstable), they have been able to be active agents in the development process of the MENA region, for instance, by implementing distributive policies and also by fostering the creation of new institutions.

7   Human capital and labour markets in the MENA region

Since independence, and more specifically from the 1990s onwards, MENA governments have embarked on a massive programme of structural reforms at all levels of education, which have led to the achievement of considerable results in the provision of schooling (almost universal at primary level), in the reduction of the gender gap, in the improvement of supply and variety of education at secondary and tertiary levels, and in the enhancement of the quality of infrastructures. Nevertheless, empirical studies show how, despite such investments and positive outcomes of the reform process, human capital is not contributing much to growth and productivity (Pissarides and Véganzonès-Varoudakis 2007). In terms of supply, this result can be attributed to the low quality of the educational system and to the misalignment of the public and private rates of return on investments in human capital, the latter being the result of educational choices that make reference to the influence of tradition and social norms, in which family background is still seen as a main determinant. In terms of demand, the main reason for the failed support to productivity lies behind the structure of the MENA region's labour markets, characterized, despite country variation, by the particular segmentation between the private sector and both the public sector and government jobs (presenting more guarantees in terms of insurance and wages). The traditional leading role of the state in regulating and setting standards by a 'public' approach, coupled with the inefficiency of the bureaucratic system, has slowed down the growth of the private sector, so that in most countries the public sector still plays a dominant role in terms of employment creation. In the past, in the presence of growing unemployment, of an overcrowded public sector, and of a constrained private sector in initiating business and in innovation the MENA region's informal labour market has been so dynamic that nowadays it represents one of the main sources of employment for the Arab labour force. The misallocation of labour across sectors and the structural imbalances between demand for and supply of skills are evident in unemployment rates (where unemployment is concentrated among the most educated people) and are also related to skill shortages at the industrial level: highly-educated people wait for a job in the public sector, while firms complain about the lack of a labour force with firm-specific technical skills (UNDP 2002; Billeh 2002; World Bank 2008b).

Starting from an overview of the connection between human capital (as a complex dimension) and the socio-economic growth process, this chapter outlines main practices related to the provision of education in the Middle East and North Africa, a process that has historically been informal, i.e. related to cultural norms and social behaviour and mainly provided through religious schooling. The evolution of educational organization, that is the gradual move towards a formal system (conditioned by colonial powers, mainly the French) at the beginning of the twentieth century, and later, when independence was gained, the transit through 'universalization' of education (following a Nasserian principle) and then the adoption of a state-funded system with the reform of the mid-1980s, highlights the variety of strategies that explain the outcomes and limitations of the policy implemented by national governments. Huge public investment in education and the positive achievement in terms of 'quantity' and of human capital across the region, has not led, on average, to an increase in 'quality', which is generally assessed as rather poor and, as such, as one of the main reasons for insufficient regional economic growth.

The inability of human capital to turn into economic growth, despite investments made by national governments in terms of enlarging education provision and relative choices, is analysed vis-à-vis the labour market's peculiar structure and growth dynamics, in particular considering the pressure facing the market because of the demographic transition (that favours the young and active labour force and increases the participation of women). As this labour market structure resulted in information asymmetry and market rigidities (so that the contribution to economic growth has been low even though the educational system has been able to produce skilled labour), this chapter tries to provide a rationale for these outcomes by making suggestions as to how to match the educational system with the labour market's needs. If the reason behind this is not the missing reform of MENA countries (since indicators of market-oriented reforms show the region's ranking is not bad in the world average), then it is the economic and institutional factors that have undermined the effectiveness of reforms. Adopting a comprehensive approach, capable of taking into account the set of incentives/disincentives presented at institutional level in order to align norms and overcome rigidities and bottlenecks, is thus a viable path for the regional economies. Additional elements to be considered are the peculiarities of the local environment (i.e. the regional market's structure, characterized by a public-private dichotomy) and the dynamism of the informal sector, without neglecting the social and cultural norms that influence individual choices (at both educational and labour-market level) and the public returns (in terms of development and growth) arising from the productive investments in such a precious resource (i.e. the skills, the know-how and the competences of the labour force).

Human capital and economic growth

The economic theory recognizes education as one of the forms of human capital that emerges, at the same time, as both the prerequisite (input) and the outcome (output) of economic growth and social development. The stock and the combination of physical and human capital, in fact, determine the output of both firms (goods and services production) and, at aggregate level, of the whole economy, given the available technology. In turn, human capital affects the capacity of a country to innovate, to absorb new technologies, to enhance quality of life, to determine social and economic transformations and to ensure a growth that is more sustainable. Education is thus a central element of modern economies: the quantity and quality of education provided by a country's institutions determines the skills and the capabilities of its citizens to be productive and efficient workers and to promote economic growth and social change.

But what is 'human capital'? In the modern literature, the first scholar to introduce the concept of human capital was Theodore W. Schultz (Schultz 1961: 2), who emphasized how skills, knowledge and on-the-job-training are not the result of a consumption process, but rather the product of deliberate investment by which people may improve their welfare, enlarge their range of opportunities and enhance the wealth of nations. Human capital can be accumulated in different ways: by attending formal schooling (education), by transfering of specific skills and knowledge to workers during work activities (on-the-job training), by training in/attending post-school programmes (Becker 1964). The concept of human capital was further investigated by the Chicago School and by scholars like Mincer (Mincer 1958) and Becker (Becker 1964), the latter distinguishing between 'specific' and 'general' human capital. The first category refers to firm exclusive knowledge (highly specific skills) which is not easily utilized in other firms, while general knowledge is more useful and adaptable to other firms. This distinction makes clear why highly specialized workers are less likely to quit their jobs and to be in an unsecure position during an economic downturn, representing a unique asset for firms (because these workers are not easily replaceable). Becker also emphasized how investment in education, although it involves initial costs in terms of time and forgone earnings, will determine higher return (in terms of wages) in the future. But empirical research highlights how many other factors may influence the rate of return of education: apart from inner ability (social and personal attitudes such as creativity, etc.), school quality, family background and income, institutional incentives, gender, time and type of skills acquired are important variables in determining differences in returns of education across countries and people (Fleischhauer 2007). Thus human capital is not easily measured as it is a set of complex interactions of different variables, some of them (the most tangible), such as years of schooling, experience and investment costs in education, are more easily 'quantifiable', while others, such as personal ability, social environment, the role of culture and of institutions, are intangible and the less observable components of the human capital stock of individuals.

If human capital theory justifies large public expenditure on education, the central economic issue is the relationship between investments of this kind in human capital and returns of education (growth externalities). In fact, investments in education imply both social and private costs and benefits. In developing/middle income-countries (i.e. most of the MENA region's economies) the private cost of education (the financial cost supported by the student's family) is lower than the corresponding social cost (the economic resources invested by a society), and this difference increases as education expands at higher levels.[1] However, the private expected benefits (not only in the increase of a more educated student's earning prospects, but also in the non-economic benefits for their family, social status and cultural tradition) gradually overtake the collective gains (the increase in productivity, facilitation of job creation, provision of competences necessary for domestic labour markets), as the level of education increases. This mismatch provides an increase in the demand of students for higher education that can result in 'market distortion', when governments allocate more and more public resources to a sector where the private benefit of the investment may be higher than the expected social return (Todaro and Smith 2012: 379-81). This situation, as we will see in the course of this chapter, is the result of inappropriate public policies of educational formation and pricing, that are blind to the allocation of human capital in line with market requirements and economic sectors' needs. In the presence of an imperfect institutional setting, where human resources are not properly allocated in the labour market by considering their costs (public expenditure and private investment in education and training) and rewards (earnings differentials to workers for higher level of education, training and skills), it means that when the economy suffers from unemployment and lack of job opportunities many distortions can occur at labour market level (Todaro and Smith, 2012: 385). This occurs, in particular, in the presence of 'excess' production of education at higher levels and of insufficient absorptive capacity of the economy (due mainly to lack of investments) because:

1   students seek jobs for which they are qualified, but that are taken by people who are even more educated. Students then become temporarily unemployed and wait to find a job which satisfies their aspirations and social status;

2   educated people adjust to labour market demand and take jobs for which they are overeducated in terms of years of schooling and skills. Thus underemployment occurs where the worker is employed but underutilizes his capacity, in terms of level of skills, experience, compensation and hours;

3 those who fail to enter the modern labour market become unemployed or shift to the informal system and self employment;

4 labour migrants, both internal (from the rural to the urban sector) and international (beyond national borders and usually from low to higher income countries), may result giving rise to 'brain drain' phenomena when migration flows become of permanent nature.

Although countries' performance and economic history demonstrate how a well-educated labour force that increases the quality of human capital can foster the development of modern economies,[2] its contribution is not an automatic outcome, as it is closely related to and conditioned by national policy orientation, educational system features and labour market structures. In particular, the expansion of educational opportunities at all levels does not always result in returns of such investments, both at micro level (extra earning for an additional year of schooling and training) and at macro level (GDP growth rates).

The educational system and educational policy in the MENA region

Historically, education in the Middle East and North Africa has been an unofficial system related to cultural norms and social behaviour, and has mainly been provided through tutorial in mosques. Thus religious schooling was the main form of education for people and primarily aimed at forming good citizens. In Egypt religious schooling dates back to 642 AD when Arab forces took control of the country and the *kuttab* (also known as *maktab* – school – or *madrasa*) was created (Sayed 2006: 24). In the wake of the Arab-Muslim conquest, *kuttab* were established in the entire region as traditional Islamic schools attached to mosques in order to provide basic education to children through memorizing the Quran and through learning the fundamental Islamic practices and beliefs. Although in the Middle Ages only a few boys could attend Islamic schools (girls were not allowed to attend), in modern times *kuttab* stood as universal schools for the poor and lower and middle classes, while upper classes used private forms of education, such as hiring tutors to educate their children at home.

Education's reform in the mid-nineteenth century led to the decline of *kuttab* and to the move towards a state-funded system of education, although in some countries these private religious schools remained an important alternative to Islamic education provided by the public system,[3] or as charitable trust foundations (*waqf*) (Campo 2009: 437). The introduction of formal education in Egypt in the early nineteenth century by the Mohammed Ali dynasty represented an alternative tool for training intellectuals, bureaucrats and soldiers with technical skills; among them, promising Egyptian students were even sent to England and France to continue their education. During the late nineteenth and early twentieth centuries, formal education was later introduced in most countries of the MENA region under European colonization: compulsory education followed Western culture and was modelled on Western institutions. The new Ottoman élites were also trained under the guidance of European teaching, and mainly through French model schools.

In the 1960s and 1970s, most MENA countries – as with many other developing countries – in line with the social changes and power reallocation that characterized the post-colonial period, became aware of the need to invest in human capital to enhance economic growth and the level of welfare of regional economies. By establishing a centralized system of education, based on government control, the MENA countries started to adopt inclusion strategies in the form of 'free education' and 'education for all' policies. This approach was based on the concept of education as a right for citizens, to be applied at all levels of education (from primary to tertiary) and to be publicly financed by local governments. Some countries, such as Egypt under President Nasser's leadership, first promoted the 'universalization' of education at primary level (i.e. full enrolment) and, once this goal had been achieved, aimed to achieve universal access at higher levels. As a result of such policies, in the 1970s the MENA countries experienced a more equal distribution of education when compared to other areas (Latin America and East Asia for example);[4] the reversal of the trend during the 1980s was considered to be inevitable by some analysts (Thomas, Wang and Fan 2001), given that at the beginning of the decade the MENA region had the lowest average years of schooling caused by:

1   the higher education access for the non-poor and urban population at all levels with respect to the poor people and the rural population, because of social motivations;
2   the increasing inequality over time as countries enlarge their education system for structural factors;
3   the fact that, with increasing enrolment at primary level, national government invested higher resources (expenditure per pupil) in secondary relative to primary education to continue the policy introduced.

Furthermore, although education was largely centralized and publicly financed with significant government's financial commitment (see Table 4.3. Chapter 4), most MENA countries have shifted to an increase in the participation of the private sector in the provision of education at all levels. This policy was in line with the prevailing developmental ideas of the 1990s, advocating structural reforms and adjustment programmes (based on market integration and privatization) as recipes to foster growth in the wake of globalization.

Enrolments in private education have generally increased across the region, although this is only in a few countries (Lebanon, Iran and West Bank and Gaza) and rather limited in the other MENA countries. At primary level the private enrolments range from a high percentage in Lebanon, UAE and Qatar (about 71 per cent for Lebanon and UAE and 54.4 per cent for

Qatar in 2009) to much lower percentages (the historical trend shows that Turkey, Israel, Oman, Tunisia and Morocco, for instance, have values below 20 per cent for the entire period 1980-2009). The same variability applies at secondary level: few countries show consistent private enrolment rates (Lebanon and Qatar with more that 50 per cent in 2009) or consistent rates at upper secondary level (Qatar and Kuwait with more than 30 per cent in 2009).

At higher education level, the available statistics from UNESCO on the status and number of MENA universities show that, in 2008, private institutions represented 36 per cent of all higher education institutions in the area (UNESCO 2010). In some countries (Lebanon, Palestine and Jordan) the higher education system is mostly private, but in others (Tunisia, Algeria, Morocco and Egypt) the private system is still modest. It is also relevant to note how privatization policies in education have been controversial, in particular when private commitment has been allowed in the provision of basic education (World Bank 2008b: 24-6), because this trend emphasizes the increase of inequality of access to education.

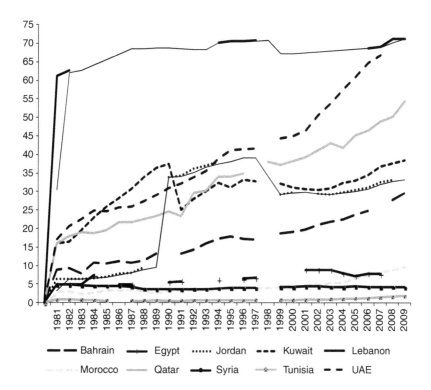

Figure 7.1a Private enrolment by level of education (% of total enrolment) for selected MENA countries: *Primary level*

Source: Authors' elaboration of data from UNESCO *Towards an Arab higher education space: International challenges and social responsibilities*, 2010.

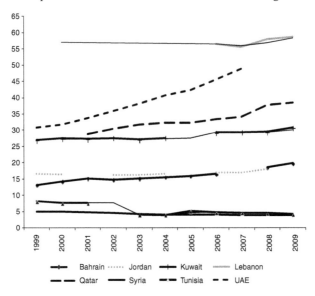

Figure 7.1b Private enrolment by level of education (% of total enrolment) for selected MENA countries: *Secondary level*

Source: Authors' elaboration of data from UNESCO *Towards an Arab higher education space: International challenges and social responsibilities*, 2010.

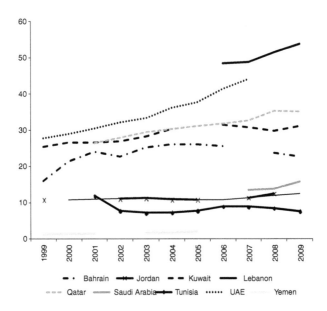

Figure 7.1c Private enrolment by level of education (% of total enrolment) for selected MENA countries: *Upper secondary/General programmes*

Source: Authors' elaboration of data from UNESCO *Towards an Arab higher education space: International challenges and social responsibilities*, 2010.

Over the last 40 years, MENA countries have been able to achieve nearly universal education and have closed the gender gap at primary level. The policy agenda of national governments has thus been enriched with new priorities, in particular focusing not only on the quantity of education provided (by increasing the enrolment rates at all levels and by promoting systematic education through reduction of the drop-out rates), but also on the improvement of quality and variety of education, in order to deliver new skills and expertise that meet market demand. In September 2010, 18 ministries of the Arab world met in Doha for the 'Quality of Education for all' Declaration. They shared the belief that:

> Improving education quality is the highest-impact and most cost effective national investment for any country in the Arab World, regardless of its level of economic development and income. The benefits resulting from successful educational reform far outweigh its costs, whatever its size, considering that the high economic output and returns of improving the performance of human resources reduces the impact of economic fluctuations and cyclical crises.
>
> (Doha Declaration 2010: 2)

The state of human capital in the Middle East

Today, as primary education is compulsory in almost all countries (except Tunisia), and as free education is now a fundamental part of the social contract in post-independence states of the region, it can be said that basic education is provided almost universally in the MENA region. Moreover, despite persistence of gender and geographical inequality, it can also be said that access to education has generally improved together with the enlargement of opportunities at secondary level. Enrolment at tertiary level, which normally requires the successful completion of secondary education, has also increased despite showing the highest country variability: the most recent data available show the highest tertiary enrolment percentage for Israel (62.5 per cent), Lebanon (52.2 per cent) and Bahrain (51.2 per cent), followed by Jordan (40.6 per cent), Tunisia (34.4 per cent), and Saudi Arabia (32.7 per cent). Among the countries that show the lowest percentages are Morocco (12.8 per cent), Qatar and Yemen (about 10 per cent) (Table 7.1).

In terms of growth of human capital stock, the Arab region presents country disparities, with some countries showing significant annual growth rates at the beginning of the twenty-first century: Tunisia (5.2 per cent), Algeria (4.7 per cent), Egypt (4.1 per cent), and Bahrain (4.1 per cent), and others with lower rates: Kuwait (2.3 per cent), Iraq (2.6 per cent), Jordan (2.8 per cent) and Syria (3.8 per cent) (Galal 2002). Despite country variability, the stock of literate persons within the adult population is substantial, with a minimum value for Morocco (56 per cent) and much higher values for the other countries: Libya (88.9 per cent), Lebanon

Table 7.1 School enrolment by level of education (%, gross)

Countries	Primary			Secondary			Tertiary		
	1980	1990	Last available year*	1980	1990	Last available year*	1980	1990	Last available year*
Arab World									
Algeria	96.83	94.30	107.69	31.25	62.02	96.48	4.93	10.49	30.62
Bahrain	104.68	108.87	106.55	57.50	99.75	96.43	3.47	17.64	51.20
Egypt	66.35	86.12	101.10	46.25	68.64	67.20	15.72	13.96	28.45
Iraq	107.27	105.85	102.54	51.52	44.87	51.47	8.39	11.90	15.52
Jordan	110.18	105.77	96.83	76.43	78.90	88.22	15.18	21.02	40.65
Kuwait	102.91	91.16	94.80	77.60	82.62	89.89	10.85	12.45	18.90
Lebanon	108.04	96.42	103.16	57.76	60.83	82.14	30.05	27.92	52.52
Morocco	79.12	67.68	107.40	23.73	37.50	55.85	4.90	10.93	12.88
Oman	45.23	82.63	83.91	8.28	39.39	91.32	0.01	3.85	26.44
Qatar	103.03	107.12	105.91	62.11	83.25	85.22	9.64	23.80	10.24
Saudi Arabia	n. a.	n. a.	98.88	n. a.	n.a.	96.81	6.38	9.65	32.78
Syria	94.74	100.46	122.21	47.55	50.97	74.74	14.03	17.97	n. a.
Tunisia	101.21	112.60	108.17	24.91	44.03	90.21	4.80	7.93	34.44
United A. E.	89.52	114.64	105.39	48.30	64.14	95.20	1.82	6.76	30.40
Libya	125.12	119.58	110.32	74.28	73.56	93.48	7.00	8.00	55.74
Yemen	n. a.	71.41	85.39	n. a.	n. a.	45.66	n. a.	4.41	10.23
Others									
Iran	93.47	10.60	10.76	43.38	52.07	83.07	3.36	5.85	36.49
Israel	98.89	9.38	111.09	81.42	90.44	89.10	30.48	32.62	62.55
Turkey	92.27	9.85	99.30	35.41	46.69	81.96	6.14	12.00	38.37

*Last available data for primary level refer to: Iraq 2007; Jordan 2008; Libya 2006; Turkey 2008; Yemen 2008. For secondary education: Iraq 2007; Jordan 2008; Morocco 2007; Oman 2003; Turkey 2008; Yemen 2008. For tertiary education: Bahrain 2010; Egypt 2008; Iraq 2004; Jordan 2008; Kuwait 2004; for all other countries data refer to 2009.

Source: World Bank (2011b), *World development indicators*.

Note: Where data is not available, the data closest to that year is used (in italics).

Gross enrolment ratios of 100% or more indicate that a country is able to accommodate all of the population of the age group that officially corresponds to the level of education shown and some additional over aged scholars.

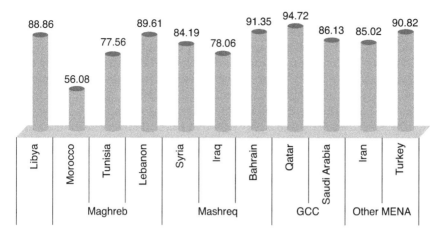

Figure 7.2 Adult literacy rates as a percentage for selected MENA countries in 2009

Source: Authors' elaboration of data from World Bank (2011b), *World Development Indicators.*

(89.6 per cent), Bahrain (91.3 per cent), Qatar (94.7 per cent) and Turkey (90 per cent) (Figure 7.2).

Some common factors can be found across the region in the educational and human capital system acquisition, as they are mainly conditioned by the shared socio-cultural and institutional context:

- *Imbalance patterns of education expenditure:* In most MENA countries, public expenditure in human capital formation is inefficient because it is biased in favour of tertiary education at the expense of secondary and primary education, which is more desirable in terms of social benefits. In addition it is not devoted to investment in physical capital, innovation and teacher training, but in teacher's wages, thus resulting in a reduction of quality of the educational system as a whole.
- *Quantity vs. quality:* Since the 1950s, MENA governments have followed a policy of 'universalization of education' at primary level (full enrolment) resulting in a remarkable increase of educational demand also at secondary level. The increase in quantity of education provided (despite continued high drop-out rates) has, on average, resulted in a decline of quality and a bias between private and public educational systems (especially at university level).

Huge public investment in education and the positive achievement in terms of 'quantity' of human capital across the region have not led, on average, to an increase of 'quality', assessed as rather poor and, as such, a main factor of insufficient regional economic growth. Among the main indicators used in the economic literature to measure the quality of education are the learning achievements of students, so that educational systems are considered to be of high quality when students demonstrate higher levels of learning in international comparison perspectives (Chapman and Miric 2009). The quality of teaching and learning (measured through student-teacher ratio, for instance), of teachers, of inputs and of physical infrastructures are other variables used as proxies for an efficient educational system; these indicators enable a country to supply a well-trained labour force. According to these indicators – and despite the effort of governments to control the supply side of education (teachers and staff) and to enhance student learning – the performance of MENA countries is still below other regions, reflecting the situation of middle-income and developing economies: only a few countries, Jordan, Morocco and Tunisia, have participated in recent international assessment studies,[5] and positive results were achieved in maths and science for Iran and Jordan. The quality of teaching and learning has also suffered, despite teaching forces in most countries expanded to meet growing enrolment. This expansion has been followed by continually low student/teacher ratios with huge urban/rural area variation. Where an oversupply of teachers has occurred, turning in lower student/ratios and in smaller class size, the advantages that lower classes offer have not been attained. The main reasons ascribed to the poor quality of the educational system are the ineffectiveness of formal training, the inability to put formal training into practice or the inability of governments, in the presence of an over-supply of teachers, to be more selective in their choices. In fact, if governments have heavily invested in teachers' salaries, monetary compensation (still perceived as low) has not been an incentive to improve teaching practice and sometimes, as has occurred in Egypt, it has also created 'perverse incentive' as private tutoring (Chapman and Miric 2009).[6] The MENA region also faces significant problems, with school facilities with multiple 'shift schools' in countries such as Egypt, Iran and Jordan and small schools in rural areas lacking laboratories and libraries. According to the World Bank and UNESCO shift schools are schools for two or more entirely separate groups of pupils during a school day; each group uses the same building and facilities, but at different times during the school day, with a common problem of deterioration of physical capital. Such indicators, which give some information on the quality of the educational system and teaching provided, and which still reflect lack of comprehensive data, cannot be used to make cross-country performance comparisons, due to the huge differences in cognitive skills and the type of education provided by local institutions (World Bank 1999: 11-13).

The educational crisis, that is, the mismatch between the output of the educational system and the labour market needs (UNDP 2002) is in fact, as in the analysis by Galal, the result of both a public accountability problem and of the need for reforms that go beyond building schools, training teachers and improving the curriculum. Such an approach would emphasize how improving human capital and educational system is a top-down process that calls for the direct participation of the civil society in the decision-making process. According to Galal, citizens can improve educational outcomes only if they gain official/political representation: if they are able to directly influence education policies and choices made by policy-makers and experts in the field, and if they can set priorities according to available resources (Galal 2002).

Some other general features that concern the educational/training system in the MENA countries include the presence of traditional schooling, of limited opportunities for retraining and for upgrading skills and, as a general tendency, of unemployment inversely related to the level of education. In fact, in most countries unemployment rates tend to increase with the level of education achieved (Billeh 2002). As Figure 7.3 shows, in the case of Morocco, Algeria, Palestine and UAE to a lesser extent, unemployment rates are higher for people with tertiary education; in Tunisia, Turkey, Israel and Iran graduates are better off and yet unemployment tends to be significant both at secondary and tertiary levels of education all over the region.

The decline in standards and the incapability of the educational system to form a highly-skilled labour force that suits the demands of the market, as we have seen, is caused by different factors, such as the rapid expansion in university enrolment rates (not balanced by investment in resources and in the quality of the system), and the traditional approach to education (with little attention toward the accumulation of knowledge, analytical capabilities and formation of 'ideas') (Fergany 2001). Therefore, in most Arab countries the educational system, developed mainly in primary and in secondary schools and mainly concentrated on humanistic formation, is incapable of foreseeing, in the medium-long term, the evolution of professional figures and of the development of the competences demanded by local labour markets. Moreover, on a personal level, the preference for university learning and the absence of training programmes can be attributed to the lack of

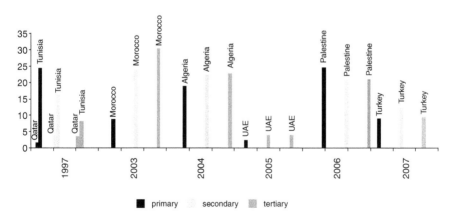

Figure 7.3 Unemployment rates by level of education for selected MENA countries

Source: Authors' elaboration of data from ILO, *Key Indicators of the Labour Market*, 2009.

information and to socio-cultural factors, such as the important role of the family in planning vocational choices of children (Wilson 1995), thus resulting in a mismatch between personal return of investment in human capital and social benefit. This dynamic is particularly marked when governments subsidize education at higher level, thus influencing investment choices at household level.

In the 1960s, MENA education attainment (the average number of school years and total population over 15 years old enroled in school) was the lowest in the world. By the end of the 1990s MENA countries had closed the educational gap with developing economies. This happened even though most countries, after the fall in oil price of the 1980s, experienced a sharp decline in GDP growth rates (due in part to the decrease in employment and incomes as well as to reduced investments) and a sharp fall in total factor productivity (TFP), which had a large impact on social and private expenditure capacity. A small recovery occurred in the 1990s, despite the cut in investments, but it was not sufficient to close the gap with the most advanced developing economies. Nevertheless, as we will see shortly, the 'paradox' of human capital in the region (i.e. the inability of human capital to turn into economic growth despite the investments made by national governments in terms of enlarging education provision and relative choices) cannot be ascribed solely to the supply side (market for education and the quantity/quality dichotomy), which is strongly related to the demand side, to the labour market's peculiar structure and institutions and to its growth dynamics.

Regional labour markets: structures and features

Despite the high investments in human capital that have occurred in the region since the 1960s, the return on human capital and the overall TFP were low. Why didn't human capital contribute to growth? Some scholars are investigating further the demand side and the structure of the labour markets to complete the picture sketched by the analysts of the supply side. According to Pissarides and Véganzonès-Varoudakis, close to the low quality of human capital it is misallocation (that is the utilization of skilled labour in low-productive and rent seeking activities, rather than in growth enhancing jobs) that is to blame (Pissarides and Véganzonès-Varoudakis 2007). This inefficient allocation of the labour force stays in the labour market structure, especially in its bias towards public sector needs. As the state is the most important job provider of these economies for socio-historical reasons, and as public jobs are perceived to be more secure in terms of wages and compensation than private sector jobs, thus this prejudice follows. The inability to provide the prospective labour force with the skills and competences required by the private sector at all levels of education, reflects this preference for public sector activities and leads to a system of formation that finances and encourages skills needed at public sector level.

With the slow growth of the public and the inability of the private sector to absorb the huge number of new entrants in the labour market, only a few countries (some of the oil-producing ones) have been able to absorb an educated population. Moreover, where governments have been unable to spur on skilled labour mobility as a balancing mechanism for market failures, open unemployment[7] has coexisted with high level of under-employment (World Bank 2008b). Furthermore, labour market distortion, due to inadequate policy and wage setting institutions[8] and scarce employment relations, has led to information asymmetry and market rigidities, so that even though the educational system has been able to produce skilled labour, the contribution to economic growth has been low.

To avoid this short-circuit some scholars propose new rules for the labour market (both private and public) to introduce flexibility: according to them, economic efficiency and worker protection could be achieved if governments set as an overarching goal 'to protect the income of workers as opposed to protect particular jobs' (see Angel-Urdinola, Kuddo, Tanabe and Wazzan 2010); other scholars propose a new social contract (World Bank 2004). These suggestions would adjust common trends behind the regional labour markets, such as:

1   *Structural imbalances*: MENA labour markets present structural imbalances between demand and supply of skills, with highly educated people waiting for a job and the inadequately educated workforce a major constraint for business establishment (Figure 7.4).
2   *Low productivity and rising job creation*: The relative growth in the absorptive capacity of the regional economies (as in the case of Egypt, Algeria and Iran) is still matched with a negative relationship between productivity growth and employment creation (due mainly to lack of investments). Moreover, in some countries, such as Algeria, Tunisia and Iran, real wages in non-agricultural activities have increased much faster than labour productivity, suggesting a rise in the unit labour cost and decreasing competitiveness.
3   *Market segmentation*: Instead of segmentation between capital intensive and labour intensive sectors, MENA labour markets present a division between the public sector and government jobs (with more guarantees in terms of insurance and wage) and the private jobs. The dominant role of the state in economic affairs and the inefficiency of the bureaucratic system have slowed down the growth process of the private sector, which is constituted by a small number big firms benefiting from state incentives, and several small firms having limited access to official credit and governmental programmes. The result is that the public sector still plays a dominant role in employment creation in most countries, from 10 per cent in Morocco to 93 per cent in Kuwait (being 70 per cent the GCC values). The slow growth of the private sector, the reduced absorption capacity of the public, together with the mismatch between demand and

supply in the labour markets, have exacerbated unemployment problems, mostly for the young labour force. One of the main outcomes has been an increase of unofficial activities (World Bank 2005).

4   *A rising informal sector*: The informal labour market, mainly constituted by small, family-owned activities and firms that require little investment and have no official insurance system, has been so dynamic in the past decades that nowadays they represent one of the main sources of occupation for the Arab labour force. More important is the fact that informal activities, in both rural and in urban areas, are becoming a form of persistent labour market, suggesting that in the presence of high unemployment rates or inaccessibility to formal business, this is not a transitory solution but rather a proper occupation (World Bank 2004). In Egypt, for example, the total establishment of small and medium informal enterprises, at 1.1 per cent before 1952 (compared to 2.3 per cent for the formal enterprises) rose to 7.5 per cent in the period from 1970 to 1979, to 16.9 per cent in the 1980-1989 period and to 35.9 per cent in 2000 and beyond (in the last period the total number of formal enterprises established was equal to 27.7 per cent) (El-Mahdi and Rashed 2009).

Figure 7.4 Percentage of firms identifying inadequate skill level as a major constraint for establishment (average values)

Source: Authors' elaboration of World Bank (2011), *Enterprise Surveys Data.*

As we have seen in Chapter 4, the demographic changes that have occurred in the Arab region in the past have, in fact, resulted in a remarkable decline in the dependent group and in the massive increase of the economically active population; projections for the 2000-2015 period suggest how employment in selected Arab countries has to rise by more than an annual four per cent with the strongest acceleration required for Algeria (five per cent) and lower targets for Egypt, Morocco and Tunisia (3.6 per cent). The market has thus been fed with a supply of new entrants (creating unemployment due to low market absorptive capacity), resulting in a window of opportunity for growth (based on the wide availability of human capital and skilled labour to employ). Among the main reasons for the increasing pressure on the labour market is the enlarged total labour force participation rates[9] (in the MENA region this grew from 49 per cent in the 1980s to 52.05 per cent in 2009) (Figure 7.5a), which is due to women's rising participation in economic activities in particular: in the region, women's participation rates increased from 21.09 per cent in 1980 to 22.2 per cent in the 1990s and reached almost 26.8 per cent in 2009. The increase has been more marked in countries like the GCC, but also in Iran (19.5 per cent in the 1980 and 31.9 in 2009), Algeria (19.35 per cent in 1980 and 37.3 in 2009), Libya (11.5 per cent and 24.5), Tunisia (19 per cent and 19.6), Jordan (12.5 per cent and 23.3) and Lebanon (15 per cent and 22.3) (Figure 7.5b, 7.5c, 7.5d). The greatest challenge for the region is thus the creation of jobs and the productive employment of available human capital. However, during the 1990s, the rate of growth of the labour force exceeded the rate of growth of employment: this is the case of Algeria, Iran, Jordan, Morocco and Yemen, which accounted for about 50 per cent of the entire region's labour force. In Tunisia and Egypt the rate of growth of employment remained almost paired with the rate of the labour force, while in only some of the GCC countries (Bahrain, Kuwait and Oman) employment growth was enough to absorb the new entrants. The region thus failed to create an environment in which the private sector could emerge as an engine of sustainable development (Keller and Nabli 2002: 4-13), especially in the presence of congestion and reduced absorptive capacity at public sector level.

However, over the last three decades, and in particular since the 1980s, MENA countries have moved towards an economic model based on private investment and trade openness, but investments did not transform the region into diversified, high performing economies, unlike what happened in East Asian countries (China, Korea, Malaysia). The reason behind this is not missing reforms in MENA countries (indicators of market-oriented reforms show how the region ranks in the world average, and how the gaps are too small to explain the difference in performance), but rather the persistence of some traditions and social behaviours which undermine the effectiveness of reforms. These include rent allocation channels, a tendency to preserve the status quo by beneficiaries that are well organized to protect their rents, the presence of policy-making institutions that lack credibility of commitment,

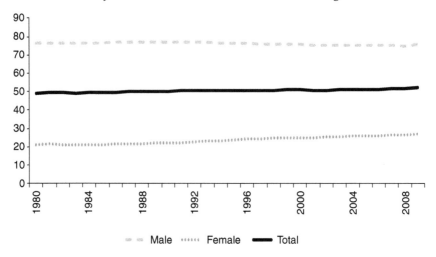

Figure 7.5a MENA labour force participation rates

Source: Authors' elaboration of World Bank, *World Development Indicators*, 2011b.

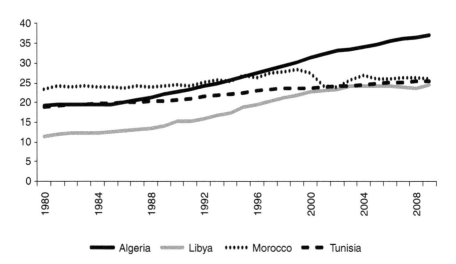

Figure 7.5b Female labour force participation rates by regional subgroups:
           Maghreb

Source: Authors' elaboration of World Bank, *World Development Indicators*, 2011b.

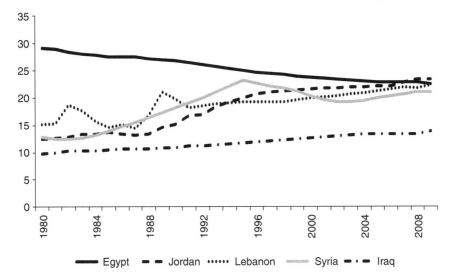

Figure 7.5c Female labour force participation rates by regional subgroups: *Mashreq*

Source: Authors' elaboration of World Bank, *World Development Indicators*, 2011b.

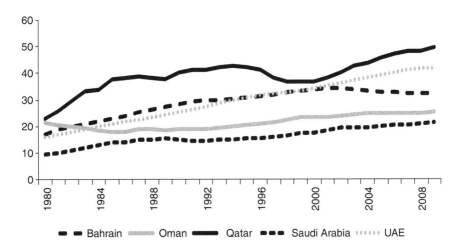

Figure 7.5d Female labour force participation rates by regional subgroups: *GCC*

Source: Author's elaboration of World Bank, *World Development Indicators*, 2011b.

and the absence of institutions that limit discretion and arbitrariness by public officials (World Bank 2009: 3-11). This would suggest that, basically, the market-oriented model and the implementation of reforms aimed at achieving openness and privatization, were less effective for the MENA economies (due to inner-institutional factors and proper ways of conducing economic activities); as a matter of fact, higher dynamism (in terms of sector growth capacity) has been shown by the region when following the proper model that, based on the insufficient growth capacity of the public sector and the inability of the public sector to provide more jobs, has moved to the informal sector and self-employment. In Table 7.2 these concurrent effects are all presented and, despite the lack of data (which means that the phenomenon of self-employment is underestimated), the labour market trends produced by the mentioned phenomena emerge. The high rate of participation to the labour force is deep-rooted in oil-rich labour-importing countries (between 47.3 per cent in Saudi Arabia and 85.8 per cent in Qatar), which is side by side the preference for public sector employment (nearly 80 per cent, UAE excepted) and the irrelevance of self-employment. The oil producers present a high population performing worse in terms of participation rate (up to 40 per cent), keeping unemployment at around 10 per cent (Yemen excepted) and these countries seem to rely more on self-employment (between 34.4 per cent of Algeria and 38.8 per cent of Iran) and on public sector jobs to account for about a third of employed people (Yemen for 12 per cent). This is due to their mixed economies that complicate the labour markets in respect to the other oil economies. As to the populous MENA countries, the relevance of young people affects the participation in the labour force (around 40 per cent) and unemployment, especially in Jordan (12.9 per cent), Tunisia (14.2 per cent) and Turkey (11 per cent); although the public employment is declining, it still reaches percentages of 38 and 28.7 in Jordan and Egypt respectively, while in Tunisia it is 20 per cent and in Turkey it is 13.8. Finally, in this group of countries the labour market problems push workers toward self-employment more in Morocco (56 per cent) but less in Tunisia (35.6 per cent) and all of the other countries are somewhere in between these.

Peasantry is still a relevant professional group in MENA region as we can see if we look at MENA economies by employment sector. This highlights that in a lot of countries peasantry is diffused over the following MENA region countries: Morocco (40.9 per cent) and Egypt (31.6 per cent) are the top agricultural economies, followed by Iraq, Iran, Turkey and Algeria, where 20 per cent of employed people are in agriculture (Table 7.3).

Syria, Algeria, Turkey and Iran also present between one third and one fourth of workers in the industry, but Egypt, Israel, Jordan and Morocco also reach around the 20 per cent.

Table 7.2 MENA employment, unemployment, self-employment and public employment ratios

Country	Employment to population ratio (% 2010)	Unemployment ratio (% of total labour force, year 2009)	Self-employment (% of total employment, year 2008)	Public employment (% of total employment, year 2008)
Algeria	38.6	10.2	34.4[b]	30.0
Bahrain	64.9	–	3.8	80.0
Egypt	44.2	9.4	41.5[c]	28.7
Iran	39.8	10.5[d]	46.8	–
Iraq	33.5	–	–	–
Israel	53.5	7.5	12.7	17.8
Jordan	36.0	12.9	8.8	38.0
Kuwait	66.2	–	2.7[b]	75.0
Lebanon	41.7	9.0[c]	37.3[c]	–
Libya	49.2	–	–	–
Morocco	45.0	10.0	56.0	9.0
Oman	54.9	–	–	–
Qatar	85.8	–	–	–
Saudi Arabia	47.3	5.4	–	83.0
Syria	39.0	8.1	38.9	29.0
Tunisia	40.7	14.2[d]	35.6[a]	20.0
Turkey	44.0	11.0	39.0	13.8
U A E	75.9	4.0[d]	4.8	23.6
Yemen	41.5	14.6	–	12.0

[a] 2003
[b] 2005
[c] 2007
[d] 2008

Source: Authors' elaboration of data from the World Bank (2011b), *World Development Indicators and Global Development Finance.*

Table 7.3 MENA countries sector employment (% of total employment) in 2008

Country	Agriculture	Industry	Services	Total
Algeria	20.7[a]	26.0[a]	53.1[a]	100.0
Bahrain	0.8[a]	15.0[a]	84.2[a]	100.0
Egypt	31.6	23.0	45.4	100.0
Iran	21.2	32.2	46.6	100.0
Iraq	23.4	18.2	58.4	100.0
Israel	1.7	21.5	76.8	100.0
Jordan	2.6	19.3	78.1	100.0
Kuwait	2.7[b]	20.6[b]	76.7[b]	100.0
Lebanon	–	–	–	–
Libya	–	–	–	–
Morocco	40.9	21.7	37.4	100.0
Oman	–	–	–	–
Qatar	2.5[d]	51.8[d]	45.7[d]	100.0
Saudi Arabia	4.3	19.8	75.9	100.0
Syria	16.8	30.3	52.9	100.0
Tunisia	–	–	–	–
Turkey	23.7	26.8	49.5	100.0
United Arab E.	4.2	24.3	71.5	100.0
Yemen	7.9[c]	–	–	–

[a] 2004

[b] 2005

[c] 2000

[d] 2007

Source: Authors' elaboration of data from the World Bank (2011b), *World Development Indicators and Global Development Finance.*

Matching demand for and supply of labour

In trying to synthesize the poor labour market outcomes of the MENA region, Keller and Nabli state that:

> […] the simplest answer is that economic growth has been insufficient, given the region's labour force growth. Labour force growth in MENA is exceptional, the result of both rapid population growth and increasing rates of labour market participation (particularly of females). At the same time, this labour force growth has barely been matched with economic growth.
>
> (Keller and Nabli 2002: 8)

Despite efforts to overcome the macroeconomic imbalances of the 1980s and policies to create a positive environment for the private sector's growth, labour market outcomes have been unsatisfactory. The main reason for this lies in the decline in accumulation during the 1990s and the lack of investment, in particular the lack of increased private investment, and the fact that the private sector, 'developed under the patronage of governments', was mainly driven by domestic demand. Together with this, it is also true that the regional economies embarked on massive reform programmes, but in some sectors (the public sector for the rationalization of resources allocated, the banking sector and the regulatory framework for easier business) light reforms have been more easily implemented, but not effective in the long run (Keller and Nabli 2002: 5-16).

Given the persistent unemployment concentrated among the more educated and those with an intermediate level of education (which, as we have seen, is the result of interrelated factors and processes linked to both state policy and culture, to the education system and labour market structures), some relevant questions need to be addressed: why did the past reforms fall short of their objectives? Why is education not meeting market demand? What can be done for the future? In trying to provide an answer to these delicate questions, Galal, referring to the Egyptian case, states that the main reason is the current approach that views education in terms of input/output or as a function of production, that is education is connected to the process of maximization of private and social returns across the population. In fact, the mainstream approach neglects the incentives for supply: governments have not been able to motivate the actors (parents, students and supervisors) in the delivery of good quality education (parents have no decision-making power while teachers are restricted by low salaries and a rigid civil service code). The centralization of the system, in fact, creates a distance between those responsible for delivering educational services and those who benefit from education. However, even if the incentives were aligned to supply, some disincentives still persist in terms of demand, especially when the demand is low or distorted by labour market rigidities, so that expansion in education does not necessarily imply growth enhancement. Moreover the market for the delivery of education, due to information asymmetries and lack of competition, fails to achieve efficiency, thus calling for the intervention of national authorities in providing solutions to the set of aforementioned disincentives. But, to overcome the false entitlement of free education and limit the subsidy only to those in need; to provide students with access to the credit market; to develop objective indicators about school performance and actual student attainment, and to prevent schools from monopolistic and discriminatory behaviour, are just some of the measures that could correct for market failures. With respect to supply, corresponding measures could be, to improve active participation to the decisional processes concerning education; to ameliorate training of teachers and the physical quality of schools; to upgrade the curriculum. As for the labour market, they need to implement reforms that activate the economy, promote labour-intensive production, and improve the overall functioning of the market (Galal 2002: 6-13).

But instead, according to Mona Said and Fatma El-Hamidi, governments should pay attention to the kind of level of education they promote. In many countries, like Egypt and Morocco, actual policies do not differ from the policies of the colonial period: most of the programmes, such as those under the initiative of international organizations, are allocated at basic and primary education level, due to the higher social returns of such investments. Moreover, while the 'graduate employment guarantee', aimed at encouraging university education, increases the number of graduates queuing for government jobs, vocational and technical education, mainly due to the influence of family background, remains a second best choice. Policies aimed at tailoring vocational programmes towards labour market needs, together with the fostering of private-public partnerships will be beneficial for the MENA countries in trying to match such structural imbalances (Said, El-Hamidi 2008).

As for the labour market, we have seen that it is its broad institutional structure (based on a large public sector) and the excessive regulation for the private sector that prevents the sector's growth and creates rigidities: wage setting institutions (high wages and non-wage incentives) induce highly qualified workers to enter the public sector, resulting in poor contribution of human capital to economic growth. However, the institutional framework for labour market regulation, which manages employment relationships, trade unions, hiring and firing rules and standards at work, is mainly aimed at the public sector and thus results in stringent restrictions that prevent private sector growth (by limiting the incentives for innovation and new businesses start ups). Finally, it is relevant to stress how social norms have a strong influence both in the choice of education (being at a familiar level, considered to be of higher value university with respect, to other forms of post-secondary education) and in the choice of future work (public sector jobs are considered to be more valuable in terms of social status, economic returns and guarantee). There is also a strong association between traditional social norms and women's participation in the labour force: at household level, men's attitudes and conservative behaviours can be barriers to women's participation. As more women are married than have children (as the case of Jordan shows), this argument is the main reason for women to withdraw from the labour market (Chamlou, Muzi and Ahmed 2011).

MENA countries policies that match the educational system and the labour market's needs should thus be based on a comprehensive approach that, taking into account the set of incentives/disincentives and needs of the socio-economic actors (those involved in the educational domain such as families, teachers and students, and those in charge of the provision of labour such as firms and entrepreneurs) should move to reform the institutional and regulatory framework for realigning the incentives. Furthermore, the political economy should try to consider not only the dichotomy between the private and the public in the formal sector, but also the dichotomy between the formal labour market and the informal sector. The incentives for small-scale businesses to start a process of 'informalization' in the private sector are, nowadays, mainly due to the higher standards of public sector employment and wage policies, preventing the informal from shifting to the formal. Also, in the need to turn human capital available into socio-economic growth, the MENA governments should take into account that currently the informal sector, which is an 'outsider' as it is still exempt from public regulation and thus less attractive and accountable to the workforce, is unable to attract the most educated. The formal public sector is, nowadays, the main 'insider', as it is able to attract the most educated workers and women (Said and El-Hamidi 2008) but incapable of turning human capital and the skilled labour force, that strives for those jobs, into growth.

8 The migration-development link in the MENA region

The Middle East and North Africa region and the European Union countries constitute one of the most important world areas as far as migration flows are concerned. Since the end of the Second World War, European countries (mid-west first and then southern) are, and continue to be, a major attraction for Arab and Turkish migrants engaged in south to north movements, driven mainly by economic reasons. Later, during the 1970s, the rapid growth of the Persian Gulf countries supplied these migrants with an alternative destination to Europe. In fact, the Arabian Gulf economies emerged as a single migration area characterized by socially, politically and culturally common features (language, religion and traditions), by similar demographic trends (low population growth, poor population density), by a homogeneous labour market structure (lacking national workforce participation, especially of women, where natives were reluctant to work in the private sector and the levels of education were inadequate) and, lastly, by the deployment of the *Khafeel* System[1] (Baldwin-Edwards 2005). At the same time that this break in development in the Arab countries occurred, as well as the advent of an economic recession, European countries, following the example set by the US, adopted policies restricting flows and favouring family reunification. Such regulations, together with the adoption of selective policies in the Gulf, made migration flows from MENA countries more difficult. Additionally, the creation of the European Union reduced the external worker flows, as the free movement of factors encouraged migration between the EU members.

Despite these recent trends affecting labour flows from and inside the MENA region, migration represents today, as it did in the past, a multifaceted feature of these economies. The high degree of complexity of the migration phenomenon (which can be attributed to its economic, social, political and demographic relevance and to its dynamic nature) shows that the central role it plays in development policies requires a methodological premise and a deep investigation to be completely understood.

The first step in this analysis is to look at how migration arises in a particular environment (the historical and institutional framework), usually involving economic and social 'push' factors – poverty, job shortage, and inequality – in origin countries, which drive the migration flow, and 'pull' factors – formal or informal recruitment mechanisms, family or social networks, immigration policies, and demand for foreign labour in specific sectors – in destination countries. Migration is generally revealed by out-flows of labour,[2] classified by duration of working abroad as 'permanent' or 'temporary' ('return' or 'circular' migration). Economists pay particular attention to returnees[3] who are considered to be the potential actors for change in domestic economy, since they mobilize different kinds of resources acquired abroad (remittances, knowledge, and know-how) to implement entrepreneurial projects and to finance expenditure in key areas for development (such as education and technical formation).

Regardless of the high diversification among MENA countries with respect to the forces that fuel migration ('pull' and 'push' factors), the empirical evidence shows, as a shared stylized fact, that strong bonds are kept with the origin communities, together with a high propensity to transfer savings in the form of remittances. This is mainly due to the fact that migration, rather than being an 'individual' decision taken by a single person – an isolated economic agent aiming to maximize his personal income – is instead the result of a process implemented by three components: 1) a family strategy, 2) an economic project made by the migrant and 3) the support of transnational, social and economic networks operating between the origin community and host country.

The hinge emerging from this framework is the family, intended as the economic unit ensuring its reproduction and preservation through the allocation of common resources (including labour and monetary income), that undergoes the whole migration process. This is due to the fact that the family strategies are aimed at balancing its available resources (such as labour and capital) and the needs of common consumption on one side, and at providing an alternative manner to generate monetary and non-monetary income on the other. Once in the host country, the behaviour of the migrant and the way he relates to his family depends on his personal motivation and intention (willingness to share part of his income with the community of origin) and, as previously mentioned, on his plans to return. The motivation to remit income can be purely altruistic, out of personal interest (inheritance motives or the will to invest personal savings once back at home), or in keeping with an informal contract made with the family on departure. The migrant, trying to diversify the 'economic risk' faced by its family or to compensate for the inefficiency of home credit and capital markets with some kind of secure income, intermediates between the family and local markets in the origin country by the network the migrants implement and share.

In such a theoretical framework, the growth of the sending country receives an important stimulus from the local development of migrant origin communities. This gives rise not only to a divergence with a purely macroeconomic view (where remittances are the only financial flow that supports home investments), but also to a trade-off in promoting development policies that manage the migration process and its effects. Indeed, according to the traditional theory, the economic relevance of migration is due only to the presence, in the balance of payments, of a monetary in-flow revealing the export of working services: so migration and trade could be considered substitutes, representing both distinctive components of the 'current account' (factor income and trade earning, respectively). Therefore, as to development policies in this framework, a greater openness of the economy to export (avoiding labour outflows and creating an increased trade balance surplus) is desirable, while instruments supporting the local development through a migrant's remittance are considered ineffective.[4]

All these issues will be developed in this chapter, which aims to demonstrate how migration in the MENA region represents a microeconomic mechanism for bottom-up development.

Migration in the MENA region: pattern and dynamics

The migration process can be viewed as a set of economic activities performed in connection with the implementation of a development path. This is the reason why international migration is not the result of the lack of development, but a condition of the development process itself, so it is true that its intensity is related to income growth. There is very little migration at low levels of development, because the poverty trap prevents people from implementing migration projects. As income reaches a certain value, the migration process starts and the workforce begins to flow out from the origin country, first increasing at growing rates, and then continuing at declining ones when the domestic economy gives people incentives and opportunities to stay (Figure 8.1). Migration does not last forever, despite the tendency to perpetuate itself over time, because it stops when a high level of income has been reached in the domestic economy. Thus, each country generally undergoes a life cycle of the movement of its people (following the stages of economic development and demographic transition), so countries that experience high levels of out-migration can sometimes eventually become receiving countries for immigrants (as the experience of Italy, Spain and Turkey reveals).

The migration/development relation, called the 'migration hump' by Martin and Taylor (Martin and Taylor 1996), brings to light the fact that middle-income developing countries are the most engaged in migration. In fact, the MENA 'exporting labour' economies first experienced a huge intra-regional migration (on average) in the 1970s, with the implementation of liberalization policies by the receiving countries and the rapid growth of some Arab economies. They then reached a peak in the 1980s, when a prolonged growth of population meant more outward flows. In the migration transition of the MENA countries, the 1990s can be seen as a turning point, because of the high volumes of returning migrants following the Gulf crisis and of the changing demands of the receiving Gulf countries (less foreign

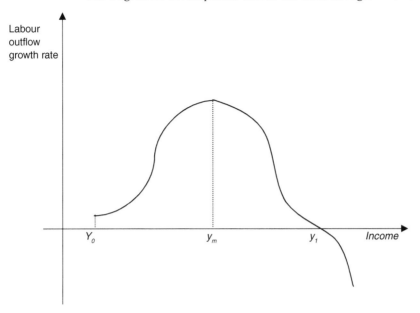

Figure 8.1 The migration cycle
Source: Authors' elaboration in accordance with Martin and Taylor 1996.

workers were required and a process of substitution of Asian migrants for South Mediterranean ones was implemented).

According to the neoclassical paradigm (Todaro 1976), the decision to migrate is the result of a rational calculation in which individual migrants consider the wage differential between the country of origin and that of their destination (or the probability of finding employment) on one hand, and the cost of physical displacement (transport costs) on the other. But the economic variables, although continuing to be a primary, stable incentive to migrate, are not sufficient to account for migration movements, unless they are incorporated into a wider dynamic frame (cultural, political and institutional). In fact, in the Mediterranean and Middle East, apart from economic differentiation of origin countries, many factors shaped labour migration movements: migration policies implemented after the Second World War that discouraged emigration from MENA countries; the massive 'guestworker' programmes starting in the 1960s and continuing to the 1980s with the expansion of the GCC countries; and the need to cope with labour shortages in specific sectors inside and outside the region. And today the surpluses in domestic labour supply and the high unemployment experienced throughout the MENA region contribute to steady migration flows (together with networks and migration policies in host countries like, for example, the family reunification mechanism). Both examples suggest that migration has turned out to be a consequence of a wider process of social, political and economic integration through international borders.

In this context, colonization emerged first as a key element in defining the direction of migration flows across international borders: the empirical evidence shows that among the countries linked by a common colonial past, a set of conditions were established that would encourage the perpetuation of flows towards the colonizing country even after independence. This is the case of many North African countries (Algeria, Morocco, Tunisia) and of West and Equatorial Africa that were colonized by France since the nineteenth century. In the early stages of this settlement, the migration flow went from France to the colonies, and it was only after the First World War that this was reversed and there were more migrants to France from the colonies (the migrants were mostly employed in the army, but later they became substitutes for French workers engaged in the conflict). Migration flows from the colonies to France continued after the war because immigration (of Algerian workers, for instance) was a strategy to cope with low population growth. So, colonial ties and international relations represent the key variables that explain why some MENA countries remain the main source for external migrants to the EU: the persistency of this vertical pattern is demonstrated by the number of first generation migrants[5] living in the EU (between 10 and 15 million people, equal to 4.8 per cent of the Mediterranean countries of the MENA region's aggregated population in 2005). Moreover, EU statistics reveal (Figure 8.2) the presence of around 5.8 million migrants of Med-MENA origin in 2005, with Germany and France as main receiving countries followed by the other members, and the pivotal role of the Netherlands, Spain and Italy acting as core countries for flows originating in the South Mediterranean (CARIM 2005). About 2.8 million of these people are from Morocco, 2.5 million are from Turkey (UNHCR 2010), and the remaining people are from Tunisia and Algeria.

If Europe is the single-largest destination for migrants from the cited Med-MENA countries, it is the Arab oil economies that exert a pull on Mashreq workers. Beginning in the 1970s, as previously mentioned, the geography of migration changed with people from the south east Mediterranean presenting a second pole of attraction (that is the Gulf area). The huge subsequent south-south movement of workers showed, over time, three main phases: 1) an intense flow in the 1970s and 1980s linked to high levels of economic growth in the Arab world, 2) a change in the composition of worker-origin countries during the 1990s with a gradual increase of the Asian presence (because of the Gulf War of 1991), and 3) the current phase of uncertainty for the future (where the external shocks related to conflicts, the wavering oil prices, the growth of domestic supply work in the Gulf countries, represent a reversal of the intra-regional migration patterns). Whereas Maghrebi workers have been mainly pulled to Europe by labour demand and the Maghreb outflows have evolved into permanent migration due largely to policies of family reunification (Baldwin-Edwards 2005), Mashreq workers have been mostly engaged in a temporary, horizontal migration[6] towards the GCC countries, supported

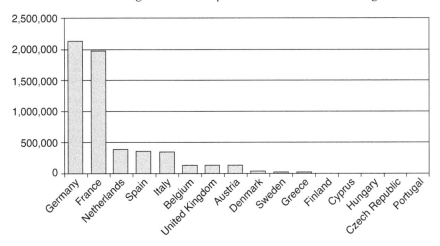

Figure 8.2 Med-MENA migrants to European countries (number of people in 2005).

Source: Authors' elaboration of statistics of countries of destination. CARIM database (2005) *http://www.carim.org/.*

by policies to prevent naturalization of migrant workers, consisting in fostering employment of natives.

As a result of these horizontal flows, the foreign-born population resident in Mashreq countries is at about 26.6 million people (11.9 per cent of the total population of the area and 13.5 per cent of the world migrants in 2010), of which 15.1 million people are temporarily hosted by GCC, 8.7 million by other Mashreq countries in which they are not resident, and less than three million are hosted by Israel (UN 2010: 205-16 in IOM 2010). Considering that East Mediterranean countries were traditionally the migrant senders, and that now an important percentage of their population is composed of immigrant people (Table 8.1), these figures highlight not only the relevance of these horizontal flows for the economy of the region, but also the starting of an intra-regional restructuring in the migration process.

As two different migration patterns coexist in the MENA region, recent economic studies in the field have started to explore the likely implication of both migration experiences (south-north vs. south-south) on the development of MENA sending countries (i.e. labour exporting countries). Comparing two experiences, of Morocco and Egypt, Collyer identifies some important variables (geography, timing and nature of migration) that reveal how different migration patterns can result in different LED (local economic development) patterns (Collyer 2004). The dominant distinction between Morocco and Egypt remains in the geography of migration, with 85 per cent of Moroccan migrants moving to Europe (and significant groups in Canada and USA) and 70 per cent of Egyptians moving to Libya or the Gulf (mainly in Saudi Arabia). Diversity can also be found in the skills endowment of migrants: in the 1970s mainly highly skilled Egyptian individuals migrated,

Table 8.1 Foreign-born people as a share of total population in selected MENA
            countries

Countries	2010
Jordan	45.9
Kuwait	68.8
Lebanon	17.8
Libya	10.4
Oman	28.4
Palestine	43.6
Qatar	86.5
Saudi Arabia	27.8
Syria	9.8
United Arab Emirates	70.0
Israel	40.4

Source: Authors' adaptation of data from IOM, *World Migration Report*, 2010: 116.

while Morocco responded primarily to demand for unskilled labour abroad
(the composition of flows has since changed, leading to a more heterogeneous
migration of the Egyptians and to a gradual increase in the number of
qualified Moroccan migrants). Regarding the duration of migration, for
Egyptians it is traditionally of much shorter nature than for Moroccans: this
should negatively affect the level of remittances sent back, since transfers
increase over time and allow for a maturity point to be reached (IOM 2002).
In spite of this effect and of similar remittance fluctuations (Diliph and
Zhimei Xu 2008), the total value of Egyptian monetary funds sent home by
migrants was much higher than the Moroccan one in the period 2000-
2007.[7] Regarding the nature of the skills of returning migrants, although it
is difficult to test whether migrants can improve their competences by taking
jobs abroad that match their skill sets, it is likely that a more heterogeneous
migration (as in the case of Egypt) can increase the training of migrants,
especially for the unskilled ones. Conversely, the integration of medium-
high skilled migrants (as in the case of Morocco) in a labour market where
the demand is mostly for low-skilled workers (as in the case of Europe), may
result in little or no human capital improvement for migrant workers. Thus,
for the aforementioned reasons, it is the south-south flows that seem to
create a more 'development friendly' pattern.

Network as an institutional bridge between the migrants' projects and the origin community

The analysis of migrant networks only emerged in the 1970s and 1980s
when scholars in the field of international migration, focusing on the role
of economic interdependence, looked at migration as a transnational
process. Exceeding the neoclassical approach (Lewis 1954; Ranis and Fei
1961; Todaro 1976), the main target of the 'network-based view'[8] was to

provide an explanation for the presence of migratory flows in the absence of significant wage differentials or of structural change in the demand for labour in receiving countries (Massey, Arango, Hugo, Kouaouci, Pellegrino and Taylor 1998). Compared to the previous theories, the network approach focuses on the distribution of incomes in the country of origin (and not only on the absolute income), on the role of family and community, on information asymmetries, and on the complex interaction between migrants and the socio-political context in which they operate. It also highlights the multiplier effects of migration, the potential that earlier generations of immigrants have on future flows (giving rise to a phenomenon of chain migration) and the dynamics of human capital improvement (Becker 1974). As a final point, the approach explains why migration may become cumulative in nature, that is 'independent' from the factors that it originated from (Sciortino and Decimo 2006). Thus the network represents, on one hand, an analytical meso-dimension (intermediate between the micro level of individual decisions and the macro-structural determinants), and on the other, an institutional set defined in the field of agents (individuals, families, companies, nation states) and of their economic and socio-political relations.

There are different approaches to the study of networks: the 'adaptive' approach considers the migration process in the short run, stressing the role of family networks in reducing the physical cost of migration, while the 'integration' approach, instead, focuses on the long-term effects and the ability of networks to structure the position of migrant communities of different ethnicities in destination countries. The network is also a powerful explanatory tool: when applied to the study of 'chain migration', it reveals its ability to lower the cost of information for potential migrants and to influence the decisions to move; however, when applied to the 'systemic framework', it emphasizes the continuous process of interaction between migrants in the country of origin and destination, regarding the exchange of information and resources, visits and eventually return (Faist 1997).

Following the categorization of Fawcett (1989), migration networks can be identified as the result of the actions made by the agents involved in the migration process (states, mass cultures, persons/families and agencies) in particular domains of activities (tangible, regulatory and relational) carried out according to different kinds of rules. Thus, these four categories of agents and the three types of behaviours produce a matrix, where each column represents an activity domain and each line a type of agent. The resulting 12 cells identify one or more networks of agents belonging to the same category operating by transnational links. The tangible state-state network, for example, includes trade in goods and services and financial flows resulting from technical, economic and military assistance programmes; the interstate regulatory cell includes migration policies, while the recruitment programmes of the workforce refer to the agency activities in the regulatory domain. Among the agent categories identified by Fawcett, families and persons build networks[9] of particular relevance, not only because they constitute tangible bonds (like remittances) or informal institutions to channel them, but also because they shape relational links affecting the remittance behaviour of migrants.

Remittance behaviour (the motivation of which is dependent on network strength intensity) finds an explanation in the 'theories of altruism' of the 1970s. This altruistic behaviour was believed to occur where the family appears as an income-equalizer (Becker 1974) and the migrant, motivated by the desire to improve family welfare, decides to relocate part of his savings in the form of remittances, equalling his own marginal utility of consumption with the marginal utility of household consumption. Assuming declining marginal utility of consumption, remittances are thus an increasing function of expected income differentials between the migrant (donor) and the relative family (beneficiary). As the weight of the utility of the recipients is determined by the migrant, both the optimal amount of remittances for each level of income (thus the degree of altruism) and the migrant satisfaction through the consumption activity (utility) are determined, the latter depending directly on the welfare of his family (that is on his consumption utility – see Clark and Drinkwater 2001).

A behavioural model of migrant remittance based on altruism had been also proposed by Funkhouser (Funkhouser 1995). Among the main predictions of the model, there are the following tendencies:

1   Migrants with more economic potential (in terms of employment status and human capital) tend to remit more, while families with middle and low incomes are the major beneficiaries of the transfers.
2   Remittances depend on the relatedness degree and on the intention to return to origin countries. The idea of the importance of proximity in terms of strength of ties between families and migrants can already be found in Edgeworth's discussion on the inverse relationship between social distance and altruism (Edgeworth 1881).
3   Remittances decrease with increasing number of migrants belonging to the same family (discouraging altruism).
4   The transfer of remittances decreases with increasing household income target.
5   Remittances tend to decrease over time because the attachment to the family (a solid network) is weakened when migrants reside in the destination country for long periods of time (Stark 1991).

Several empirical studies, based on the MENA region, have attempted to test the hypothesis of altruism linked to the existence of a familiar network, not only as the main motivation behind migrants transfer, but also as an explanatory variable for some stability of cash flows. In a recent study, Bouhga-Hagbe, defining altruism as 'the will of the migrant worker to give financial assistance to family members in situations of economic distress', showed that this reasoning is relevant in explaining the transfer of remittances to Egypt, Jordan, Morocco, Pakistan and Tunisia. Using agricultural production as an indicator of the economic performance of considered countries, the study shows that in the long run, when farm income falls (leading to a deterioration in economic conditions of communities dependent on these activities), migrant remittances tend to increase (Bouhga-Hagbe 2004). The inverse relationship between agricultural output and the volume of transfers confirms the importance of altruistic motives in sending remittances, suggesting that in these countries such financial flows provide a source of steady income and a form of insurance that can mitigate the shock of the economic system. The same results were seen in a previous study on Morocco, where Bouhga-Hagbe developed a model in which the altruism of the migrant, together with a certain degree of attachment to the country of origin, helps explain the stability of flows over time. In the case of Morocco, however, it is the attachment to the motherland that presents the greatest explanatory power, because the desire to maintain ties with the community of belonging is reflected in the investment of remittances in real estates. In the long run, the empirical evidence demonstrates the existence of a positive relationship between remittances and the purchase of non-financial assets, as the altruistic migrant, linked somehow to the country of origin through remittances, diversifies its portfolio by allocating financial resources between consumption in the host country, household consumption and purchase of non-financial assets in the country of origin. Other empirical results, confirming the hypothesis of altruism, emerge from a study of Schiopu and Siegfried on the basic determinants of remittance transmission from 20 European countries to Morocco, Egypt, Turkey, Lebanon and Jordan (among top ten recipients of remittances in the period taken into account) (Schiopu and Siegfried 2001). The study, using a database built on the flows of remittances (which were bilateral in order to control other variables, such as differences in the costs of transfer between countries and the possible presence of the financial network), shows that income differentials among countries of origin and destination increase the volume of remittances transferred, confirming the reasons for altruism.

Finally, some scholars have seen altruism as one of the main reasons behind non-market exchanges. If individuals perceive altruistic-informal transfers as better (or more satisfactory) than formal exchanges regulated by the market, they tend to preserve such a system even when the economy becomes more oriented to markets (Stark 1995). This is especially true in developing countries where altruism is a dynamic force that, in the presence of market failures and high transaction costs, emerges as an alternative trade arrangement. Such networks neutralize or substitute markets in allocating resources and transfers of public nature (such as spending on education and state benefits in the event of unemployment), with important effects on policy distribution of national governments. The aforementioned

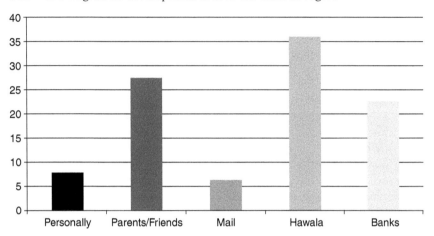

Figure 8.3 Channels of international remittances (2006)

Source: Authors' elaboration of CAPMAS, Egypt Labour Market Panel Survey (ELMPS), 2006.

considerations become particularly true in the case of MENA countries, where empirical evidence shows that, despite the existence of different institutional networks, migrants prefer the informal money transfer system known as *Hawala* (Figure 8.3).

The origin of *Hawala* dates back to the Middle Ages and to the need of facilitating commercial transactions between contracting parties resident in distant regions. It consists of an informal monetary transfer based on trust and agency. Despite the diversity of definitions (*Hundi* in Pakistan and Bangladesh, *fei Ch'ien* in China, *Padala* in the Philippines, *Phei Kwan* in Thailand), the traditional channels of remittance transfer mechanisms have similar 'modus operandi', with a simple transaction taking place in presence of a remitting agent, a receiver and a service provider in the person of a financial intermediary (see Figure 8.4). If an Egyptian immigrant who works in Abu Dhabi wants to send remittances to family members who live in Cairo, he will make a payment in Egyptian pounds (or convert it to another currency, usually US dollars) to an agent present in the host city who, in turn, will contact an agent in Cairo. The latter will pay the family recipients the sum equivalent to the payment made by the migrant, but in the local currency. As a form of identification the migrant will receive a code (to be sent to the family) that will be sufficient to receive the funds. The presentation of a valid identity card is optional. Once the transaction takes place, the agent in Abu Dhabi will pay off its debt with the agent in Cairo in person or using a series of intermediaries.

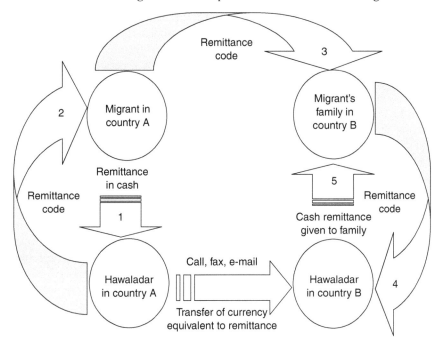

Figure 8.4 The *Hawala* system

Source: Authors' elaboration in accordance with El Korchi, M., Maimbo M. S. and John W. F. (2003).

Such a system, alternative to banks and international funds transfer services (like MoneyGram and Western Union), presents some specific features:

1   Today *Hawala* involves mainly the sending of remittances from employment with most cases occuring on international routes.
2   Transactions are made using more than one currency.
3   Each transaction requires intermediaries. Transactions made using the *Hawala* system, in fact, require a *Hawaladar*, that is, an improper broker or banker who anticipates the amount the migrant has decided to send, drawing on personal reserves.
4   This mechanism, based on trust and agents, provides a way for the repayment of debts incurred by the intermediary and, in many cases, allows remittances to be paid to the beneficiaries even before the *Hawaladar* has received the equivalent amount from the migrant.[10]
5   *Hawala* represents a kind of debt transfer to an agent. Both the institutions (transfer and agency), unknown in the Roman law, were accepted by the Islamic law and by the later common law as obligations (Badr 1977).

Despite the introduction of new technologies and numerous services for trans-national government and attempts to formalize these channels in order to make the banking system more competitive (in terms of cost and time) and safer, MENA migrants still prefer the informal networks of transfer based on number of operational characteristics of the *Hawala*, including its speed, cultural convenience, versatility, anonymity and moderate costs (El Korchi, Maimbo, and John 2003). Furthermore, informal channels show a strong stability and even a tendency for growth, especially in times of political and economic instability (such as during periods of overvaluation of the official exchange rate, which represents an implicit tax on those who send remittances to formal channels).

Although the *Hawala* transactions show mainly the importance of networks as an economic (tangible and regulatory) link between the migrants and their origin communities, it is relevant to stress that, from the host country's perspective, such transactions prove the capability of transnational networks to improve access to host labour markets by favouring selection and integration mechanisms. There is such a strong connection between the existence of networks and the success of the migration experience, that networks can increase the likelihood of finding employment, receiving higher wages and investing in entrepreneurial activities (Portes, Guarnizo, and Haller 2002; Munshi 2003). Several empirical studies have confirmed the power of networks in influencing migration patterns and migrants' destinations (first and second generation), favouring, for example, flows of highly skilled migrants rather than low-skilled migrants (Bauer, Epstein, and Gang 2000; Pedersen, Pitlykova and Smith 2004).

The particular tie between migrants and families (forming tangible, institutional and relational social capital networks[11]) (Coleman 1988), emerges from applied analysis on the beneficiaries of remittances. In Egypt, the major beneficiary of migrants' remittances (mainly from the Gulf) is the spouse, followed by parents and other familiar members outside the nuclear family (Figure 8.5). Furthermore, for recipient households remittances are the main form of non-work income: in 2006 four per cent of interviewed households had received remittances from members living abroad (Wahba 2006). Regarding beneficiaries, it is worth noting that in Egypt, although the nuclear family is the main recipient, parents and others are also beneficiaries, supporting the idea of income transfer in the form of remittances as a welfare share mechanism.

Meyer and Brown identified another interesting typology of migrant networks in the regulatory (institutional) domain (Meyer and Brown 1999) in a series of countries including the MENA region (see Table 8.2). Called *TOKTEN* (Transfer Of Knowledge Through Expatriate Nationals) and supported by the United Nation Development Programmes, they take the form of 'distant cooperative work' within an intellectual diaspora. These formal networks, linking countries to their skilled nationals abroad, are systematic and well-established networks that involve people and assist

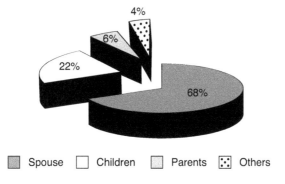

Figure 8.5 Relationship between the remitter and family members

Source: Authors' elaboration of CAPMAS, Egypt Labour Market Panel Survey (ELMPS), 2006.

skilled expatriates in engaging in various development projects. In the form of student/scholarly networks, local associations of skilled expatriates, pooling expert assistance and intellectual and scientific diaspora, they are utilized, among other functions, for skilled labour recruitment and movement outside of the homeland (Vertovec 2002). *TOKTEN* programmes create long distance networks and serve as knowledge and information channels throughout in exchange of capital, skills and managerial know-how (Meyer and Brown 1999).

Table 8.2 MENA diaspora networks

Country	Name of network	Type of network
Arab Countries	The network of Arab Scientists and Technologies Abroad (ASTA)	Intellectual/Scientific Diaspora Network
Lebanon	TOKTEN for Lebanon	TOKTEN Programme
Morocco	Moroccan Association of Researchers and Scholars Abroad (MARS)	Student/scholarly network
Palestine	Programme of Assistance to the Palestine People	TOKTEN programme
Tunisia	Tunisian Scientific Consortium	Intellectual/Scientific Diaspora Network

Note: Only MENA networks/diaspora organizations have been reported in the table.

Source: Authors' selection/elaboration of Meyer and Brown, 1999.

Migration, remittances and local development

From a macro perspective, the study of remittances generally aims to analyse in the short term the impact that these financial flows have on the macro-economic variables of the destination country (on prices, production, exchange rates, trade and national spending) and on the economic performance of recipient countries in the long term. In the case of the latter, the focus is on the structural change of remittance relationships, as economic development is based on the accumulation of financial, physical and human capital, leading to changes in the composition of demand, production, trade and employment. Remittances, as a strong currency, can act as a prerequisite for structural change by favouring not only the accumulation of physical and human capital, but also causing a shift in production from the non-tradables to tradables, thus affecting national competitiveness. In addition, in countries with high rates of emigration (and experiencing the upward phase of the migration cycle, see Figure 8.1), remittances have economic implications on poverty, income distribution and public welfare, consumption patterns and the propensity to save, remaining relevant when the development moves along. As for the importance of remittances for the MENA economies, Table 8.3 shows their high contribution to income in the case of two small countries (Lebanon and Jordan), but also in the case of other bigger countries (like Morocco and Egypt): with respect to the GDP of Morocco and Egypt, the lower share of remittances does not prove their top position among MENA recipients (because of the different dimensions of the economies) and the fact that the total value of their remittances is more than the double of the value received by the Lebanon and Jordan (World Bank 2008a: 14).

Contrary to what happened in the past, today the attention on the role of migration as a development tool for sending countries has increased, addressing the potential of the returnee in improving brain gain and transfer of capital in particular, and at local level especially (Olesen 2002). However, not all return migrants (short-term seasonal workers or permanent

Table 8.3 Remittance inflow (as % of GDP) in MENA countries in 2008

Country	Remittances
Algeria	1.3
Egypt	5.3
Jordan	19.0
Lebanon	25.1
Morocco	8.0
Syria	1.5
Tunisia	4.7
Yemen	5.3

Source: Authors' elaboration of data from IOM, *World Migration Report*, 2010: 136 and 208.

migrants) can promote local development. According to Cesare (Cesare 1974), returnees can be classified by the reason of return. So a returnee migrant is someone who couldn't find a job with wages he could survive on and also use to send remittances home ('return of failure'); a returning migrant tends to preserve the status quo in the host country and does not contribute to changing the environment in which he reintegrates ('return of conservatism'); a migrant who comes back to retire in his homelands ('return of retirement'); and a migrant who returns to utilize resources accumulated abroad and realize his projects in his country of origin ('return of innovation'). The last classification here, which is described by Cesare as the most dynamic, is also the most interesting when dealing with the relationship between return migration and development. Nevertheless, it has to be stressed that the influence of return migrants on the development path of origin countries depends on many factors: on one hand it depends on the returnees' level of preparedness (as well as willingness to return), on pre-return conditions (motivation, status, length of stay and resource mobilization), and post-return conditions (reintegration process) (Cassarino 2004). On the other hand, it depends on the local environment, that is, on the economic and institutional factors that shape the development path in origin communities (the educational background of economic agents, work experience and the capability of innovation).

Regarding pre-return conditions, it must be pointed out that in the MENA region, due to the imbalance in the local educational system that favours tertiary education at the expense of technical formation and professional schools, the majority of migrant workers have little chance of acquiring adequate professional training before leaving the country and after return. Furthermore, few of them engage in training during the migration experience, as MIREM data on returnees to the Maghreb countries (Algeria, Morocco and Tunisia) show. In 2007, only 17.5 per cent of the total returnees to the Maghreb have followed some professional training in the main country of immigration, while 80 per cent have not. On return, only four per cent of migrants have engaged in some form of training course (see Table 8.4). The previous considerations suggest that working abroad is the main training for return migrants: entrepreneurial ideas and specific know-how that represents scarce resources in origin countries are mainly acquired in the host labour market through learning by doing. Migration is thus a strategy for achieving some form of specific human capital (demanded by the markets in the migrants' homelands) improving the possibility of implementation of economic projects upon return, as confirmed by overseas returnees who invested in human capital in the host countries (Dustmann 2001).

Even if migrants become engaged in similar patterns of employment when they return to their origin countries, there are noticeable changes in the sector of employment (private vs. public) and in the share of migrants engaged in technical, scientific and management occupations. In Egypt, for example, at the beginning of the 1990s, the returnees from the Gulf countries

Table 8.4 Professional training acquired in the main country of immigration and in the origin country by returnees to the Maghreb (2007)

Answers	Did you follow any professional training courses in the main country of immigration? (% of 992 answers)	Did you follow any professional training courses in your country of origin after return (% of 992 answers)
Yes	17.5	3.9
No	79.7	94.1
No reply	2.8	2.0
Total	100	100

Source: Authors' elaboration of data from CAPMAS, *Egypt Labour Market Panel Survey* (ELMPS), 2006.

were more likely to invest in partnership and joint ventures and to provide good jobs (e.g. jobs that offer paid leave), which suggests how human capital acquired in more advanced environments increases cooperation among economic agents, and improves the quality of the business environment (Wahba 2004).

Migration experience, as a means of human capital formation, has been explored in the literature on this subject following two different perspectives. Under 'investment hypothesis', where the remittances correspond to an investment in education repaying the training the migrant received by his family before he settles abroad, migration reveals an 'a priori mechanism of selection' of both educated and beneficiary migrants based on 'educational endowment' (Kugler 2005). In this approach migration, through remittances, results in spill over effects on the local labour market, increasing the probability of creating new professional figures and reducing the gap between demand and supply of skills.[12] In a second, more complex perspective of major relevance for investigating the relationship between migration and development, remittances, skills and learning by doing acquired in the host countries act as an 'a posteriori selection mechanism' for occupational choices of return migrants, channelling this resources towards sectors or 'job positions' that require some specific technical competences (Kugler 2005).[13]

The MENA region's experience gives evidence of both hypotheses, shown in studies that compare individual characteristics of return migrants (such as human capital endowment and job position/sector of employment) with non-migrants. For example, in Egypt in 2006, returnees seemed to be more educated than non-migrants, on average. By taking into account data referring to the male head of household, despite the fact that both groups are endowed with a largely similar basic level of education, the percentage of people with post-primary education is higher for return migrants:[14] 9.3 per cent of returnees had attended technical school or secondary schools

Table 8.5 Characteristics of return overseas migrants and non-migrants in Egypt
(2006)

Education	Non-migrants	Returnees
Level of education (%)		
None	62.00	46.00
Basic	23.00	26.70
Primary [a]	7.60	11.60
Secondary [b]	5.00	9.30
Tertiary	2.00	5.50
Other	0.40	0.90
Total	*100.00*	*100.00*

[a] including preparatory school

[b] high school and technical institutes

Source: Authors' elaboration of data from CAPMAS, *Egypt Labour Market Panel Survey (ELMPS)*, 2006.

Note: Data refer only to family 'first member', i.e. the male head of household.

(compared to five per cent for non-migrants) while 5.5 per cent of return migrants had a university education (the percentage decreases to two per cent for non-migrants) (Table 8.5). Most of the migrants with university education had experienced migration to Saudi Arabia and Kuwait, those with secondary education to Libya, Iraq, Kuwait and non-Arab countries, while those with technical education chose Saudi Arabia and Iraq as destination countries (ELMPS 2006).

As for job positions, according to Wahba (Wahba 2009), although the share of waged workers is very similar for both groups of people, the proportion of employers among returnees is much higher than among non-migrants (around 21 and 12 per cent respectively). It is also interesting to note the higher participation of return migrants to formal sector activities: 55.46 for returnees and 41.93 for non-migrants (Table 8.6).

Return migration has a more pervasive role in promoting local economic development (LED), since returnees tend to transfer their savings to origin communities rather than invest or consume in destination countries. In the MENA region, due to limited access to formal credit and minimum wages in many sectors, remittances constitute an additional form of liquidity that can have positive effects at household level, both if consumed or invested. In the presence of liquidity constraints, the combination of remittances and human capital acquired abroad generally presents a positive impact in promoting occupational change and in increasing the probability of self-employment upon return (McCormick and Wahba 2000; Ilahi 1999). The amount of economic projects financed through savings accumulated abroad by Tunisian entrepreneurial returnees in the 1980s has been significant, so that it peaked at 87 per cent of all the projects carried out in the region (Mesnard 2004).

Table 8.6 Characteristics of return overseas migrants and non-migrants in Egypt (2006)

Professional features	Non-migrants	Returnees
Job position (%)		
Agriculture	23.96	17.44
Other productions	26.40	20.22
Services	8.55	3.30
Sales	8.80	3.17
Technical and scientific	20.72	32.20
Management	5.21	16.38
Clerical	6.36	7.29
Total	*100.00*	*100.00*
Employment status (%)		
Waged	65.93	64.12
Employer	12.11	21.15
Self-employed	9.59	13.17
Unpaid family worker	12.37	1.56
Total	*100.00*	*100.00*

Source: Authors' adaptation of Wahba, 2009.

More recent studies on return migration and enterprise development in the Maghreb show that in 2007 a significant share of migrants did invest in projects and business after return (around 34 per cent invested in at least one project). Regarding the features of projects or businesses owned by returnees, it can be said that they are concentrated in a small number of sectors (wholesale and retail trade, followed by hotels and restaurants, agriculture and manufacturing) and that most enterprises owned by return migrants are rather small (less than 10 employees). However, as the share of medium-sized enterprises (between 11 and 50 employees) is equal to 14 per cent, it is possible to say that returnees are significant as local employers (Nordman and Gubert 2008).

As for the use of remittances for consumption purposes, it is generally believed that migrants' savings can result in a dependency effect if they induce changes in labour supply discouraging participation, especially in agricultural activities. Empirical studies have found that in some MENA countries, such as rural areas in Morocco (de Haas 2006), the 'dependency effect' has instead resulted in a 'substitution effect', because, thanks to remittances, migrants' households do not perform agricultural works anymore but hire external labour to carry out agricultural activities. Thus the overall effect is the creation of new jobs in farming activities.

If spent on investment goods, such as building material, light machinery and fertilizer, remittances promote local economic development (LED) through increasing productivity and through making the agricultural sector more capital intensive. In the latter cases, migration represents an important tool for local development of origin communities, since it speeds up the process of labour substitution in specific sectors and of change in consumption behaviour of recipients, increasing the probability of expenditure in key areas for development (intermediate goods, import of capital).

As a general rule, the main constraint for the implementation of self-employment and entrepreneurial activities in migrant origin countries is the local environment. In the MENA region this limit is represented mainly by institutional factors like the formal banking system, state incentives and market information for small entrepreneurs, but lack of experience, market conditions and administrative constraints can also cause failure. Among the main reasons for not investing in the country of origin after return, the MIREM survey shows how, for about 60 per cent of the interviewed returnees, insufficient financial means are the main hamper, followed by lack of experience (29 per cent) and institutional hindrances (25.7 per cent) (MIREM 2008). As for financial resources used to carry out investments by returnees to the Maghreb countries (Algeria, Morocco and Tunisia), self-financing represents the main capital for undertaking some economic activities once back home (for 90 per cent of returnees), with only a small percentage of the total referring to bank loans. Parental networks are another form of support for investment projects, representing about 10 per cent who provided help for migrants that decided to go back.

Finally, it is worth stressing that in the long run returnees have a pervasive role on the growth process, since remittances are used to finance the formation of another form of productive investment: human capital. The 2008 survey on Maghrebi returnees confirms that, for about 30 per cent of the sample surveyed, investments in children's schooling are considered a priority, second only to the acquisition of some form of assets[15] (MIREM 2008, see Table 8.6). Investments in education, in turn, result in a virtuous circle for the LED process, since human capital has both economic and non-economic outcomes (social externalities), leading to improvements in well-being and the status of individuals.

The economic literature on the reasons that push migrants to become entrepreneurs underlines how the migration experience gives the migrant access to credit and to 'superior' information on the market and on relative profit opportunities (scarce in origin countries), providing them with an economic advantage in respect to non-migrants. Although few studies have focused on the possibility for returnees to the MENA region of becoming entrepreneurs, the main findings emphasize how the amount of savings and the time spent abroad have significant and positive effects on the probability of becoming entrepreneurs: in the case of Egypt, individuals who have spent one year abroad and saved 6,000 EGP (Egyptian Pound) have a 27 per cent probability of becoming an entrepreneur, but if they stay for two years and save 10,000 EGP, the probability increases to 32 per cent. Concerning returnee's activities, those investing in non-agricultural enterprises are, on average, more educated with respect to those investing in the agricultural sector, suggesting the benefit of skills acquired overseas. The main differences between small enterprises owned by returnees and by those who do not migrate, are found in the higher value of the capital invested, in the higher number of employees, and in the fact that returnees are more likely to invest in partnership and joint investments, to establish formal business and to provide good jobs (Wahba 2004).

All the findings presented emphasize how, for the returnees, remittances are a means of reducing the opportunity cost of capital (with respect to non-migrants that have to borrow from the local market), and how working overseas is a relevant strategy for the acquisition of new skills and ideas that can result in a breaking of the environmental constraints and of the way of behaving. This is particularly marked when return migrants turn to new standards and ways of conducting economic activities (for example, giving more guarantees and higher wages to workers, or licensing business).

That migration, and in particular return migration, represents an instrument to support the development of sender countries, is a stylized fact that is increasingly acknowledged alongside the need for appropriate policies to be implemented in order to manage the migration process in a more virtuous way. The *World Migration Report 2010*, supporting this view, suggests ten policies to reach this aim:

1   Mainstreaming migration in development plans;
2   Optimizing formal remittance flows;
3   Enhancing the developmental impacts of remittances;
4   Engaging diasporas;
5   Consolidating knowledge networks;
6   Strengthening the links between return and development;
7   Promoting circular migration;
8   Training to retain;
9   Developing ethical recruitment policies;
10 Institutional capacity-building.'

(International Organization for Migration, 2010)

9 The openness of the MENA economies

Beyond lost regionalism, en route to a new regional arrangement

There is a wide consensus among researchers on the lack of openness to international markets for MENA countries, whose trade volumes are 'significantly lower than what would be expected given their economic, cultural and geographical characteristics' (Bhattacharya and Wolde 2010). Recent applied studies have also shown that, for intra-regional trade, common borders seem to have a less positive impact on exchange among MENA economies, suggesting that both cooperation on procedures and infrastructures, and harmonization of policies may be more unfavourable to trade than elsewhere. The specific reasons behind the poor trade performance of the MENA region have been mainly attributed to market distortions and insufficient institutional development, inward-oriented policies, high tariff barriers, lack of competitiveness, polarized market structure, traditional products and bottlenecks in the transport sector (Ahmed 2010).

This situation is persistent despite the several initiatives undertaken to increase trade, such as the unilateral trade liberalization, the signing of agreements with individual or group of countries, the joining of WTO and the partnership with the European Union. The desire of restoring an economic regionalism in Arab world, dating back to the 1950s, is witnessed by a long history of integration attempts unravelled by multilateral agreements like the Arab Economic Unity Agreement signed in 1957, the Cooperation Council for the Arab States of the Gulf (later Gulf Cooperation Council or GCC) created in 1981, the Arab Maghreb Union established in 1989, and the Greater Arab Free Trade Area or GAFTA declared in 1998. The hope of taking advantage of integrating national economies in a more globalized world, instead, is shown by the bilateral treaties signed, like the accession to the WTO agreements and to the Barcelona declaration proposed by the European Union in 1995.

Nevertheless, the agreements supported by the Arab League were affected by the difficulties of political interstate cooperation, so that joining free trade areas was ineffective in stimulating both the openness of the MENA economies and the participation to the world economic regionalization, because of the international relations environment promoting them. In fact:

[...] the historic policy of key foreign actors in the region, especially the United States and European countries, while ostensibly touting regionalism and regional cooperation, were in fact largely bilaterally based, while in many cases specifically designed to counter the goals of their fellow competitors. US unilateralism needs no explanations, but I have found equally divisive the competition of the previous colonial powers in the region (the UK and France) and the aggressive bilaterally-focused action of players in the economic scene, notably Germany, Italy and Spain.

(Harders and Legrenzi 2008: xi)

This environment, without providing an excuse for the unsuitability of national policies to pursue a more open economy, raises questions concerning both the mainstream concept of openness (neglecting the export of labour services, that is migration flows), and the inability of trade agreements to encourage the integration in world markets. Thus the chapter moves from the approach to trade analysis in a narrow sense (as merely elimination of tariffs, quotas and custom procedures to create an open economy) to a call for a closer look at deep integration of the region, that is a more comprehensive approach involving the institutional and the political levels together with the strengthening of all market flows' relevance. In this respect, the stress is on the unique role played by regional labour markets and by migration movements as the most dynamic features of integration, with the assessment of the relation between trade and migration as a complementary component of the balance of payments current account, rather than as a substitutive one. The deep integration perspective also reveals, for the MENA countries, an unexpected dynamism in the renewal of small-scale agreements and of bilateral trade treaties that seem to have had more relative success with respect to the joining international protocols.

The openness of MENA economies: trade patterns

From the applied analysis of the openness of the MENA economies, it emerges that the matter is at least questionable, because some so-called stylized facts show contradictory trends. On one hand, the regional trade value/GDP ratio (the measure that is used more for the openness of an economy), after a sharp climb up to a percentage score of 105 in 1980, declined below 65 per cent in 1986 and settled around this value for the following 15 years before regaining points close to 100 per cent in 2008. But despite this rise and fall in trade patterns, MENA openness not only remained in line with (or higher than) the other world developing regions over the entire period (Figure 9.1), but in 2008 it was even wider than 'the world on average' (Behar and Freund 2011: 9). On the other hand, with this expanding openness there has been a declining MENA share in world exports since 1995: in fact, total MENA exports, representing 2.2 per cent of the global value in that year, dropped to 1.8 per cent in 2008. If this specific result could be explained by the rapid growth of world exports, especially in developed countries, it is also true that estimates of gravity models for the region demonstrate that, on average, 'MENA exports to the rest of the world were at only a third of their potential' (Behar and Freund 2011: 9), considering the level of GDP produced. In addition, the oil and natural resources' relevance to regional exports and the volatility of their prices affect the MENA trade heavily, avoiding the appraisal of the structural current openness of those economies. Thus, a deeper analysis of MENA international trade that goes beyond these misleading appearances is needed.

The aforementioned issues have been tackled in recent studies, providing statistics that exclude oil trade and look to the traditional MENA countries sub-groups (Maghreb, Mashreq and GCC) for further disaggregate evidence. The main result is that half of the openness of the MENA region depends on oil, given that the ratio between the total trade (with the world and within the sub-regional groups) and the GDP accounted in 2007 for 76.3 per cent with oil, and for 36.9 per cent without. This dependence on oil and natural resources is confirmed by the analysis of the international market integration for the different sub-regional groups, as on average the countries' openness in 2007 dropped from 92.9 per cent to 43.2 per cent in the GCC, from

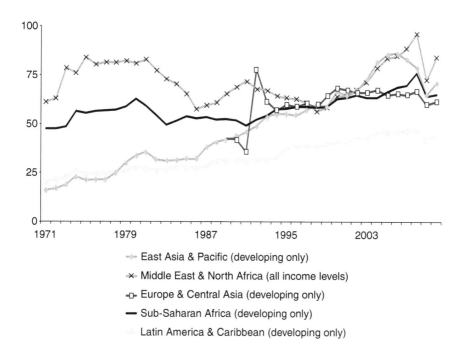

Figure 9.1 Trade (% of GDP) in selected regions

Source: World Bank (2011b), *World Development Indicators and Global Development Finance*.

67.2 per cent to 32.7 per cent in Maghreb (to which Algeria and Libya belong), and from 66.0 per cent to 29.7 per cent in Mashreq (including also Iraq) (World Bank 2010a: Table A2.2 and A2.4). An additional check of the trend is provided also by the shares each sub-regional group retained on the total regional exchange in 2007: the GCC countries (the most important MENA exporters of oil) accounted for 60 per cent, the Maghreb for 15-17 per cent and the Mashreq for about the same share (the remaining quota being due to Iran and Yemen) (World Bank MENA Region 2010a: 4).[1] Finally, the composition of MENA-world exports by products and services in 2008 also shows this trend (Table 9.1).

If the MENA world trade exchange exhibits the excessive reliance on oil and natural resources productions, what is about intra-regional trade among the other environmental and institutional impediments, the concentration of the export structure/polarized market structure? In the last two decades the intra-MENA exports fluctuated around 10-11 per cent of the total exports, a value that grew to 32-33 per cent without oil and natural resources. But these values are 10-15 per cent lower than the potential of the economies, except for the Mashreq countries that 'present a higher level of intra-group trade' (Bhattacharya and Wolde 2010: 4). Thus, both MENA-world and intra-MENA trade presents a lower development in relation to their potential, a feature bringing back the constraints that inhibit the integration in world markets.

In applied analysis, two kinds of barriers have been identified. The first set of barriers is connected to the structure of MENA economies, such as insufficient and expensive transport systems,[2] an unfavourable business environment (due to poor education and overbearing governments) and a lack of competitiveness in home productive systems. All these items reveal an unsatisfactory endowment of infrastructures, human capital and institutions, whose provision requires medium to long term investments and targeted policies; thus they are not specific barriers to trade, but general conditions for the development of an economy. The second set of barriers to

Table 9.1 Composition of MENA-world trade by products and services in 2008

Productions	Exports (%)	Imports (%)
Fuel	58	9
Food	2	9
Manufactured goods	17	50
Other goods	11	7
Tourism	6	5
Other services	6	20*
Total	*100*	*100*

* Eight per cent of which represents transportation.

Source: World Bank, *World Development Indicators 2011b*.

MENA integration are related the financial costs and procedures that can be executed by trade, that is the level of tariffs, the overvaluation of exchange rates, the number of days for clearing exports through customs, the number of documents required for trading, all elements whose removal, according to some analysts, could improve the regional export even of a 10-15 per cent (Bhattacharya and Wolde 2010: 15). Regarding these elements, steps forward have been taken by MENA countries during the last two decades, not only because of structural adjustment policies, but also as a consequence of trade agreements. Table 9.2 shows a general reduction regards both the tariffs (aligned below 10 per cent with the exception of Tunisia, and able to dismiss an high protectionism like in the case of Morocco) and non-tariff constraints (the procedures and the time required to trade).

These policies of trade liberalization succeeded in increasing, mainly since 2000-2002, the exchange of goods and services of the non-oil countries that implemented them. In addition to the trend presented in Figures 9.2 and 9.3 regarding merchandise, 'there are indications that MENA's exports of services have grown faster than its exports of goods – both in percentage terms and relative to middle-income countries' (Behar and Freund 2011: 27). Services, in fact, is the stronger sector in regional perspective: during 1998-2008, MENA's share in world exports of services grew by nearly 30 per cent compared to 15 per cent for middle-income countries excluding China. The same comparison in exports of non-oil goods suggests a slower growth of MENA (17 per cent) with respect to the middle income countries except China (26 per cent), revealing a better performance and better competition of MENA firms in exporting services rather than goods (World Bank 2011a and b). Among the success cases, Tunisia and Egypt appear to be the most relevant. Tunisia has become an 'outsourcing hub' in the MENA region, having successfully attracted foreign direct investments in textile production, car assembly and food processing over the past several years and, more recently, in information technology (IT), customer service and aeronautics (Ahmed 2010: 26). These results were obtained simply by simplifying regulations, implementing suitable policies (government incentives), structural conditions (modern infrastructures) and creating the right environmental atmosphere (commitment to a knowledge-based economy that generates well-trained, low-cost workers). Also Egypt has attracted 'global IT investment from firms such as Microsoft, Oracle, Vodafone and IBM [thanks to improvements in business environment and investments in infrastructures]. Much of Egypt's IT industry is housed in the so-called "Smart Village" in Cairo, which currently employs 22,000 workers' (Ahmed 2010: 26).

Despite success in exports, the most recent available data show how MENA countries are paying attention to deficits in current account balances, which are more stressed in sectors that are essential for development (like the food sector, where the MENA imports are four times greater than

Table 9.2 Tariff and non-tariff barriers to trade for selected MENA countries

Country	Years	Documents to export (number)	Documents to import (number)	Average days to clear exports through customs	Time to export (days)	Time to import (days)	Tariff rate, weighted mean, all products (%)	Cost of exports (US$ per container)
Egypt	1991	–	–	–	–	–	–	–
	1996	–	–	–	–	–	16.7 (1995)	–
	2001	–	–	–	–	–	23.7 (2002)	–
	2006	8	9	4.8 (2004)	20	25	13.3 (2005)	1014
	2010	8	9	5.8 (2007)	12	12	8.0 (2009)	613
Jordan	1991	–	–	–	–	–	–	–
	1996	–	–	–	–	–	–	–
	2001	–	–	–	–	–	12.3	–
	2006	6	7	3.8	19	22	5.6	680
	2010	6	7	–	14	18	5.2 (2009)	825
Lebanon	1991	–	–	–	–	–	–	–
	1996	–	–	–	–	–	–	–
	2001	–	–	–	–	–	8.36	–
	2006	6	11	6.8	25	34	4.48	969
	2010	5	7	7.6	25	35	–	1000
Morocco	1991	–	–	–	–	–	45.4 (1993)	–
	1996	–	–	–	–	–	17.3 (1997)	–
	2001	–	–	–	–	–	24.6	–
	2006	7	9	2.2	17	30	10.8	577
	2010	6	8	1.1	13	17	7.1 (2009)	577

Country	Years	Documents to export (number)	Documents to import (number)	Average days to clear exports through customs	Time to export (days)	Time to import (days)	Tariff rate, weighted mean, all products (%)	Cost of exports (US$ per container)
Tunisia	1991	–	–	–	–	–	26.0 (1992)	–
	1996	–	–	–	–	–	27.4 (1995)	–
	2001	–	–	–	–	–	26.4 (2002)	–
	2006	4	7	–	16	29	18.3	760
	2010	4	7	–	13	17	16.0 (2008)	773
Turkey	1991	–	–	–	–	–	6.1 (1993)	–
	1996	–	–	–	–	–	5.6 (1997)	–
	2001	–	–	2.9 (2002)	–	–	1.9 (2003)	–
	2006	8	13	6.0 (2005)	20	25	1.6	713
	2010	7	8	5.2 (2008)	14	15	2.4	990

Source: Authors' elaboration of data from the World Bank (2011b), *World Development Indicators and Global Development Finance*.

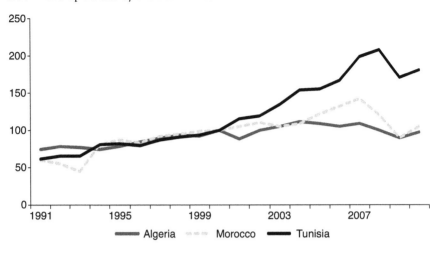

Figure 9.2 Export volume index (2,000 = 100) for selected Maghreb countries
Source: World Bank (2011b), *World Development Indicators and Global Development Finance.*

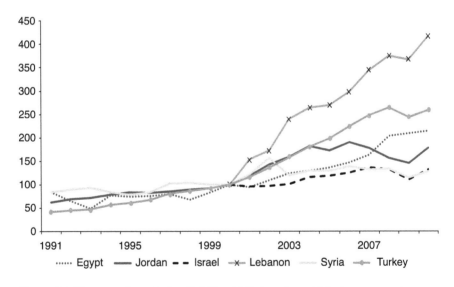

Figure 9.3 Export volume index (2,000 = 100) for selected Mashreq countries
Source: World Bank (2011b), *World Development Indicators and Global Development Finance.*

exports, as shown in Table 9.1). However, the capital account of the same countries records inflows of foreign direct investments (results of a good environment for entrepreneurship) that do not always offset the current account balances (Figures 9.4 and 9.5). So the openness of the region must face a trade-off between a deeper internationalization and a higher current account deficit and this must be managed by policies.

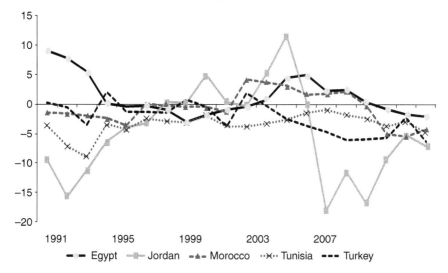

Figure 9.4 Current account balance (% of GDP) for selected MENA countries

Source: World Bank (2011b), *World Development Indicators and Global Development Finance.*

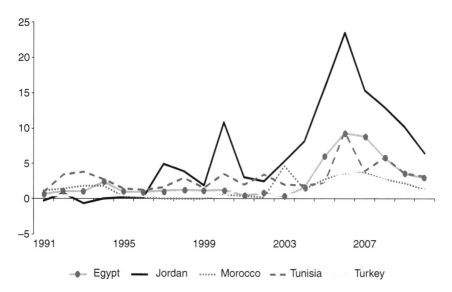

Figure 9.5 Foreign direct investments inflow (% of GDP) for selected MENA countries

Source: World Bank (2011b), *World Development Indicators and Global Development Finance.*

Coming back to impediments blocking the openness of MENA region, the third group of constraints is represented by the features of trade, that is, by the relatively low number of exported goods and by the high polarization of commercial partners (Dasgupta, Nabli, Srinivasan, and Varoudakis 2004; World Bank 2010a). Considering the low number of exported goods in the period 1985-2007, the number of products exported has increased less than the volume of exports, both for the whole region (from 156 to 192) and for sub-regional groups (from 174 to 214 in GCC, from 123 to 165 in Maghreb and from 177 to 203 in Mashreq). These export volume indexes are derived from UNCTAD's volume index series and are the ratio of the export value indexes to the corresponding unit value indexes (export volume index [2000 = 100]). As a result, the product concentration of exports (measured by the Herfindahl-Hirschman index ranging from 0 to 1) increased for the MENA region (from 0.51 to 0.59), emphasizing the predilection for fuel and gas exports in GCC (from 0.69 to 0.82), in Maghreb (from 0.42 to 0.44) and in Mashreq (from 0.28 to 0.29) (World Bank MENA Region, (2010a). Conversely, considering the regional countries that had a more dynamic approach to export during the last decade, Morocco, Tunisia and Jordan reduced their concentration to low values (about 0.18-0.15), while Egypt and Lebanon increased the export concentration to values of 0.31-0.37 (World Bank MENA Region 2010a: Table A2.6). Finally, as to the territorial polarization, the EU is the main trade partner of the Mediterranean Arab countries, accounting for 52 per cent of the total exchange in 2003. Turkey represents about one third of the total Mediterranean trade, followed by Algeria (15 per cent), Israel (about 13 per cent), Morocco and Tunisia (almost 10 per cent each), while Egypt, Syria, Jordan and the Palestine Territories shared the rest (20 per cent). Considering the sub-regional aggregates in 2008, Maghreb traded mainly with the European Union while Mashreq traded mainly with the rest of the world, followed by the European Union and other MENA countries (Table 9.3).

Although this concise analysis of the openness of MENA region has deepened the features of exports and imports and highlighted successes and failures, structural inefficiencies, short-term policies, trade-offs and side effects, the fact-finding framework provided still could not be considered sufficient for an appraisal of the internationalization of the economies. The reason for this is due to the fact that, when countries become open to exchanges, both goods and services are traded, in particular labour services. As the MENA countries are involved in flows that are internal and external to the region, migration must be considered as a constituent of the openness of the economies, just like exports. After all, in macroeconomic accounting, remittances represent money inflows due to payments for labour services sold abroad (just like those due for exported goods) and registered in the current accounts of the balance of payments as one of the entries enhancing the foreign currency reserves of an economy. However, according to international trade theories, these payments represent the value of elements

Table 9.3 Destination of exports and origin of imports for MENA countries in 2008

Countries (or groups of countries)	Destination of exports (%)					Origin of imports (%)				
	MENA	EU27	USA	Rest of the world	Total	MENA	EU27	USA	Rest of the World	Total
MENA[a]	5.9	55.9	11.7	26.5	100.0	5.1	40.6	6.3	48.0	100.0
Maghreb	3.3	63.1	13.4	20.2	100.0	5.4	52.7	4.7	37.2	100.0
Morocco	2.1	59.3	3.9	34.7	100.0	4.2	51.8	5.1	38.9	100.0
Tunisia	8.7	72.1	1.7	17.5	100.0	8.9	57.3	3.0	30.8	100.0
Mashreq[b]	18.4	24.2	6.0	51.4	100.0	6.4	26.0	5.5	62.1	100.0
Egypt	12.6	35.5	4.8	46.1	100.0	2.8	27.1	10.8	59.3	100.0
Jordan	11.1	4.2	16.8	67.9	100.0	7.7	20.9	4.6	66.8	100.0
Lebanon	15.5	15.3	1.4	67.8	100.0	5.8	36.5	11.8	45.9	100.0

[a] Turkey, Iran, Iraq and GCC excluded

[b] Without Egypt but with Palestine

Source: Authors' elaboration of Richter 2012: 4–5.

traded in different markets (the market of goods in the case of exports, the market of production factors in the case of migration), thus reacting differently to a wider mobility chance due to international liberalization. So, in this context the theoretical problem is to understand if, once two economies are interacting, both migration and export contribute to increase exchange (so they are complements) or compete in doing so (thus are substitutes), while the policy implications concern the desirable level of migration in relation to the level of trade and the measures to be adopted to manage it (Schiff 2006).

Trade, migration and foreign direct investment (FDI): complements or substitutes?

The analytical framework used to identify if there is a substitute relationship or rather a complementary factor between trade and migration, is the Hecksher-Ohlin-Samuelson (HOS) theory of international trade. This model explains exchange by assuming that two countries, characterized by different endowments of capital and labour, specialize in and export the goods produced by the relatively more-abundant factor (that is, the more capital-intensive or the more labour-intensive products, respectively). In the presence of international mobility of labour and of unrestricted international markets, the exchange pattern identifies a relationship of substitution between migration and trade, due to the fact that progressive protectionist policies are followed by a decrease in trade and increase in migration while, conversely, lowering trade barriers produces an increase in trade and a decrease in migration. But Mundell demonstrated that, based on this theoretical framework, migration and trade are perfect substitutes because in the long run a perfect competition equilibrium is achieved and the incentive to migrate is annulled (because trade results in the equalization of factor prices and in the absence of a wage differential), and as in a perfect labour mobility situation trade is absent (because the comparative advantages in production and exchange are cancelled – see Mundell 1957).

In spite of these theoretical results, the empirical evidence has shown that migration and trade may be complements rather than substitutes because, since 1850, migration has increased on a global scale and so has trade, and there has been growing trend for both macroeconomic variables since the Second World War (O'Rourke and Williamson 2005). This complementarity can be explained by the fact that in a world where, in addition to the factors capital and labour, the most marked differences between countries are in the endowment of technology (embodied in capital) and of skills (whose labour is gifted), neither the comparative advantages of the more technological productions nor the wage differentials in service labour markets are cancelled.

Following this evidence, subsequent theoretical developments, that are based still on a HOS model but assume identical relative factors endowments and unleashing some of the assumptions of the basic version, show how the relationship between migration and international trade is complementary rather than substitutive. In particular Markusen, relaxing the hypotheses of perfect competition, of identical technology and preferences, of constant returns to scale, and of domestic distortions absence, verified that complementarity is obtained by means of the increase in the endowment of labour of the country's export sector (due to immigration), that in turn produces more exports (Markusen 1983). In general, in the presence of a degree of factor mobility and of changing protectionism, because of technological advantage and quality of workers:

1   Migration and trade are substitutes when there are high barriers and they are complements if they are low.
2   A change in the level of trade barriers determines complementarity or substitution in dependence on the barrier value and on the corresponding wage differential between migrants' origin and destination countries.

While Mundell's substitution 'holds for any initial value of the barriers to migration and trade and for any change in these barriers, [...] this is not the case for Markusen's complementarity result' (Schiff 2006: 7). Thus, in the Markusen model, the trade liberalization moves the economy from a region of substitutive status to a region of complementary status when, beyond a certain threshold in the level of migration costs, lower barriers go together with a positive wage differential: factors of production will move to areas where they are used intensively, leading to an increase in migration and trade in both countries. These results suggest that if a country has a relative technological advantage in a particular area where barriers remain high, the increase or decrease of migration depends on the level of initial protection. Therefore policies aimed at maximizing social welfare will determine the optimal level of migration associated with a certain degree of trade liberalization (Schiff 2006: 9).

In Turkey and Jordan the shift from a region of substitution to a region of complementarity occurred with the internationalization of economies. Turkey has traditionally been a country of emigration with distinct periods of labour movements, as labour recruitment to Western Europe (1961-74 period) was followed by migration to MENA countries and Australia, due to a shortage of labour demand in Europe (1974-80) (Baldwin-Edwards 2005). From the 1990s a new phenomenon occurred and Turkey became not only a growing exporter country but also a transit route for irregular migrants from Afghanistan, Bangladesh, Iraq, Iran and Pakistan and, largely, a destination for refugees and asylum seekers and economic migrants. Labour migration flows have been shaped both by Turkey's efforts to become a member of the European Union (thus a more attractive destination for migrants) and by the growing of its irregular and small-scale commercial, construction and tourism sectors, as well as by the increasing number of EU member-state nationals engaged in professional activities in Turkey.

As to Jordan, the country has traditionally been both a country of origin and destination for migrant workers. From the mid-1970s to the mid-1980, hundreds of thousands of well-educated and highly skilled Jordanians migrated mainly to oil-producing countries to find work, and during the same period (thanks to policies favouring the immigration) Jordan became attractive for semi-skilled workers from Egypt, Syria and especially Asian countries, meeting the needs of highly segmented domestic markets (in particular, those of agrarian, semi-industrial, manufacturing and service-oriented activities). Besides this phenomenon, in recent decades the country has also experienced a progressive export flow.

The traditional HOS model in the Markusen version is also used to analyse the relationships between capital and trade, thus to establish if foreign direct investments (FDI) help integration in world markets (as complements to exports) or not (being their substitutes). According to some scholars (Brainard 1993; Horstman and Markusen 1992), they are substitutes when, in the presence of geographical proximity to export markets, firms adopt a market-seeking strategy: a producer located near its export country can satisfy the foreign demand for its product by FDI instead of by more exports, unless goods could be produced more efficiently by a concentration of production at home because of scale economies. In this case FDI is connected to import substitution policies. But, according to Helpman and Krugman (Helpman and Krugman 1985), in the presence of differences in factors endowment and specialization, a complementary relationship can be set in motion, because FDI pushes the host country's export sector, which in turn requires services from the trading partner. When exports and FDI are complements, important policy implications derive from the causal link between them: an export-led model is supported if successful export attracts foreign investments, while incentives to attract FDIs are needed if foreign capitals are the precondition to develop competitive sectors.

Regarding the relation between trade and FDI in the MENA region, applied studies (Backer 2005) point out that the Euro-Mediterranean Partnership produced an increase both in FDI and in exports, but less than expected. This seems due to the fact that 'foreign investors follow the traditional step-by-step sequence of servicing these markets: in the first phase of commercial relationships they test the ground exporting before investing directly through FDI (in fact MPCs (Most Preferential Countries) imports grew more quickly than MPCs exports)' (Favara, 2006: 180). More than a substitution effect, this situation could reveal a complementary relationship between trade and FDI creating dependency, a 'vicious circle, where foreign investors open up firms in the South just to benefit from lower wages and produce semi-finished items, in order to re-export them to Europe for further treatment' (Favara 2006) and retain all the value added produced in the investing country.

Finally, considering the potential relationship between migration and FDI in developing countries, several empirical studies have focused on the attempt to understand whether the influence of foreign capital could have a substitution effect or encourage migration. Although the literature is unanimous in finding that the influx of foreign capital can generate positive externalities in recipient countries in terms of increased demand for skilled labour (thus reducing migration), several studies show that there is a complementarity between capital inflows and migration flows. In fact, by reducing the constraints of income and positively influencing the formation of human capital of migrants, capital input (especially if comprising remittances) may lead to increased migration among skilled workers who decide to move, attempting to qualify for the best opportunities in the market labour of their destination countries (Ivlevs 2005). FDI can also have an indirect, ambiguous effect on migration through their contribution to the formation of human capital: this can happen when corporations relocate production to developing countries and support the training of the local workforce. If the contribution in terms of human capital formation (through learning by doing or technical training) is positive, the presence of foreign firms may upgrade the local labour market (improvement of standards, increase of employment), replace migration and reduce the out-flows. There is, however, a strong effect of complementarity when transaction costs and information for potential migrants are reduced: as the influx of foreign capital increases the flow of bilateral information about the opportunities, practices, skills, and organizational procedures of the foreign firms in the labour market abroad, further migration is encouraged (D'Agosto, Solferino and Tria 2006).

At this point we should stress that not only the structural features of economies, but also the institutional and political variables (such as relations between countries and harmonization of standards), together with the types of migration flows, may affect the relationship between trade and international migration. As suggested by the OECD, even if trade and migration policies can be implemented in a complementary regime as policies to attract external forms of capital (aid and FDI), they tackle different targets and development opportunities (Table 9.4).

The theoretical debate on substitutive or complementary relationships between trade, migration and FDI provides an important support to the thesis that an appraisal of the openness of MENA economies cannot be presented without considering labour flows and foreign investments, given the generalized contribution to the internationalization of the economies they show both in theoretical and in applied studies. In the framework of increasing integration, the MENA region appears typical and less upstream than claimed. Perhaps the institutional structure of trade agreements affects the process more than the upgrading of technical instruments necessary to open the economies (tariff and non-tariff barriers). Thus an analysis of the integration path is needed.

Table 9.4 International and migration policies: complementarity regime

Domains	Aid	Investments	Migration	Trade
Policies	Promote growth and poverty reduction	Expand productive capacities	Enhance income opportunities	Expand consumption possibilities
Aid		Reduce investments costs; promote human and physical capital growth	Enhance capacity building and market integration in origin countries	Promote trade capacity and competitiveness; create demand for developed countries' goods and services
Foreign investment	Increase human and physical capital stock; promote local enterprise development and business start ups		Expand employment opportunities	Enhance linkages to foreign markets, increase export capacity and quality standards; develop business networks
Migration	Enhance bottom-up growth through remittances and skills acquired through migration experience	Encourage savings and productive investments; brain circulation and technology transfer		Encourage trade opportunities and business networks
Trade	Promote growth	Enhance market access	Increase wages	

Source: Authors' elaboration in accordance with OECD, 2006.

The steps towards integration: from multilateral to bilateral small scale agreements

The countries of the Middle East and North Africa have a long history of attempts to open their economies, witnessing on one hand the signing of treaties to reduce tariffs (for limited goods) and the implementation of more comprehensive programmes for creating pan-Arab market institutions on the other. Such attempts reflect their hopes to increase the bargaining power of the region to achieving a better standard of living of member countries and a better economic performance in a more globalized world (Galal and Hoekman 2003). The intended processes undertaken by the governments have been the traditional harmonization path for a geographical entity (already homogeneous in socio-cultural features) through state agreements supporting an economic regionalism (see Chapter 1), or the creation of a free trade area regardless of the regional dimensions. Since the 1950s, Arab economic integration was pursued through a set of attempts implemented by the Economic Council – EC – of the Arab League, an institution coordinating and supporting initiatives aiming at enhancing socio-economic cooperation among Arab states. The first initiative taken by the Council was in 1953, when a treaty organizing transit trade among members of the Arab League, was created, followed by the Arab Economic Unity Agreement (AEUA) of 1957 (endowed with its own operative Council), that went on to support an agreement for the creation of an Arab Common Market in 1964[3] including the Arab Republic of Egypt, Iraq, Jordan, and the Syrian Arab Republic (later joined by Libya, Mauritania and South Yemen[4]). But these efforts did not produce the expected results, owing to political events and to differences in economic structures, in the tax systems and in the level of development achieved by the members.

Following the oil boom of the 1970s a renewed phase of regional integration was launched, by implementing some sub-regional economic unions as an alternative and viable solution to succeed in opening and integrating the regional economies. Pursuing this objective, 18 members of the Arab League signed the Trade Facilitation and Trade Promotion Accord of 1981, and in the same year the Gulf Cooperation Council (GCC, between Bahrain, Kuwait, Oman, Qatar, Saudi Arabia and the UAE) was created. In 1989, the Arab Magreb Union (AMU, between Algeria, Libya, Mauritania, Morocco, and Tunisia) and the Arab Cooperation Council (ACC, for a short period involving Egypt, Iraq, Jordan and Yemen) were set up. In 1997, the Agreement on the Greater Arab Free Trade Area (GAFTA) was signed, being considered as the way by which to fill the gap between 'the hope of an higher internationalization of the economies and the reality of a limited success of the small-scale grouping of the 1980s' (Romagnoli and Mengoni 2009: 70). More recently, in 2004, Jordan, Egypt, Tunisia and Morocco signed the Rabat the Agadir Agreement, a free trade area among the four Mediterranean Arab countries (see Table 9.5). Despite the commitment to eliminate both tariff and non-tariff barriers, the GAFTA, as an expression of such desire, remained 'a traditional (shallow) preferential trade agreement, limited to trade in merchandise. Services and investments are excluded [...] highlighting how non-tariff measures are likely to remain important barriers to regional integration, unless further reforms are undertaken' (Galal and Hoekman 2003:5).

As a result of the disillusion towards the regional integration policies all MENA countries, although unwilling to comply with the wave of

Table 9.5 MENA international economic policies and agreements

Kind of policy	Agreement	Date
Regional integration policies	*Multilateral General Agreements*	
	League of Arab States	1945
	Economic Unity Agreement Among States of the Arab League (AEUA) and Council	1957
	Arab Common Market [a]	1964
	Trade Facilitation and Trade Promotion Accord	1981
	Gulf Cooperation Council (GCC) [a]	1981
	Maghreb Arab Union MAU	1989
	Greater Arab Free Trade Area (GAFTA)	1997
	Agadir Agreement (MAFTA) [a]	2004
Liberalization policies	*Bilateral Agreements*	
	Euro-Mediterranean Partnership (EMP) & Association EU-Tunisia (1998), EU-Israel and EU-Morocco (2000), EU-Jordan (2002), EU-Egypt (2004), EU-Algeria (2005), EU-Lebanon (2006)	1995
	Membership of WTO (excepted Algeria, Iran, Iraq, Lebanon, Libya)	1995– 2006
	US-Middle East Free Trade Area Initiative (MEFTA) [b] US-Morocco (2006), US-Bahrain (2006), US-Oman (2009), US-Jordan (2010)	2003
Trade and co-operation policies	*Bilateral Agreements for Economic co-operation*	
	Egypt-Tunisia, Egypt-Lebanon	1998
	Morocco-Tunisia	1999
	Morocco-Egypt	2002
	Turkey-Israel	2000
	Egypt-Iraq	2001
	Iraq-Lebanon	2002
	Jordan-UAE, Morocco-UAE	2003
	Bilateral Agreements for Trade co-operation	
	Egypt-Kuwait, Egypt-Jordan, Morocco-Jordan	1998
	Egypt-Saudi Arabia	2000
	Egypt-Libya, Kuwait-Jordan, Syria-Jordan	2001
	Morocco-Syria	2001
	Iraq-Qatar, Iraq-Saudi Arabia, Syria-Iraq	2002
	Syria-Saudi Arabia	2002
	Israel-Jordan, Lebanon-GCC, Morocco-Turkey	2004
	Syria-GCC, Turkey-Tunisia	2004
	Turkey-Egypt	2005
	Syria-Iran	2011

[a] Agreement aiming at creating a common market

[b] US-Israel (1985)

Source: Authors' elaboration of national sources.

globalization, during the 1990s adopted a trade liberalization policy by stipulating bilateral commercial treaties with the 'northern' countries, after joining trade organization agreements or proposals. This phase started in 1995 when the European Union issued the Barcelona Declaration, a protocol promoting a new approach in economic relations with neighbouring countries of the Mediterranean, based on free trade principles and on WTO rules, a framework reasserted in the 2004 European Neighbouring Policy (ENP), and revamped in 2008 with the creation of the Union for the Mediterranean. In addition to these policies, the United States promoted the Middle East Free Trade Area Initiative (MEFTA) in 2003, signing free trade bilateral agreements with Morocco, Jordan, Bahrain and Oman. Both programmes are based on a multi-targeted protocol (whose accession involves the acceptance of general principles, as well as trade liberalization policies leading to a free trade area between partners), implemented only with respect to bilateral trade agreements.

The phase of trade liberalization just presented is quite different from the regionalism pursued by the Arab League through multilateral general agreements, not only because of the aims of the treaties (mainly the creation of a free trade area and the activation of a development/cooperation process in a framework of expanding international exchanges and national economies, respectively), but also because of the differences in the building process of agreements and in the model of exchange underlying them. As to the first element, the accession to WTO, MEFTA and EMP subdues subscribers to rules elaborated by committed international organizations (or groups of states), while in creating common regional trade institutions all the partners can participate in the elaboration of trading rules from a parity position. Regarding the trading models, one-sidedness liberalization policies tend to create commercial regimes (efficient according to the international trade theory) and virtual regions, harmonizing quite different economies (considered, by definition, partners who are featureless and equal) through the imposition of a unique institutional set of common, symmetric, reciprocal and not preferential trading rules. On the contrary, multilateral economic and cooperation agreements build their trading institutional assets taking into account the different needs and conditions of economic partners, so that all of them could gain from trade.[5]

Among the aforementioned protocols, the Barcelona Declaration is particularly important for Southern East Mediterranean countries, not only because more than a half of their international exchanges are with the EU, but also because the European Community intended to base on this document a new political, social, economic and cultural order in the Mediterranean. The partnership proposed to Arab Mediterranean countries was centred on three pillars:

1   Political and security partnership: aiming at establishing a common area of peace and stability (free from nuclear proliferation, war, terrorism),

where the rule of law, democracy, human rights and fundamental freedoms were respected and promoted.

2   Economic and financial partnership: intended to create an area of shared prosperity, where sustainable and balanced economic and social development were reached by economic and financial cooperation and by setting up a free trade area.

3   The partnership in social, cultural and human affairs developing human resources, promoting the understanding between cultures and the exchanges between civil societies.

Except that the 'economic logic behind this Partnership is based on the conventional economic wisdom on trade liberalization, [that] should increase the competitive pressure in the economy and facilitate the reallocation of production factors [...] from non-competitive industries [...] to more competitive ones' (Martin 2007: 116-7) resulting in the increase of resources productivity and economic growth rates, some important features of the pillars regarding exchanges appear to conflict both with the claimed spirit of the proposal and with deep integration. In particular, on one hand agricultural productions (that could present comparative advantages for Southern East Mediterranean countries) are excluded from the free trade area, and on the other, migration isn't considered a labour service that could move inside the free trade area, but a socio-cultural problem for which the partners agree 'to strengthen their cooperation to reduce migratory pressures' and 'to adopt the relevant provisions and measures, by means of bilateral agreements or arrangements, in order to readmit their nationals who are in an illegal situation' (Barcelona Declaration 1995). Finally, the Barcelona Declaration does not take into account some advice that the economic theory of free trade areas made by arguing that regional integration would increase partners' welfare if intra-regional trade relations were high prior to integration and if the economies of members were competitive in the pre-integration stage and potentially complementary, which are all features lacking in Mediterranean Arab countries.

Apparently the European Neighbourhood Policy (2004) seemed to compensate for these inconsistencies, as explicitly it recognizes both 'the differences in capacity and priorities in the context of bilateral economic cooperation between the EU and its neighbours' and the 'need to complement binding treaties with "soft law"' (Hoekman 2007: 14). In addition, it declared to support the national development strategy of partner countries, to partially integrate them into EU economic and social systems and to implement the association agreements. Nevertheless, the spirit of the protocol is not centred on the Mediterranean but rather on Europe itself, as the 'accession model' proposed by the EU calls for the institutional harmonization to the European regulations, directives, social legislation, technical rules, standards and competition policies (the so-called 'Community acquis'). Neither the 'four freedoms' (the movement of products, services, capitals and migrants) came into effect, nor the new institutions (and in particular, the Secretariat) established by the European Union for the Mediterranean (2008) succeeded in revitalizing a European policy for Mediterranean countries.

Despite this, and with the aim to liberalize trade between both the EU and Southern Mediterranean economies (north-south trade implementation) and Southern Mediterranean countries themselves (south-south trade implementation), Southern countries were asked to implement long transitional mechanisms and secure safeguards, to obtain improved access for their agricultural exports, to increase financial flows and to receive community help to accelerate modernization of socio-economic systems. Apart from Syria, all Mediterranean countries belonging to the Euro-Mediterranean partnership have concluded Association Agreements with the EU, and Libya started negotiations in 2008. From the south-south perspective, the EU supported the strengthening of intra-regional agreement through the opening up of the Agadir Agreement between Tunisia, Morocco, Jordan, and Egypt (in place since 2007) to other Arab countries, as well as the signing of a bilateral agreement between Turkey and Egypt, Israel, Morocco, the Palestinian Territories, Syria and Tunisia, the establishment of free trade agreements (FTA) between Israel and Jordan and other similar initiatives, so contributing to enlarge 'the complicated web of institutional arrangements' (World Bank 2011a: 270), which Figure 9.6 presents.

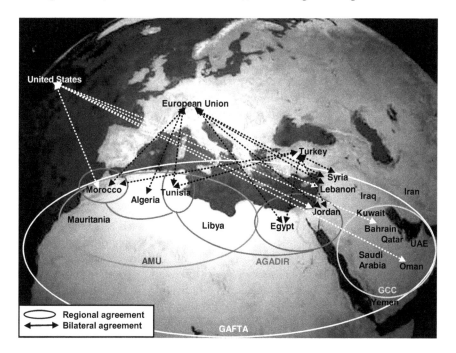

Figure 9.6 Regional and bilateral agreements including MENA countries

Source: Authors' elaboration of *World Development Indicators*, 2011b.

An appraisal of MENA international economic integration and outcomes

The ups and downs of Arab countries in the path towards the international integration of their economies (leading them to sign regional/sub-regional multilateral agreements and to access free trade agreements one after the other) reflect the main debate of 1990s that was based on the contrast between regionalization and globalization. While some scholars considered the creation of a trading block (standing on intensive intra-regional trade flows) to be a step towards the globalization process, others thought the open trade regime was a premise for intra-regional trade (Zarrouk 1998: 7). Thus, an appraisal of the openness of the MENA economies cannot distract from the fact that in the last two decades two different international trade arrangements were in conflict to be considered the best way to develop.

Under the EU Mediterranean framework, MENA countries achieved a decline in external tariffs, mainly as a reflection of unilateral reforms and WTO commitment, limited liberalization of agricultural trade and slow implementation of agreements on service trade and investment. To sum up, in Hoekman's words, 'a compelling case cannot be made that the EMP has had a significant economic impact. Although it is difficult to determine the counterfactual' (Hoekman 2005), on the trade front overall non-oil growth was lower in 1995. Since then, intra-regional (intra-Mediterranean) trade shares have increased somewhat and there has been a (small) rise in intra-industry trade, indicating greater diversification.

On the international level, the move to the adoption of the WTO regime also showed the limited chances in terms both of export diversification and global market integration (despite the efforts to reform trades) and of attempts to exploit the rise of China and India[6] (World Bank 2011a), leading to insufficient gains from trade. The Euro-Mediterranean Free Trade Agreement (EU-MFTA) confirms this trend: comparison of MENA with the rising new trading blocs showed its bad performance, avoiding the possibility for Arab countries of developing the economies by a broad and comprehensive regional trade agreement and to take the opportunities offered by a large and privatized market (foreign direct investments, for example). Nevertheless, it has to be underlined how Middle East and North African trade policies and diversification outcomes are influenced by the diversity of countries whose economic structures are resource-poor but labour-abundant, resource-rich and labour-abundant, resource-rich and labour-importing, together with countries endowed with natural resources. The differences in 'size, level of development, market structure and level of protection suggest that regional liberalization of trade in goods is not likely to be the best way to integrate Arab countries' (Galal and Hoekman 2003: 8). But as factor mobility and trade in services have been a substitute in the Arab region for trade in goods, 'trade liberalization and concerted reform of service markets may be more successful' (ibid).

The bad performances in opening MENA economies produced by this recent phase of economic interstate liberalization policies is probably due to the fact that those policies did not produce gains from trade. From a theoretic point of view, to rely on the 'traditional' (WTO 'extended') preferential trading arrangements would cause static effects such as an increasing welfare through an efficient allocation of resources, leading to processes of 'trade creation' and 'trade diversion'. But the economic theory indicated necessary conditions for succeeding in opening the economy in the pre-integration stage, such as a high intra-regional trade relations, high competition and complementarities of trading members (De Melo and Panagariya, 1993). Also, the dynamic effects emerging from the internationalization process (increasing rates of investment, higher intra-industry trade, reduced balance of payments distortions) were subordinate to the warning that their intensity would be higher as the level of industrial development is higher, the per-capita income is similar, industry is specialized and the supply side of the member economies is flexible (Edwards 1998). But these conditions were absent in MENA economies. Applied analysis, in fact, reported the heterogeneity of economic conditions among countries (the diversity index presented evident differences in welfare – Hebbers 1999), ascribing the unfeasible implementation either of static or of dynamic effects to a range of economic and institutional factors.

Denying the prediction that the smaller the economies are, the more they tend to open their markets, in particular in a phase of increasing globalization where the trade off between size and heterogeneity moves in favour of smaller and more homogeneous countries (Alesina et al. 2002), empirical evidence shows how the MENA region has not really integrated. The main reasons behind this poor integration are:

1   market distortion and insufficient institutional development as a legacy of colonial power (Saidi: 2004);
2   inward-oriented policies and protectionism (particularly marked from the 1960s to the early eighties) and, more recently, the delay of entering into the WTO;
3   high tariff barriers still in place (the Arab market is segmented by physical barriers and bottlenecks in the transport sector[7]);
4   security and political issues, including bilateral conflicts and economic sanctions;[8]
5   structural features: differences in per capita income, lack of product differentiation, homogeneity of exports and geographical features hampering intra-regional trade.

If Arab integration with the rest of the world is still low (thus presenting room for further integration), a look at intra-Arab exports shows an interesting dynamism: from 1990 to 2009, as the GAFTA case has shown, merchandise exports of regional sub-blocks (such as GCC and the Arab

Common Market) had been more dynamic (Table 9.6), especially if oil is excluded (this means that oil producing countries send most of their non-oil products to other countries in the region). It is also interesting to note how the acceleration was more marked after the creation of bilateral economic and cooperation agreements: trade between Egypt, Jordan, Morocco and Tunisia, for instance, shows a higher dynamism after the creation of the Agadir agreement, with a considerable increase in the value of exports within blocks (from 635 million USD in 2005 to 1.046 in 2007) (World Bank 2011b).

Furthermore, and despite the existence of many factors hampering intra-regional trade, the proportion of intra-Arab trade within subgroups is significantly higher than overall intra-Arab trade. Nearly two thirds of Maghreb trade with the Arab world goes to other Maghreb countries; three quarters of GCC trade goes to other GCC countries and one third of Mashreq trade goes to other Mashreq countries (World Bank 2002c). Mashreq countries show higher diversification in terms of destination: in 1997, 37 per cent of Egyptian exports (to total trade) went to Saudi Arabia; 28 per cent of Jordanian exports to Iraq and 28 per cent to Saudi Arabia; while 21 per cent of Syrian exports went to Saudi Arabia. What is more, by disaggregating the region into subgroups, empirical results show that while trade in the Maghreb and in the GCC is less than expected, Mashreq has achieved a higher level of intra-regional trade and it is also more integrated with the global economy, compared to the other two subgroups. The higher dynamism of the regional sub-system thus opens the perspective of Mashreq countries as a middle group between AMU and GCC, acting as a bridge between east and west Arab countries in promoting the overall integration in the region.

Table 9.6 Merchandise exports within MENA sub-regional trade blocks (millions USD)

Agreements	1990	1995	2000	2005	2009
A.C. MARKET (1964)	911	1.368	1.312	–	–
GCC (1981)	6.906	6.832	7.958	15.408	21.849
AMU (1989)	958	1.109	1.041	1.885	3.422
GAFTA (1997)	13.204	12.948	16.188	41.659	61.881
Agadir Agr. (2004)	156	226	294	635	2.075

Source: Authors' elaboration from *World Bank* 2011b; *World Development Indicators* 2011b.

Note: Agadir Agreement, Egypt, Jordan, Morocco and Tunisia; Great Arab Free Trade Area (GAFTA), Jordan, Bahrain, United Arab Emirates, Tunisia, Saudi Arabia, Syria, Iraq, Oman, Qatar, Kuwait, Lebanon, Libya, Egypt, Morocco, Sudan, Yemen, Palestine; Arab Maghreb Union (UMA), Algeria, Libya, Mauritania, Morocco, and Tunisia; Gulf Cooperation Council (GCC), Bahrain, Kuwait, Oman, Qatar, Saudi Arabia, and the United Arab Emirates; Arab Common Market, the Arab Republic of Egypt, Iraq, Jordan, Libya, Mauritania, the Syrian Arab Republic, and the Republic of Yemen.

The current economic structures of MENA countries emphasize two main trends: 1) the lack of intra-regional integration and, 2) the diversity of the major macroeconomic indicators. The picture changes if we consider the sub-regional clusters identified according to kind of exports and relative income (oil exporting countries with relatively high incomes, diversified economies with average incomes and primary exports economies with low incomes) and, in particular, if we consider groups of countries on the basis of trade agreements. According to the latter criteria, we can see how trade among regional economies that are joining some kind of bilateral agreement is in line with trade among developing economies in similar trade blocks (this is the case of AMU trade in goods compared with CARICOM and COMESA), with trade even higher within Mashreq countries. However, the economies exporting more of their shares of domestic products in the region do not have significant percentages of intra-Arab trade, while the major exporters direct their production mainly from the outside which is, of course, a sign of the different trade policies implemented at country level.

As for the economic heterogeneity of the Arab countries it should also be noted that each of the institutional aggregates presents different indexes of regional diversity (0.27 for EU-12 and 0.38 for the GCC, 0.45 for the Mashreq and 0.5 for UMA), limiting the possibility of enjoying dynamic effects. Moreover, the fragmentation in a large number of small economies and the similarities in the production structure of the countries are considered to be factors that limit the incentives to open up the economies. However, some interesting trends have come about in the last two decades, confirmed by empirical evidence, such as a rising cross-border trade shown, in the case of Mashreq, by a high trade-intensity index (much higher than in other trading blocs (Hebbers 1998: 69-70); a composition of inter-Arab trade dissimilar in respect to the Arab countries' total trade, connected with different demand structures; an 'inter-Arab trade positively affected by the size of the trading countries, whether they are members of either GCC or AMU' (Limam and Abdalla 1998: 19). Moreover, a lot of trade agreements have been signed (most of them bilateral) and some others had been improved, especially by adjacent countries (Hamoudeh M. 2002; Zarrouk and Zollio 2000), making this process consistent with the institutional developments occurring in the area to support internationalization, thus suggesting to economists that they need to extend their vision of integration process and adopt a broader approach, emphasizing the economic and political value of geographical contiguity.

In this framework, if we move beyond the traditional concept of economic integration (*shallow integration*), as merely openness in trade of goods and elimination of relative barriers (tariffs, quotas, customs procedures) to a more comprehensive concept – (*deep integration*, implying a higher degree of integration at both economic and socio-political level), the growth profile of MENA countries shows interesting (although scattered) outcomes both focusing '*outward*' integration (with the global economy) and '*inward*' integration (strengthening of regional ties). Deep integration implies:

- *at economic level:* a real openness involving liberalization of cross-border flows in all markets, so that not only the exchange of goods and services must be taken into account, but also the international financial markets (Foreign Direct Investments; Banking and Capital flows) and the labour markets. Encouraging factor mobility means the dismantling of formal and informal barriers, such as tariffs and NTBs (non-tariff barriers) to trade in goods, services, capital and labour.
- *at institutional/political level:* a real openness calls for the harmonization of domestic policies that affect production and trade incentives on one side, and for the homogenization of trade related legal regulation. In addition to this, the establishment of institutions to manage integration at all levels and to modernize communication and transport infrastructures.

If we consider the integration of Arab countries with the global economy in recent decades by having in mind this broader and more comprehensive framework, and if we take into account all forms of transactions, the data available show that merchandise trade has increased since 2004 almost in all countries, which is particularly marked in the Maghreb countries, but also in Kuwait, Oman, UAE and Iran (Table 9.7). The data from 2009 confirm the worsening economic situation and the significant drop of imports from and exports to the Middle East and North Africa. It also has to be stressed how, despite trade in goods, trade in services has shown higher dynamism and a relative increase in 2009 (with respect to 2004) in almost all countries, with the exception of Mashreq ones (Yemen excluded).

In recent years an increasing number of research papers have been devoted to the study of relationships between institutional building processes and economic development (Beck and Laeven 2005; Chang H.-J. 2005). In this respect also international trade agreements have been studied to identify the requirements they must have to support increasing flows of international exchanges. Such institutions must present:

- procedures and rules of conduct for the agencies that promote development;
- protection of interests of the market entities;
- dispute settlement systems;
- market culture and mentality.

Reviewing the agreements signed in the MENA region in this respect (see Table 9.8) means to consider, in particular, the presence (or the absence) of certain elements: trade liberalization policies and custom duties, rules of origin, non-tariff barriers, agricultural protection and sector cooperation,

Table 9.7 MENA region integration with the global economy

Countries	Trade in goods (% on GDP)			Trade in services (% on GDP)			Gross private capital flows (% on GDP)		
	1990	2004	2009	1990	2004	2009	1990	2004	2009
Kuwait	59.8	73.1	75.9	25.2	19.6	18.0	19.3	35.8	–
Oman	70.1	91.4	99.0	6.7	14.7	15.9	3.5	8.6	–
Qatar	64.6	–	–	–	–	–	–	–	–
S. Arabia	58.6	68.2	76.6	21.8	12.6	22.1	8.8	20.0	–
U. A. E.	103.2	125.1	136.8	–	–	–	–	–	–
Algeria	36.6	59.7	60.1	2.9	–	–	2.6	–	–
Libya	64.2	91.0	73.4	5.2	7.6	8.7	7.3	24.5	–
Morocco	43.4	54.7	51.2	13.4	20.3	21.1	5.5	7.6	–
Tunisia	73.5	79.6	84.8	20.6	19.9	21.4	9.5	6.6	0.1
Egypt	36.8	26.0	36.1	22.6	28.2	18.8	6.8	13.3	1.4
Jordan	91.1	104.9	81.5	67.5	36.9	33.3	6.3	18.1	–
Lebanon	106.5	51.2	60.1	90.4	–	90.4	–	–	2.7
Syria	53.7	46.7	51.2	14.3	19.1	13.3	18.0	1.6	0.1
Yemen	46.9	65.0	53.5	16.3	11.1	12.8	16.2	1.6	–
Iran	32.9	48.4	38.8	3.7	–	–	2.6	–	–
Israel	55.0	69.6	49.8	18.1	23.5	20.0	6.5	18.7	–
Turkey	23.4	53.1	39.5	7.4	11.7	8.2	4.3	12.8	1.7

Note: Data for Bahrain not available.

Source: Authors' elaboration of *World Development Indicators* 2011b.

Table 9.8 Transparent contents in selected agreements signed by countries of the MENA region

Countries	Customs & Sector Policies	Rules of Origin	Health & Standards	Agricultural Products	Services (Labour)	FDI
Multilateral general agreements						
AEUA	–	x	x	x	x	x
GCC	x	–	x	x	x	x
MAU	x	x	x	x	x	x
GAFTA	x	x	x	x	–	x
MAFTA	x	x	x	x	–	x
Bilateral econ. and trade agreements						
Egypt-Tunisia	–	x	x	–	–	–
Egypt-Lebanon	–	–	–	x	–	–
Morocco-Egypt	–	x	–	–	–	–
Egypt-Iraq	–	–	–	–	x	–
Iraq-Lebanon	x	–	–	–	–	–
Jordan-UAE,	x	–	–	–	–	–
Morocco-UAE	x	–	–	–	–	–
Egypt-Jordan,	x	–	–	–	–	–
Morocco-Jordan	–	x	–	–	–	x
Egypt-S. Arabia	x	x	x	x	x	–
Egypt-Libya	–	–	–	–	–	x
Morocco-Syria	x	–	–	–	–	x
Syria-Iraq	x	–	x	x	x	x
Syria-S. Arabia	–	x	x	x	–	–
Syria-GCC	x	–	–	–	–	–

Source: Authors' elaboration of data from www.arabicnews.com/economics

trade in services (especially labour and FDI), intellectual property rights protection, competition laws and policies and dispute settlements.

A search for these specific contents in selected agreements signed in the MENA region returns some interesting results:

- almost all agreements have been signed in the last decade;
- there is generally a gap between planned and actual implementation;
- bilateral agreements prevail, but they are interested only in particular trade flows;
- bilateral agreements present regular committee meetings to solve problems;
- multilateral agreements tending to create trading blocks present all the pillars but also delay and lack of implementation;

In addition, considering the structure of the agreements, it is noticeable that:

1   there are difficulties in the liberalization of agricultural products trade (due to Farmer's Almanac and negative lists);
2   there are disputes about the rules of origin between countries with and without diversified and sophisticated industrial production;
3   only Egypt, Jordan, Morocco and Tunisia, among the selected agreements, have competition laws;
4   the dispute settlement is not active because of the lack of courts.

Although the multilateral trade agreements appear suitable (from an institutional point of view) to promote development, they are not implemented in some aspects, and this is the reason why they have relatively little success in comparison to bilateral agreements. Some authors (Afifi 2005; Escribano and Jordàn 1999; Regnault 2002), in fact, argue that only Euro-Med and intra-Arab agreements (south-south trade) can support the development of the MENA region through the 'creation/diversion' and 'gravity' effects.

It is relevant to stress how regional integration and active participation in global markets do not present exclusive or opposing choices. Many successful countries have built up their strategies around a paradigm of 'open regionalism', which implies negotiating reciprocal preferences with regional partners while opening up to international markets. Moreover, regional agreements can complement multilateral reforms as they can make a contribution toward harmonization of rule-making. Some arrangements contain provisions in areas such as investment protection or labour migration that go beyond current multilateral trade law in terms of their integrative ambition (so-called WTO-plus arrangements) (OECD 2003).

Conclusion

At the end of the present work on the development process in the Middle East and North Africa, two main conclusions arise; the former emerging from methodological and theoretical perspectives, the latter from the regional experience. The first deduction is, in fact, the complexity of the development process and the second is its continuity regarding the historical and social legacy of the countries. Although such deductions seem trivial, they are on the contrary worthwhile if compared with the idea that some strategies that are conveniently exploited can lead rapidly and successfully to development.

Nevertheless, the aim of the development is not simply the improvement of the material conditions of life, since its realization implies changes in several other domains. Generally speaking, the awareness of development, which by introducing a new socio-economic system transforms the human lives far beyond the improvement of material conditions or modifies the environment where the human beings live, seems in fact to be rather lacking. Development implies a more profound change that sees all the old social routines discarded in the course of time, the whole production system rearranged and refashioned, and even human minds eventually adapting to innovations (the fact that the idea of progress was not born in Western culture until the eighteenth century is proof that development is also a mindset). In such a framework development isn't an end, but a means of improving the human condition through the rearrangement of all the aspects of life, it is a process determining the transition from one socio-economic setting to another. Thus time, learning and relationships are relevant constituents of development, necessary for the phenomenon to come about and essential for the phenomenon to be understood.

What is more, this process is irreversible, as it introduces scenarios previously unknown, where socio-economic features, different from those of the old system, seem to be permanent. Economists and scholars from other disciplines who analysed the experience of the 'first comers' and of the 'latecomers' were aware both of the social nature of the process and of the features of the new system that they called 'capitalism'. One of the stylized facts that they considered to be crucial for the exploitation of the development process is the co-evolution of the new political subject (the state) and of the new arrangement of economic activities (production/distribution systems). In addition, another point they took into account is that, although the development process ferries societies towards a new states of affairs, both the path and the new setting betray the legacy of the origin conditions in such a way that the stronger the legacy, the more influential it will be.

This representation of development includes all the key concepts that enabled the appraisal of the process that the MENA region experienced in the last 50 years: colonial legacy, political instability, incomplete regionalism, social contract, rent seeking attitudes and demographic and human capital issues.

The first element that influenced the MENA development during the last 50 years has been the legacy of old colonialism and the emergence of geo-economics, not only because these phenomena affected for a long time the exploitation of local resources, but also because they shaped some other environmental conditions such as regionalism and political stability. The presence of European powers in the MENA region dismantled the old regionalism, both establishing the boundaries of new states without regard to the ethnic and historical conditions of people living in the territories, and linking them to the motherland; in fact, nowadays the first commercial partner of most regional countries is the European Union. But this would not be a negative aspect if Europe, contrary to what is actually happening, could implement trade and development policies suitable to improve MENA economies. The geo-economic interests for provision of energy resources have already been crucial, causing in particular from the 1980s, on the one hand the direct intervention of armies that isolated important states like Iraq and Iran, on the other the Western preference for (and the tolerance of) authoritarian regimes. Despite this framework, some recent trade agreements enforced intra-regional exports that could help the development in the area; the integration process in the Arab peninsula, thanks also to oil rents, improved the economic conditions of the GCC countries, providing them with the chance to finance investments all over the Arab world through their sovereign funds (Quadrio Curzio 2011).

The other environmental variable affecting the development process is the political instability, fostered both by the state-society relation and by the international order established in the area. As to the first cause the centralized state, although introduced at the time of colonialism, could not strengthen its position after the independence because of the absence of acceptance by the traditional Muslim societies, that were self-sufficient and autonomous communities acknowledging only the *umma*, as a greater aggregating unit. The way by which the state could be entitled to sovereignty was to take on the traditional functions of the social units (like the clan, for example), i.e. the protection against foreigners, the promotion of the redistributive principle and the provision of social welfare. The 'social contract' thus represents the agreement by which the state commits to be interventionist and redistributive (and thus to lead the development process) and the people who support it even sacrifice some personal rights. With the worsening of the economic conditions the states, defaulting with respect to their welfare obligations, strengthened their apparatus (the army, the bureaucracies), thus preventing the institutional change or improvement and slowing development. The failed evolution of the political domain gave rise to a 'development model based on a leviathan state and greased by oil and aid windfalls' (Malik and Awadallah 2011: 1).

Political instability has encouraged the rent-seeking attitude of the classes supporting the state (bureaucrats, armed forces, parties, trade unions, etc.) and also of economies of the area, more than a half of which are forced to rely on oil rents. Meanwhile, entrepreneurial initiatives have faced insufficient support and even human capital formation has resulted in a biased attitude as the preferences for education are oriented towards public jobs.

Despite this environment the outcome of the MENA economies present satisfactory results in the first phase (up to 1980) in terms of GDP per capita, investment, education, health care and industrialization. The following two decades showed a slowing down of development, but an endurance in terms of purchasing power parity, of human development and also of trade. All these indicators improved up to the 2008 when development restarted, but in the last decade youth unemployment, which is also a result of the demographic transition experienced by the region, emerged as an important hindrance. Undoubtedly, the Arab revolts arose from the fact that 'the rising costs of repression and redistribution is calling into question the long-term sustainability of this development model' (Malik and Awadallah 2011: 1), or because of specific national aims, as 'while Tunisia and Egypt grapple in their own ways with building political/institutions, constitutions, political parties, and electoral systems, Libya will need to begin by constructing the rudiments of a civil society' (Anderson 2011: 7).

The experience of MENA's economies in the last 50 years in searching for a proper path of development (a path influenced both by the rapid change of the ancient, well-established regime and by the evolution of its international relations framework) has thus gone along with a changing dialectic between state and society, with the progressive weakening of the former and the empowering of the latter. In this framework the betrayal of the 'social contract' by the states that are unable to provide employment, that is to give a chance to human resources (labour) protected by Muslim social rules elimina as the crucial constituent of the society, probably represents the essential trigger for the present uprisings and socio-political transformation.

Notes

1 The Middle East and North Africa

1 A more recent similar view, 'sees regions simply as a method of classification – a descriptive tool defined according to particular criteria, with as many regions as there are criteria to define them. In this scheme, a particular approach is to identify regions according to their function, thus distinguishing functional regions from the formal regions mentioned above. A functional region is one that displays a certain functional coherence – an interdependence of parts – when defined against certain criteria' (Taylor 2004: 6).

2 In effect, the theoretical assessment made by the author reduced all the attributes of the region to the requirements necessary to analyse its contents in terms of regional system. 'In concluding this exercise in explication, I have proposed that the necessary and sufficient conditions for the regional subsystem are as follows:
   a. The actors' pattern of relations or interactions exhibits a particular degree of regularity and intensity to the extent that a change at one point in the subsystem affects other points.
   b. The actors are generally proximate.
   c. Internal and external observers and actors recognize the subsystem as a distinctive area or "theatre of operation".
   d. The subsystem logically consists of at least two and quite probably more actors' (Thompson 1973: 101).

3 To examine these concepts see Hurrell 1995: 39-45.

4 For more information see Hurrell 1995: 46-71.

5 See, for example, Fawcett 2004; Marchand, Boàs and Shaw 1999.

6 See on these arguments de Melo and Panagariya 1993. In particular, this article stated that, although a regional agreement is discriminatory 'because under regionalism preferences are extended only to partners [...at] the same times it represents a move towards free trade among partners'(1993: 4).

7 In the case of an economic union (like the European Union) the idea of region behind the economic analysis is widened to include not only the international harmonization of all kinds of markets, but also a common currency and common economic institutions and policies.

8 This argument will be developed in Chapter 8.

9 The structure of Arab societies in past and present times is a debated argument in different fields of social sciences. In particular, the relation between state and society in the Arab world constitutes the starting point both to discuss some relevant problems (like modernization, democracy, and development) and to apply different theoretical explanatory paradigms to Muslim countries. In this part of the book our interest is directed to sketch the basic social units of the traditional Arab societies.

10 '...market relations are efficient when there is little ambiguity over performance, so the parties can tolerate relatively high levels of opportunism or goal incongruence. And bureaucratic relations are efficient when both performance ambiguity and goal incongruence are moderately high' (Ouchi 1980: 135).

11 Ouchi 1980:135. After the presentation of the analyses by Weber (Weber 1978) and Durkheim (Durkheim 1933) Ouchi goes back on the study of the clan to compare its efficiency with that of the market and of the bureaucracy in terms of the transaction costs.

12 For this ambiguity see Lapidus 1990: 26.

13 Some scholars 'have reported on modern industrial organizations which closely resemble the clan form, [...] these organizations are typically in technologically advanced or closely integrated industries, where teamwork is common, technologies change often, and therefore individual performance is highly ambiguous' (Ouchi 1980: 136).

14 For the analysis of modes of production and for the analysis of corporatism see Ayubi 1995.

15 'Such an involvement clearly altered the nature of the relationship between tax-collectors and tax-payers. [...] This determination to protect his own investment in the land was only a symptom of a much more deep-routed change: for some *multazima* at least, their appropriation of the surplus was now as much by means of the economic exploitation of the rural population as it was by sheer political coercion' (Owen 1981: 13).

16 '... there was a tendency for some tax farmers in some places to enter the process of production more directly, lending money to the peasants and interesting themselves in the sale of their crops for their own additional profit' (Owen 1981: 13).

17 On the contrary, regional import/export was prosperous until that time. In the eighteenth century towns and cities of the Middle East, centres of administrative activities were important industrial and commercial sites. 'Most of the larger towns tended to specialize in the production of articles [...] that were sufficiently well known to be traded over a wide area' (Owen 1981: 45-46). This was the case of the muslins from Mosul, of the damask from Damascus, of the fine silks and of the cotton stuffs from Aleppo, of the olive oil soap from Nablus, and of the glass from Hebron. 'Each of the major cities of Anatolia, Syria, Iraq and Egypt lay at the intersection of a number of important routes along which goods were carried across the region' (Owen 1981: 47).

18 'Historians cite the fact that throughout the Qujar history, governors were powerless outside the provincial capitals and communities were virtually autonomous'. [...] Qujars 'only intervened in the economy to prevent urban insurrections when prices rose too high [and] auctioned off governorship to the highest bidders, who then sub farmed out tax collection in districts and cities' (Gelvin 2005: 83).

19 That the MENA territories were no more a coherent socio-political unit but a set of new political entities was confirmed by the League of Nations, that on one side denied to the Arabs a distinct statehood at the San Remo Conference in 1920, and on the other dashed their hopes of self-determination splitting their lands 'among the victorious Powers as a new form of colonial state known as mandates' (Rogan 2005: 17) and assigning also to them the settlement of state boundaries.

20 '..with the coming of Mako/Jumel new systems of rotation were developed to accommodate a crop which was planted in the spring and picked in the autumn; peasants now laboured most of the year round while their wives and children joined them at harvest time when their particular skills at picking the bolls from the cotton plants was much in demand. In addition, during the few remaining slack months these same peasants were required to work in the corvèe gangs,

cleaning out the mud deposited by the slowing moving waters in the existing deep-level summer canals, and digging new ones' (Owen 1981: 68).

21 By this key can be explained 'the decreasing salience of Pan-Arab discourse, the growing recognition of Israel as a legitimate regional player, the stability of secular Arab regimes in the region after the Iranian Islamic revolution, and the ups and downs of economic cooperation and integration in the region' (Gregory Gausse III 1999: 29).

22 The predominance of the trans-state identity principle can explain why: 'In the 1950s and 1960s Egypt's Nasser used Pan-Arabism to put normative constraints on the ability of Arab states to conduct sovereign foreign policies. Since the 1970s, political Islam has sought to Islamize states from below, aggregate them for Islamic causes, and mobilize Muslims against Western threats' (Hinnebusch 2005: 152). In some ways the revolts against political regimes spread all over the Arab world at the beginning of 2011 can also be traced back to a trans-state identity, that is to a common feeling due to moral factors (dignity, lack of freedom because of repression and corruption, lack of perspective for youths).

23 It is important to notice that the shift from the geo-politics to the geo-economics (accompanied by a vanishing of the importance of the territory and of its boundaries) goes hand in hand with the shift from a geographic region towards a virtual region (based on the concept of market instead of territory).

24 '... while the Cold War had a major impact upon the states and societies of the Middle East, to a considerable degree the states and social movements of the region also pursued individual policies' (Halliday 2005: 98).

25 'Talks of "human rights" and "democracy", later "reform", was seen as another pretext for imperialism, a simplification that was encouraged by rather too many, unfocused and irresponsible voices in the west' (Halliday 2005: 98).

2 The economic development of 'latecomers'

1 For a debate on the meanings of the term see K. P. Moseley and I. Wallerstein, 1978.

2 For an extended analysis of these theoretical models see Chapters 3 and 4 of the book by Todaro and Smith 2012.

3 'As subsistence is, in the nature of things, prior to conveniency and luxury, so the industry which procures the former must necessarily be prior to that which ministers to the latter. The cultivation and improvement of the country, therefore, which affords subsistence, must, necessarily, be prior to the increase of the town, which furnishes only the means of conveniency and luxury. It is the surplus produce of the country only, or what is over and above the maintenance of the cultivators, that constitutes the subsistence of the town, which can therefore increase only with the increase of this surplus produce. The town, indeed, may not always derive its whole subsistence from the country in its neighbourhood, or even from the territory to which it belongs, but from very distant countries; and this, though it forms no exception from the general rule, has occasioned considerable variations in the progress of opulence in different ages and nations' (Smith 1776: III.1.2). For the relation between agricultural surplus and market see Smith 1776: I.3.1.

4 'As the accumulation of stock must, in the nature of things, be previous to the division of labour, so labour can be more and more subdivided in proportion only as stock is previously more and more accumulated' (Smith 1776: II.1.3).

5 'The greatest improvement in the productive powers of labour, and the greater part of the skill, dexterity, and judgment with which it is any where directed, or applied, seem to have been the effects of the division of labour' (Smith 1776: I.1.1). 'This division of labour, from which so many advantages are derived, is

not originally the effect of any human wisdom, which foresees and intends that general opulence to which it gives occasion. It is the necessary, though very slow and gradual, consequence of a certain propensity in human nature which has in view no such extensive utility; the propensity to truck, barter, and exchange one thing for another' (Smith 1776: I.2.1).

6 Some scholars, on the contrary, support Smith's debate on transition to the capitalism and the dispute on exogenous or endogenous causes determining its upsurge. See, for example, Nunes and Valèrio stating that in Smith's analysis 'the transformation of the traditional economy is propelled by exogenous stimuli, and this implies that a market capitalist economy, or at least an embryo of its structures, must exist before the transition process starts' (Nunes and Valèrio 2001: 102).

7 'In insolent conflict with king and parliament, the great feudal lords created an incomparably larger proletariat by the forcible driving of the peasantry from the land, to which the latter had the same feudal right as the lord himself, and by the usurpation of the common lands. The rapid rise of the Flemish wool manufactures, and the corresponding rise in the price of wool in England, gave the direct impulse to these evictions. The old nobility had been devoured by the great feudal wars. The new nobility was the child of its time, for which money was the power of all powers. Transformation of arable land into sheep-walks was, therefore, its cry'. (Marx 1867: vol. 1, part VIII, chapter 27).

8 This is a fundamental feature of the new socio-economic system, insomuch as the employment contract can be considered the main institution of capitalism: 'I defined capitalism as an economic system in which surplus value is extracted from the production process by using wage labour and is utilized in the circulation process for sustaining capital accumulation' (Screpanti 2001: 258). For the analysis of the different forms of capitalism according to this approach see Chapter 6 in the book.

9 For the discussion of such an argument see Potts 2000: 112-31.

10 Every economic system can be represented as 'a set of institutions for decision making and for the implementation of decisions concerning production, income, and consumption within a given geographic area. According to this definition, the economic system consists of mechanisms, organizational arrangements and decision-making rules' (Gregory and Stuart 2004: 19).

11 Schumpeter shares the classical approach according to which 'it is not possible to explain *economic* change by previous *economic* conditions alone. For the economic state of a people does not emerge simply from the preceding economic conditions, but only from the preceding total situation' (Schumpeter 1955: 58). 'It is just the occurrence of the "revolutionary" change that is our problem, the problem of economic development in a very narrow and formal sense' (Schumpeter 1955: 63). 'Development in our sense is then defined by the carrying out of new combinations' (Schumpeter 1955: 66), that is of different methods and means combining materials and forces in a changed way to produce new or old goods.

12 Also, in Rostow's view, economic development is a phenomenon that is in some way connected to the general change in society. In fact he writes that 'this should be clear: although the stages-of-growth are an economic way of looking at whole societies, they in no sense imply that the worlds of politics, social organization, and of culture are a mere superstructure built upon and derived uniquely from the economy. On the contrary, we accept from the beginning the perception on which Marx, in the end, turned his back and which Engels was only willing to acknowledge whole-heartedly as a very old man; namely, that societies are interacting organisms. While it is true that economic change has political and social consequence, economic change is, itself, viewed here as the consequence of political and social as well as narrowly economic forces. And in terms of human motivation, many of the

most profound economic changes are viewed as the consequence of non-economic human motives and aspirations' (Rostow 1960: 2).

13 According to Todaro and Smith '[...] the linear stages-model emphasizes the crucial role that saving and investment play in promoting sustainable long-run growth. The Lewis two-sector model of structural change underlines the importance of transfers of resources from low-productivity to high-productivity activities in the process of economic development [...] The empirical research of Chenery and his associates seeks to document precisely how economies undergo structural change. [...] The thoughts of international-dependence theorists alert us to the importance of the structure and working of the world economy and the many ways in which decisions made in the developed world can affect the lives of millions of people in the developing world. [...] Although a good deal of conventional neoclassical economic theory needs to be modified to fit the unique social, institutional, and structural circumstances of developing nations, there is no doubt that promoting efficient production and distribution through a proper, functioning price system is an integral part of any successful development process'(Todaro and Smith 2012: 131-2).

14 'The term "general-purpose technology", or GPT, has seen extensive use in recent treatments of the role of technology in economic growth, and is usually reserved for changes that transform both household life and the ways in which firms conduct business. Steam, electricity, internal combustion, and information technology (IT) are often classified as GPT's for this reason. They affected the whole economy'. (Jovanovic and Rousseau 2005: 1184).

15 For the presentation of these theories see Todaro and Smith, 2012: Chapter 4.

3 Institutions and development in the Middle East and North Africa

1 'Out of 1,689 projects with institutional development goals approved between 1971 and 1991, only 29 per cent had a substantial impact on ID, according to evaluations by the World Bank's Operations Evaluation Department (OED). The impact on ID was modest in 45 per cent of the projects and negligible in the remaining 26 per cent.' (Kapur and Webb 2000: 9).

2 Anyway, according to Alchian, the capacity of institutions to achieve certain goals is conditioned by (and depends on) the unique environment in which they play (as stressed by the cultural approach too), so that only in a given period and in a given place efficient institutions survive (Alchian 1950).

3 In continental countries of Europe also the Catholic confessional parties were influential in promoting the new state institutional asset.

4 The agency view is based on the definition of institutions as behavioural constraint while the structural view, common in sociology, considers institutions as properties of societies.

5 'When we understand institutions as systems we are recognizing that they are complexes composed of elements of social behaviour' (Potts 2000: 75-76).

6 A 'complex adaptive system' is a particular species of functional systems that may be themselves elements of systems of higher order and whose elements may be in turn systems of lower order. The dynamic of this system enable them to adapt to the environment (see Potts 2000: 68).

7 This comparison will be discussed in Chapter 6.

8 This historical interpretation (following Owen 2002 and Gelvin 2005) contrasts some other explanations. As to arbitrary taxation and weak property rights Kuran, for example, maintains that these phenomena were connected to the 'fiscalism' and to the 'provisionism', 'pillars of the economic governance in the Ottoman Empire after it reached maturity. But they apply with equal force to earlier Muslim-governed states' (Kuran 2004: 74, footnote and text).

9 The Maghribi trader's debate is a long-lasting dispute between Greif and Edwards-Ogilvie about forms of organizations, beliefs and behaviour of two different groups of merchants in the Mediterranean see around the tenth-eleven century. The different trading institutions and their connected ability or failure to evolve and adapt were crucial to ensure the Genoese survival and the Maghribi disappearance in the new capitalist era.

10 'The Arab state is not a natural growth of its own socioeconomic history or its own cultural and intellectual tradition. It is a "fierce" state that has frequently to resort to raw coercion in order to preserve itself, but it is not a "strong" state because (a) it lacks [...] the "infrastructural power" that enables states to penetrate society effectively through mechanisms such as taxation for example; (b) it lacks ideological hegemony (in the Gramscian sense) that would enable it to forge a "historic" social block that accepts the legitimacy of the ruling stratum' (Ayubi 1995: 3).

4 Demographic dynamics and development implications in the Middle East and North Africa

1 'Population growth rates in the More Developed Countries raised about a half percent above those in the Less Developed Countries in the century before 1950. But after World War II, population growth surged in the Less Developed Countries, with the growth rate peaking at 2.5 percent in the mid-1960s, then dropping rapidly' (Lee 2003:178).

2 The rate of natural increase is defined in demography as the crude birth rate minus death rate of a population.

3 In the statistics and as discussed in this chapter, MENA aggregate refers to the Arab countries (Algeria, Bahrain, Egypt, Iraq, Jordan, Kuwait, Lebanon, Libya, Morocco, Palestine, Oman, Qatar, Saudi Arabia, Syria, Tunisia, United Arab Emirates) plus Iran and Turkey (other MENA countries). Israel has not been included in the aggregated MENA region, nor has Mashreq for its peculiar demographic transition pattern as explained in the course of the chapter.

4 An analysis of the phases prior to 1950 is not carried out in this chapter due to unavailability of data.

5 The Western experience of boom and bust was instead a post-war phenomenon. In Egypt, too, a surge in fertility during 1973-1979 (the so-called Sadat middle years) appears to have taken place well after the October War with Israel was over. Yet, Iran's recent experience of baby boom coincided largely with the war years with Iraq (1980-88)' (Hakimian 2001: 8).

6 The youth dependency ratio is defined as the economic proportion of youths (0-14) to the adult population.

7 The population momentum occurs in the first phase of the demographic transition, when the baby boom generation reaches the reproductive age, thus creating a successive baby boom

8 Adult unemployment refers to the labour force population aged 25+; youth unemployment to the group aged 15-24.

5 The performance of MENA economies between internal conditions and external shocks

1 The term has been used to indicate a regional status of uncommon involvement in world economic trends, like globalization or integration (Aarts 1999). In this case it is used to mark some specificity in the development process.

2 They have also run the risks just mentioned, but this aspect will be treated in the next paragraph.
3 These countries are Bahrain, Kuwait, Libya, Oman, Qatar, Saudi Arabia, United Arab Emirates, Algeria, Iran, Iraq, Syria, Yemen, Egypt and Tunisia.
4 The 'seven sisters' is a nickname assigned to the seven major oil companies: Anglo-Persian Oil Company (now British Petroleum); Gulf Oil, Standard Oil of California and Texaco (now Chevron); Royal Dutch Shell; Standard Oil of New Jersey and Standard Oil Company of New York (now ExxonMobil) operating in the world market during the first half twenty century.
5 But the oil enabled them to consolidate the state system as well as their independence.
6 The watershed moment representing the turning point in the involvement of United States in the region came in 1979: 'That year was marked by five landmark events: (1) the peace treaty between Egypt and Israel; (2) the Islamist revolution in Iran; (3) the takeover of the Grand Mosque in Mecca, Saudi Arabia, by Islamist militants; (4) the Soviet invasion of Afghanistan, and (5) the emergence of Saddam Hussein as the sole ruler of Iraq. Each in its way posed new challenges for American policymakers' (Hudson 2005: 291).
7 As to the duration of the political regimes in the region the problem is pertinent for few countries, as eight have a system of hereditary rule (Bahrain, Jordan, Kuwait, Morocco, Oman, Qatar, Saudi Arabia and United Arab Emirates), four have multiparty electoral regimes (Iraq, Israel, Lebanon and Turkey), one is an Islamic republic (Iran) and, up to 2011, six were one-party regimes (Algeria, Yemen, Tunisia, Libya, Egypt, Syria, of which the last three might be classified as 'quasi-hereditary').
8 In the literature on this subject, different groupings of MENA countries (collecting sometimes only some of them) have been proposed in order to appraise the development of the region. In order to consider commercial policies and economic integration a geographic distinction has been provided (some cooperation agreements have also been used, see Chapter 9): Maghreb (Morocco, Algeria, Tunisia and Libya), Mashreq (Egypt, Jordan, Israel, Lebanon, Syria, Turkey and Iraq) and Gulf Cooperation Countries (Saudi Arabia, Kuwait, Bahrain, Qatar, United Arab Emirates, Oman). To highlight the economic structure of the countries, instead, the following grouping has been proposed (Elbadawi 2005): oil economies (Libya, Saudi Arabia, Kuwait, Bahrain, Qatar, United Arab Emirates, Oman), mixed oil economies (Algeria and Iraq), diversified economies (Morocco, Tunisia, Egypt, Lebanon, Jordan and Syria), and primary exports economies (Yemen).
9 They have been indirectly affected through the migrants hosted in oil countries and through their remittances (see Chapter 8).

6 'Social contract', human development and welfare in the MENA region

1 As emphasized by Kuran, inequality may emerge anyway from Islamic inheritance law, which may create fragmentation of resources and unequal wealth distribution among families across generations (Kuran 2012).
2 'In addition to foreign influences, much of the impetus for the consolidation of interventionist–redistributive social contracts came from within the region. The resilience of these social contracts as frameworks for the management of MENA political economies reflects the local conditions in which they arose, specifically the timing and sequencing of four processes: the rise of nationalist movements, the emergence of mass politics, the incorporation of labor into the political arena, and the introduction of electoral institutions as a by-product of the colonial presence in MENA states' (Yousef 2004: 9).

3 According to the World Bank the definition of the poverty gap is the average gaps between poor people's living standards and the poverty line. It indicates the average extent to which individuals fall below the poverty line (if they do). The poverty gap index expresses the poverty gap as a percentage of the poverty line.

4 As pointed by Adams and Page (2001), without survey data on either employment or wages for the poor it is impossible to identify how much labour-intensive growth has contributed to poverty reduction in the Middle East. Similarly, in the absence of information on the poor's access to areas of public interventions (such as health and education, that help to increase the human capital of the poor and the transferring of resources through social safety net) it is difficult to assess the contribution of state institutions to poverty reduction in the Middle East.

5 'In the process of development, economic growth modifies the distribution of resources across sectors, relative prices, factor rewards (such as labor, physical capital, human capital and land) and the factor endowments of agents. These changes are likely to directly impact on the distribution of income, regardless of whether factor and goods markets are perfect or not. In effect, ever since Kuznets and Lewis, the theoretical constructs about the effect of growth on the distribution of income focused on one or several of these basic mechanisms. Labor-market imperfections and productivity differentials across sectors with changing importance in the economy were the main theoretical explanation of Kuznets' celebrated inverted-U curve relating inequality and development almost 50 years ago. Individual accumulation behavior and subsequent aggregate changes in factor rewards due to the falling marginal product of capital explained the same evolution in Stiglitz' (1969) neoclassical model of growth and distribution. Since then, many other channels based directly or indirectly on these basic mechanisms – the "segmentation" of the economy and changes in prices and factor rewards – have been uncovered, which do not always lead to the inverted-U effect of growth on inequality. Institutional change is also closely linked with the process of economic growth in the sense that growth tends to modify institutions, social relations, culture, etc.' (Bourguignon 2004:11).

6 Adams and Page's sample includes MENA countries that, since the eighties, have conducted nationally representative households surveys, namely: Egypt, Jordan, Morocco, Tunisia and Iran.

7 The Human Development Index is a combined indicator of life expectancy, educational attainment and income that, ranging between 0 and 1, set for each dimension the relative position of a country/world area in the ranking.

8 Although local autonomy and a certain degree of decentralization was present in the Empire (as in the Egyptian case), the Arab people never knew the establishment of the state. Under the Ottoman Empire, in fact, the region was divided into administrative units, as in the case of Sham, who joined Palestine, Lebanon and Jordan in a single region. Beyond these initial configurations, the sense of belonging meant to be a member of the Muslim community and therefore the only border between the Arab world and the outside was represented by the borders of the Empire. The division of the region, ending with the formation of the independent states, started from the late 19th century, the First World War (and the beginning of the partition of the Ottoman Empire by Great Britain and the Allies) and Sikes Picot agreements that sanctioned the respective spheres of foreign influence in the area. Paradoxically, it was the foreign occupation to feed patriotic movements and nationalist ideas while at the same time, Pan-Arabism was a reaction to the disillusionment with the policies of the Empire and the dissatisfaction with the consistent presence of non-Muslims in the area. What followed in the region in the 20th century was influenced by what was happening in neighboring European countries, such as the outbreak of the Second World War, the creation of the United Nations and the beginning of the process of decolonization in the second half of the century, with the exception of Palestine.

7 Human capital and labour markets in the MENA region

1 The social costs of education are, more specifically, the opportunity costs of a society derived from the allocation of (limited) resources in the financing of higher education rather than in the investment of such funds in other (more productive) economic sectors.
2 Above all other variables (accumulation of physical capital, the institutional environment and openness to trade), the quality of human capital has been the driver of the impressive growth of emerging Asian economies in the 1970s.
3 In Egypt the University of Al-Azhar, founded by the Fatimids in 969 AD, is still the leading institution for Islamic studies in the Arab world.
4 Calculated by Thomas, Wang and Fang as standard deviation from the mean of education in the adult population, the MENA region stood at 3.40 in the 1970s (against 3.69 for Latin America and 3.77 for East Asia) and started to experience a reversal trend from the mid of the 1980s. In 1985, the standard deviation rose to 4.37 and went on to reach 5.02 and 5.05 in 1995 and 2000 respectively.
5 The most-widely used are TIMMS (Third International Mathematics and Science Study) or IAEP (International Assessment of Educational Progress).
6 According to Chapman and Miric, negative incentives occur when teachers supplement their income by offering special instruction for those students who are able to pay. This creates a negative incentive, as teachers have a financial motive to withhold their expertise during their regular teaching as a way of encouraging students (and their families) to invest in remediation outside of school hours. (Chapman and Miric 2005).
7 It is also relevant to stress how, in addition to structural unemployment, other forms of unemployment coexist in MENA labour markets such as invisible underemployment (in which the labour force's personal skills are underutilized and where the labour force receives minimum wage), and the 'moonlighting' phenomena. In the latter, the worker performs different types of employment during 24 hours: an 'official' job during the day and another 'informal' job (e.g. they might work as a taxi driver or take on small retail activities especially in local *suq*) during non-working hours.
8 Wage setting institutions are defined as wage bargaining institutions that affect the overall wage level but also non-wage outcomes; for instance, such institutions are trade unions and government policy (OECD, 2004). 'The framework that regulates employment relations, including the legal framework for standards of work, minimum wages and trade unions recognition is likely to be the result of government policy but workers organization have their own rules on hiring and firing. In the MENA region, labour market regulations have historically been stringent compared with other developing regions, introducing rigidities in labour market' (Pissarides and Véganzonès-Varoudakis 2007: 137-57).
9 The labour force participation rate, measured as the ratio between the labour force and the working age population, gives an idea of the supply of labour available for the economy. It also explains how unemployment rates can occur with increases in employment when there is an increase in participation rates (new entrants in the market) which are only partially employed.

8 The migration-development link in the MENA region

1 The *Khafeel* or *Kafala,* used both by the GCC and the Mashrek states, is a system of temporary 'guestworkers'. Also known as the 'sponsor-employer contract', it guarantees that migrant workers receive an entry visa and residence permit but only if a citizen sponsors them. The *Khafeel* is responsible financially and legally for the worker, and signs a document from the Ministry of Labour to that effect

while the worker is tied to a particular employer. If the worker breaks the contract he/she has to leave the country immediately at his or her own expense (Longva 1999). The 1970-1980s regional migration flows, mostly regulated by a series of temporary guestworker programmes, attracted labour from Egypt, Yemen, Jordan, Palestine, and also increased the migration of Turkish workers to Germany on temporary work contracts.

2 Adopting UN definition, labour migration is 'the movement of migrants whose express purpose is to pursue an economic activity remunerated from the country of destination'.

3 According to UN definition, returnees are 'persons returning to stay in their country of citizenship after having been international migrants in another country, and who plan to stay in their own country for a year or more'.

4 This is the reason why, in the Barcelona Declaration (1995), which was the building block of the Euro-Mediterranean Partnership and which was inspired by traditional economic principles, migration is considered as a socio-cultural problem instead of an economic one.

5 Foreigners born abroad who have acquired nationality of the host country.

6 Although of different magnitude, today both groups of countries experience flows that are temporary in nature as, despite permanent installation, Maghrebi migrants (following current temporary migration schemes with Europe) have engaged in considerable return (Boubakri 2001).

7 The different magnitude of the migrant stock to total population (3.2 per cent in Egypt against 8.6 per cent in Morocco in 2007), was fairly compensated by the different population (about 80 million for Egypt and 31 million for Morocco).

8 The economic network, in particular, is inserted as sub-type of social networks, that is as 'set of nodes (people, organizations) and links between them' that have intended economic effects (Zucherman 2003).

9 Familiar and personal networks refer to the correspondence between migrants and families or home communities in terms of direct transfer of remittances, written notices and gifts.

10 In many cases the transfer of the sum of money (equivalent to the remittance sent by the migrant) is performed within a few hours. In exchange for providing a service to the migrant, the *Hawaladar* (both in country A than in country B) receives a commission that ranges from a minimum of 0.25 per cent to a maximum of 1.25 per cent of the amount of remittance sent in local currency or foreign. The 'debt' of the *Hawaladar* in country A (the migrant host country) is bonded with a transfer of currency or an item of remittance (sum equivalent) in the opposite direction (Buencamino and Gorbunov 2002). In such transactions, the money never crosses the national borders of a country or enters through modern banking system, since the sending of remittance is based on communication between the two *Hawaladar* and it is not defined by contractual arrangements in writing.

11 According to Coleman, social capital, defined by its function, consists of some aspects of a social structure that facilitate certain actions of individuals who are within the structure (Coleman 1988).

12 In fact when remittances sent back home help finance education of second generation, they help to create educated workers resulting in brain gain (but also in brain drain if they migrate on permanent bases).

13 Return can result both in direct effects (in terms of an increase of average productivity and of human capital stock) and indirect effects (brain gain dynamics). Recent studies, aiming at investigating the empirical effects of international migration on human capital and labour market outcomes in middle income countries with considerable migration (especially of skilled workers), have found evidence of a significant contribution of returnees to improvement in

average productivity and wages in home countries. In particular, not only does average schooling increase with free mobility (as a form of investment in the prospect of future migration) but workers with international experience receive considerable wage premium, compared to non-migrants (Mayr and Peri 2008; Co, Yun and Gang 1998; Barrett and O'Connell 2000).

14 This trend, evolving from one generation of migrants to the other, appears more marked in Wahba 2009 (see Table 5.6, where a particular dataset is used).

15 One of the main achievements of return migrants in the MENA region is investments in housing (Adams 1991). Although considered to be unproductive (since they might result in a negative effect for the whole economy if they lead to an increase of prices in the real estate sector), they have an undeniable positive welfare effect at household level, increasing health and living conditions.

9 The openness of the MENA economies

1 The differences of values of openness between Figure 9.1 and those just referred to are due to the different grouping of countries.

2 'It is interesting to note that relaxing the transport constraints and increasing the efficiency of customs clearance procedures would have particularly strong effects on exports of the MENA region relative to other regions of the world' (Bhattacharya and Wolde 2010: 15).

3 The Arab Common Market (ACM) was founded in August 1964 on the basis of a resolution passed by the Council of Arab Economic Unity (CAEU), an organization that the Economic Council of the Arab League had established in 1957. The ACM is not an independent organization and its implementation was overseen by the CAEU. In 1999, Egypt, Iraq, Jordan, Libya, Mauritania, Syria, and Yemen belonged to the ACM.

4 This specific institutional experiment became less relevant by the 1990s, due to the closure of borders between member countries during the political unrests of previous decades and to the suspension of Egyptian membership when the country signed the Camp David Accord with Israel in 1979 (Miniesy, Nugent and Yousef 2003: 42).

5 A special case about this problem, discussed from a political, economic and legal point of view, is treated by some scholars (Schiff 1996; Bhagwati and Panagariya 1996) who show how, under particular conditions, a small country (not influential in respect to the terms of trade) joining a great free trade area can anyway gain from trade.

6 No MENA countries have signed a free trade agreement with China (World Bank 2010a).

7 Air transport, which, together with shipping, is the main mode of transportation of goods and people, is concentrated in few key airports and mainly state-owned. Restrictive bilateral agreements between governments is the main concern, as only Jordan, Morocco and Lebanon have gradually moved towards a more open skies regime. If the liberalization of cross-border traffic rights is the priority for air transport, maritime transport is hampered by lack of private participation and competition in the port system. The same concerns can be applied to network of roads, that account for the vast majority of land based freight transport.

8 As pointed out by Miniesy, Nugent and Yousef, since the 1970s there have been numerous bilateral conflicts such as diplomatic crises, border disputes and open wars that have hinder intra-trade in particular in the Maghreb (between Libya, Algeria and Morocco) and in the Mashreq (Iran versus Iraq, Syria versus Lebanon) (Miniesy, Nugent and Yousef 2003).

Bibliography

Aarts, P. (1999) 'The Middle East: a region without regionalism or the end of exceptionalism?', *Third World Quarterly*, 20 (5): 911–25.

Abdelkhalek, T. (2005) 'La pauvreté au Maroc', contribution to the *Rapport du Cinquantenaire sur 50 ans de developpement humain au Maroc*, (RDH50). Available at: <http://www.rdh50.ma/fr/pdf/contributions/GT7-1.pdf>.

Acemoglu, D. and Robinson, J. (2008) 'The role of institutions in growth and development', *The World Bank Commission on Growth and Development Working Paper*, 10.

Acemoglu, D., Johnson, S. and Robinson, J. A. (2005) 'Institutions as the fundamental cause of long-run growth', in P. Aghion and S. N. Durlauf (eds) *Handbook of Economic Growth*, vol. 1, Amsterdam: North-Holland, pp. 385–472.

Adams, R. (1991) *The Effects of International Remittances on Poverty, Inequality and Development in Rural Egypt*, International Policy Food Research Institute.

Adams, R. and Page, J. (2001) Holding the Line: Poverty Reduction in the Middle East and North Africa, 1970–2000, paper presented to the Annual Conference of the Economic Research Forum for the Arab Countries, Iran and Turkey, Manama, Bahrain, October 25–27.

Adams, R. and Page, J. (2003) 'Poverty, inequality and growth in selected Middle East and North Africa countries, 1980–2000', *World Development*, 31(12): 2027–48.

Afifi, T. (2005) *Egypt in an Arab-African-sandwich: Are GAFTA and COMESA to be implemented?*, EcoMod Network, Free University of Brussels, Belgium.

Ahmed, M. (2010) 'Trade competitiveness and growth in the MENA region', *World Economic Forum's Arab World Competitiveness Review, IMF*.

Akder, H. (2000) 'Agricultural trade around the Mediterranean', in B. Hoekman and K. El-Din (eds) *Trade Policy Development in the Middle East and North Africa,* Washington D.C.: The World Bank, pp. 102–11.

Akhtar, S. and Rouis, M. (2010) 'Economic integration in MENA: the GCC, the Maghreb, and the Mashreq', *MENA Quick Notes 33*, World Bank.

Akyol, M. (2007) 'Is Islam compatible with modernity?', *Turkish Daily News*, 24 November.

Al-Atrash, H. and Yousef, T. (1999) 'Intra-Arab Trade: is it too little?', *IMF Working Paper*, 00/10.

Alchian, A. (1950) 'Uncertainty, evolution and economic theory', *Journal of Political Economy*, 58: 211–21.

Alesina, A., Spolaore, E., and Wacziang, R. (2002) 'Trade growth and size of countries', *Stanford Graduate School of Business Research Paper Series*, 1774.

Ali, A. G. (2002) 'Building human capital for economic development in the Arab countries', *ECES Working Paper*, 76.

Ali, A. G. (2009) 'The political economy of inequality in the Arab region and relevant development policies', *ERF Working Paper*, 502.

Anderson, L. (2011) 'Demystifying the Arab Spring. Parsing the differences between Tunisia, Egypt and Libya', *Foreign Affairs*, 90 (3): 1–7.

Angel-Urdinola, D. F., Kuddo, A., Tanabe, K. and Wazzan, M. (2010) 'Key characteristics of employment regulation in the Middle East and North Africa', *World Bank SP Discussion Paper*, 1006.

Aoki, M. (2007) 'Endogenizing institutions and institutional change', *Journal of Institutional Economics*, 3 (1): 1–31.

Aron, J. (2000) 'Growth and institutions: a review of the evidence', *The World Bank Research Observer*, 15 (1): 99–135.

Ayubi, N. N. (1995) *Over-stating the Arab State. Politics and Society in the Middle East*, London: J. B. Tauris.

Backer A. (2005) 'The impact of the Barcelona Process on trade and foreign direct investment', Middle East and North African Economies Conference on *Past Perspectives and Future Challenges*, Brussels, 2–4 June.

Badr, G. M. (1977) 'Islamic Law: its relation to other legal systems', *The American Journal of Comparative Law*, 26 (2): 187–98.

Baldwin, R. E. (1952) 'The New Welfare Economics and gains in international trade', *Quarterly Journal of Economics,* 66: 91–101.

Baldwin, R. E. and Venables, A. (1995) 'Regional economic integration', in G. K. Grossman and K. Rogoff (eds) *Handbook of International Economics*, Vol. III, Amsterdam: North Holland, pp. 1597–1640.

Baldwin-Edwards, M. (2005), *Migration in the Middle East and Mediterranean*, Regional Study for the Global Commission of International Migration, Mediterranean Migration Observatory, Greece: Panteion University.

Barcelona Conference (1995) *Final Declaration of the Barcelona Euro-Mediterranean Ministerial Conference of 27 and 28 November 1995*, Barcelona.

Barrett, A. and O'Connell, P. J. (2000) 'Is there a wage premium for returning Irish migrants?' *IZA Discussion Paper*, 135.

Bauer, T., Epstein, G. and Gang, I. N. (2002) 'Herd effects or migration network? The location choice of Mexican immigrants in the U.S.', *IZA Discussion Paper*, 551.

Bayat, A. (2000) 'Social movements, activism and social development in the Middle East', *UNRISD Paper*, 3.

Beck, T. and Laeven, L. (2005) 'Institution building and growth in transition economies', *World Bank Policy Research Working Paper*, 3657.

Becker, G. S. (1960) 'An economic analysis of fertility', *Demographic and Economic Change in Developed Countries*, Princeton: National Bureau of Economic Research.

Becker, G .S. (1964) *Human Capital: a theoretical and empirical analysis with special reference to education*, New York: Columbia University Press.

Becker, G. S. (1974) 'A theory of social interaction', *Journal of Political Economy*, 82 (6): 1063–93.

Behar, A. and Freund, C. (2011) 'The trade performance of the Middle East and North Africa', *Middle East and North Africa Working Paper Series*, 53.

Bhagwati, J. N. (1991) *The World Trading System at Risk*, Princeton: Princeton University Press.

Bhagwati, J. N. and Panagariya, A. (eds) (1996) *Free Trade Areas or Free Trade? The economics of Preferential Trading Agreements*, Washington D.C.: AEI Press.

Bhattacharya, R. and Wolde, H. (2010) 'Constraints on trade in the MENA region', *IMF Working Paper*, 31.

Bibi, S. and Nabli, M. (2010) 'Equity and inequality in MENA', *ERF Working Paper, 33*.

Billeh, V. (2002) 'Matching education to demand for labor in the Middle East and North Africa region', in H. Handoussa and Z. Tzannatos (eds) *Employment Creation and Social Protection in the Middle East and North Africa*, Cairo: AUC Press, pp. 1–19.

Binder, L. (1958) 'The Middle East as a subordinate international system', *World Politics*, 10 (3): 408–29.

Birdsall, N., Kelley A. C. and Singing S. W. (eds) (2001) *Population Matters: Demographic change, economic growth, and poverty in the developing world*, New York: Oxford University Press.

Bloom D., Canning D. and Sevilla J. (2002) *The Demographic Dividend: a new perspective on the economic consequences of population change*, Santa Monica: RAND, MR–1274.

Bloom, D. and Freeman R. B. (1986) 'The effects of population growth on labor supply and employment in developing countries', *Population and Development Review*, 12 (3): 381–414.

Boeri, T. and Bruker, H. (2005) 'Why are Europeans so tough to migrants?', *Economic Policy*, 20 (44): 629–703.

Boubakri, H. (2001) 'Le Maghreb et les nouvelles configurations migratoires internationales: mobilité et réseaux', *Correspondances*, 68: 8–15.

Bouhga-Hagbe, J. (2004) 'A theory of worker remittances with an application to Morocco', *IMF Working Paper*, 04/194.

Bourguignon, F. (2004) *The Poverty-Growth-Inequality Triangle.* Paper presented at Indian Council for Research on International Economic Relations, New Delhi, 1–30.

Brach, J. (2009) 'Technology, political economy, and economic development in the Middle East and North Africa', *Review of Middle East Economics and Finance*, (5) 3: 1–23, ISSN (Online) 1475–3693, DOI: HYPERLINK "http://dx.doi.org/10.2202/1475-3693.1240"10.2202/1475-3693.1240, February 2010.

Brainard, S. L. (1993) 'A simple theory of multinational corporations and trade with a trade-off between proximity and concentration', *NBER Working Paper*, 4269.

Buencamino, L. and Gorbunov, S. (2002) 'Informal money transfer systems: opportunities and challenges for development finance', *UN Discussion Paper Series*, November.

Bystrof, E. and Soffer, A. (2008) *Israel, Demography and Density: 2007–2020*, Haifa: Chaikin Chair in Geostrategy, University of Haifa.

Campo, J. E. (2009) *Encyclopedia of Islam*, New York: Facts On File Inc.

CAPMAS (2003) *Statistical Yearbook, Labour Force Sample Survey*, Cairo. Available at <www:capmas.gov.eg>. Date accessed 2011.

CAPMAS (2006) *Egypt Labour Market Panel Survey 2006 Database* (ELMPS).

Caroll, L. C. (2002) *Alternative Remittance Systems: Distinguishing sub-systems of ethnic money laundering in Interpol Member Countries on the Asian Continent*, INTERPOL, 27 February.

Cassarino, J. P. (2004) 'Theorising return migration: the conceptual approach to return migrants revisited', *International Journal on Multicultural Societies*, 6 (2): 253–79.

Casson, M. C., Della Giusta, M. and Kambhampati U. S. (2010) 'Formal and informal institutions and development', *World Development*, 38 (2): 137–41.

Castanheira, M. and Esfahani H. S. (2001) 'Political Economy of Growth: lessons learned and challenges ahead', in G. McMahon and L. Squire (eds) *Explaining Growth: a global research project*, New York: Palgrave Macmillan, pp. 159–212.

Cesare F. P. (1974) 'Expectations and reality: a case study of return migration from the United States to Southern Italy', *International Migration Review*, 8: 245–62.

Chamlou, N., Muzi, S. and Ahmed, H. (2011) 'Understanding the determinants of labour force participation in the Middle East and North Africa region: the role of education and social norms in Amman', *AlmaLaurea Working Paper Series*, 31.

Chan, K. K. and Gemayel, E. R. (2004) 'Risk instability and the pattern of foreign direct investment in the Middle East and North Africa region', *IMF Working Paper*, 04/139.

Chang, H.-J. (2005) 'Understanding the relationship between institutions and economic development'. Paper presented to *WIDER Project on Institutions and Economic Development – Theory, History and Contemporary Experiences*, Helsinki, June.

Chang, H.-J. (2007a) 'Institutional change and economic development: an introduction', in H.-J. Chang (ed.) *Institutional Change and Economic Development*, Tokio: United Nations University Press, pp. 1–14.

Chang, H.-J. (2007b) 'Understanding the relationship between institutions and economic development – some key theoretical issues', in H.-J. Chang (ed.) *Institutional Change and Economic Development*, Tokyo: United Nations University Press, pp. 17–34.

Chapman, D. W. and Miric, S. L. (2009) 'Education quality in the Middle East', *International Review of Education*, 55: 311–44.

Christopher, A., Pissarides, A. C., and Véganzonès-Varoudakis, M.A. (2005) 'Labor markets and economic growth in the MENA region' in J. B. Nugent and M. H. Pesaran (eds) *Explaining Growth in the Middle East,* Amsterdam: Elsevier, pp. 137–57.

Clark, J. A. (2004) *Islam, charity and activism: Middle class networks and social welfare in Egypt, Jordan and Yemen*, Bloomington, IN: Indiana University Press.

Clark, K. and Drinkwater, S. (2001) *An Investigation of Household Remittance Behaviour*, School of Economic Studies, University of Manchester.

Cloke, P. J., Philo, C. and Sadler, D. (1991) *Approaching Human Geography. An introduction to contemporary theoretical debates*, London: SAGE.

Co, Y. K., Yun, M. and Gang, I. (1998) 'Return to returning: who went abroad and what does it matter?', *IZA Discussion Paper Series*, 19.

Coleman, J. (1988) 'Social capital in the creation of human capital', *American Journal of Sociology*, 94: 95–120.

Collins, K. (2004) 'The logic of clan politics evidence from the Central Asian trajectories', *World Politics*, 56 (2): 224–61.

Collins, K. (2006) *The Logic of Clan Politics in Central Asia. The impact on regime transformation*, Cambridge: Cambridge University Press.

Collyer, M. (2004) 'The development impact of temporary international labour migration on southern Mediterranean sending countries: contrasting examples of Morocco and Egypt', *Sussex Centre for Migration Research Annual Report*, University of Sussex.

Cowen, D. and Smith, N. (2009) 'After geopolitics? From the geopolitical social to geoeconomics', *Antipode*, 41 (1): 22–48.

D'Agosto, E. Solforino, N. and Tria G. (2006) 'The migration FDI puzzle: complements or substitutes?', *CEIS Working Paper*, 90.

Daniele, D. and Marani, U. (2006) 'Do institutions matter for FDI? A comparative analysis for the MENA countries', in A. M. Ferragina (ed.) *Bridging the Gap: the role of trade and FDI in the Mediterranean,* Napoli: CNR, pp. 483–512.

Dasgupta, D., Nabli, M. K., Srinivasan, T. G. and Varoudakis, A. (2004) 'Current World Trade Agenda: issues and implications for the MENA region', *Middle East and North Africa Working Paper Series*, 35.

Dayıoğlu M., Kırdar M.G.and Koç (2009) The impact of schooling on the timing of marriage and fertility: evidence from a change in compulsory schooling law. Economic Research Forum Working Paper 470. 1-27.

de Haas, H. (2006) 'Migration, remittances and regional development in Southern Morocco', *Geoforum*, 37 (4): 565–80.

de Melo, J. and Panagariya, A. (1993) 'Introduction', in J. de Melo and A. Panagariya (eds) *New Dimensions in Regional Integration*, Cambridge: Cambridge University Press, pp. 3–21.

de Melo, J. and Panagariya, A. (eds) (1996) *New Dimensions in Regional Integration*, Cambridge: Cambridge University Press.

Decimo, F. and Sciortino, D. (2006) *Stranieri in Italia: Reti migranti (Foreigners in Italy: Migrant networks)*, Bologna: Il Mulino.

Dhonte, P., Bhattacharya, R. and Yousef, T. (2000) 'Demographic transition in the Middle East: implications for growth, employment, and housing', *IMF Working Paper*, March.

Diamond, L. (1994) 'Rethinking civil society. Toward democratic consolidation', *Journal of Democracy*, 5 (3): 4–17.

Diliph, R. and Xu, Z. (2008) *Migration and Remittances Factbook*, Washington: The International Bank for Reconstruction and Development/The World Bank.

Diwan, I., Yang, C. P. and Wang Z. (1998) 'The Arab economies, the Uruguay Round predicament, and the European Union Wild Card', in N. Shafik (ed.) *Prospects for Middle Eastern and North African Economy: from Boom to Bust and back,* New York: St. Martin's Press, pp. 47–95.

Dixit, A. K. (2004) *Lawlessness and Economics*, Princeton: Princeton University Press.

Dobb, M. (1946) *Studies in the Development of Capitalism*, London: Routledge and Kegan Paul.

Docquier, F. and Rapoport, H. (2005) 'The economics of migrant remittances', *IZA Discussion Paper*, 1513.

Doha Declaration (2010) *Quality of education for all, Ministerial colloquium on quality of education in the Arab World*, 21–22 September.

Domar, E. (1946) 'Capital expansion, rate of growth and employment', *econometrica*, 14: 137–47.

Dunning, J. H. (2006) 'Towards a new paradigm of development: implications for the determinants of international business', *Transnational Corporations*, 15 (1): 174–227.

Durkheim, E. (1933) *The Division of Labor in Society*, New York: Free Press.

Dustmann, C. (2001) 'Return migration, wage differential and the optimal migration duration', *IZA Discussion Paper*, 264.

Eaton, J. W. (1972) *Institution Building and Development: from concepts to application*, Pittsburgh: Sage Publications.

Edgeworth, F. Y. (1881) *Mathematical Psychics: an essay on the application of mathematics to the moral sciences*, London: Kegan Paul.

Edwards, S. (1998) 'Openness, productivity and growth: what do we really know?', *Economic Journal*, 108: 383–398.

Ehteshami, A. (2007) *Globalization and geopolitics in the Middle East. Old games, new rules*, London: Routledge.

Elbadawi, I. (1999) 'Can reforming countries perform an Asian miracle? Role of institutions and governance on private investment', in I. Limam (ed.) *Institutional Reform and Development in the MENA Region*, Kuwait: Arab Planning Institute and Economic Research forum for the Arab Countries, Iran and Turkey.

Elbadawi, I. (2005) 'Reviving growth in the Arab World', *Economic development and cultural change*, 53 (2): 236–93.

El-Erian, M. A. and Fischer, S. (1996) 'Is MENA a region? The scope for regional integration', *IMF Working Paper*, 30.

El Korchi, M., Maimbo M. S. and John W. F. (2003) 'Informal funds transfer systems: an analysis of the informal hawala system, *IMF/WB Working Paper*, 24.

El-Mahdi, A. and Rashed, A. (2009) 'The changing economic environment and the development of the micro and small enterprises in Egypt 2006', in R. Assaad (ed.) *The Egyptian Labor Market Revisited*, Cairo: American University in Cairo Press, pp. 87–116.

ERF, (2002) *Economic Trend in MENA Region 2002*, Cairo: Economic Research Forum for the Arab Countries, Iran and Turkey.

Escribano, G. and Jordàn, J. M. (1999) 'Sub-Regional Integration in the MENA Region and the Euro-Mediterranean Free Trade Area', *Mediterranean Politics*, 4 (2): 133–48.

Esfahani, H. S. (2009) 'Understanding common trends and variations in the growth experience of MENA countries', in G. McMahon, H. S. Esfahani, and L. Squire (eds) *Diversity in Economic Growth. Global insights and explanations*, Cheltenham: Edward Elgar, pp. 161–210.

Faist, T. (1997) 'The crucial meso level', in T. Hammar, G. Brochmann, K. Tamas and T. Faist (eds) *International Migration, Immobility and Development*, Oxford: Berg, pp. 187–218.

Fargues, P. (ed.) (2005) *Mediterranean Migration Report*, CARIM.

Favara, M. (2006) 'FDI inflows and trade in the MENA region: complementary-substitution issues' in F. Praussello (ed.) *Sustainable development and adjustment in the Mediterranean countries following EU enlargement*, Milan: Franco Angeli, pp. 165–86.

Fawcett, J. T. (1989) 'Networks, linkages and migration systems', *International Migration Review*, 23 (3): 671–80.

Fawcett, L. (1995) 'Regionalism in historical perspective', in L. Fawcett and A. Hurrell (eds) *Regionalism in World Politics. Regional organization and international order*, Oxford: Oxford University Press, pp. 9–36.

Fawcett, L. (2004) 'Exploring regional domains: a comparative history of regionalism', *International Affairs*, 80 (3): 429–46.

Fergany, N. (2001) *Aspects of Labor Migration and Unemployment in the Arab Region*, Cairo: Almishkat Center for Research.

Fernandez, R. and Portes, J. (1998) 'Returns to regionalism: an analysis of non-traditional gains from regional trade agreements', *World Bank Economic Review* 12 (2):197–220.

Fleischhauer. K. J. (2007) 'A review of human capital theory: microeconomics', *VWA Discussion Paper*, 01.

Funkhouser, E. (1995) 'Remittances from international migration: a comparison of El Salvador and Nicaragua', *Review of Economics and Statistics*, 77 (1): 137–46.

Gadir Ali, A. (2001) *Internal sustainability and economic growth in the Arab states*, Kuwait: Arab Planning Institute.

Galal, A. (2002) 'The paradox of education and unemployment in Egypt', *ECES Working Paper*, 67.

Galal, A. and Hoekman B. (2003) *Arab Economic Integration: between hope and reality*, Cairo: ECES.

Gallup, J. L., Sachs, J. D. and Mellinger, A. D. (1999) 'Geography and economic development', *International Regional Science Review*, 22 (2): 179–232.

Gates, S., Hegre, H., Nygard, H. M. and Strand, H. (2010) *Consequences of Armed Conflict in the Middle East and North Africa Region*, PRIO, October.

Gelvin, J. L. (2005) *The Modern Middle East. A history*, Oxford: Oxford University Press.

Glaeser, E., La Porta, R., Lopez-De-Silanes, F., and Shleifer, A. (2004) 'Do institutions cause growth?', *Journal of Economic Growth*, 9: 271–303.

Gregory Gausse III, F. (1999) 'Systemic approaches to the Middle East international relations', *International Studies Review*, 1 (1): 11–31.

Gregory, P. R. and Stuart, R. C. (2004) *Comparing Economic Systems in the Twenty-First Century*, Boston: Houghton Mifflin Company.

Greif, A. (1993) 'Contract enforceability and economic institutions in early trade: the Maghribi traders coalition', *The American Economic Review*, 83 (3): 525–48.

Greif, A. (2003) 'Reputation and coalition in medieval trade: evidence on the Maghribi traders', *The Journal of Economic History*, 49 (4): 857–82.

Greif, A. (2012) 'Maghribi traders: a reappraisal', *The Economic History Review*, 65 (2): 445–69.

Hakimian, H. (2001) 'From demographic transition to population boom and bust: the experience of Iran in the 1980s and 1990s', *ERF Working Paper Series*, 09.

Hakimian, H. and Nugent, J. B. (eds) (2003) *Trade policy and economic integration in Middle East and North Africa*, New York: Routledge.

Halliday, F. (2005) *The Middle East in International Relations. Power, politics and ideology*, Cambridge: Cambridge University Press.

Hamilton, G. and Biggart, N. (1997) 'Market, culture and authority: a comparative analysis of management and organization in the Far East', in M. Orru, G. Hamilton and N. Biggart (eds) *The Economic Organization of East Asian Capitalism*, London: Sage, pp. 111–50.

Hamoudeh, M. (2002) *The Agadir Process*, Mediterranean Academy of Diplomatic Studies, University of Malta, June.

Harders, C. and Legrenzi, M. (eds) (2008) *Beyond Regionalism? Regional cooperation, regionalism and regionalization in the Middle East*, Aldershot: Ashgate.

Harrod, R. F. (1939) 'An essay in dynamic theory', *Economic Journal*, 49 (March): 14–33.

Hartshorne, R. (1939) *The Nature of Geography*, Lancaster PA: Association of American Geographers.

Hayek, F. A. (1976) *Law, Legislation and Liberty Vol. II: The mirage of social justice*, London: Routledge and Kegan.

Hebbers, H. (1999) 'Economic Integration in the Middle East and North Africa: factors explaining readiness for and failure of regional integration', in A. Al-Kawaz (ed.) *New Economic Developments and their Impact on Arab Economies*, Amsterdam: Elsevier Science, pp. 57–79.

Helpman, E. and Krugman, P. R. (1985) *Market Structure and Foreign Trade*, Cambridge MA: MIT Press.

Henderson, J. V., Shalizi, Z. and Venables, A. J. (2001) 'Geography and development', *Economic Geography*, 1 (1): 81–105.

Herbertson, A. J. (1905) 'The major natural regions: an essay in systematic geography', *Geographical Journal*, 25: 300–12.

Hicks, J. (1969) *A Theory of Economic History*, Oxford: Oxford University Press.

Hickson, C. R. and Thompson, E. A. (1991) 'A new theory of guilds and European economic development', *Exploration in Economic History*, 28: 127–68.

Hifazatullah, H., Badshah S.N., Farooq H., Shafiq R., and Nasir-ud-Din (2011) 'Islamic society: a conceptual frame-work', *International Journal of Education and Social Sciences*, 2 (1): 1–6.

Hinnebusch, R. (2005) 'The politics of identity in Middle East international relations', in L. Fawcett (ed.) *International Relations of the Middle East*, Oxford: Oxford University Press, pp. 151–71.

Hodgson, G. M. (2004) 'What are institutions?', *Journal of Economic Issues*, 40 (1): 1–25.

Hoekman, B. (2005) 'From Euro-Med partnership to European Neighbourhood: deeper integration "a la carte" and economic development', *ECES Working Paper*, 103.

Hoekman, B. (2007) 'Regionalism and development: the European Neighbourhood Policy and integration à la carte', *The Journal of International Trade and Diplomacy*, 1 (1): 1–55.

Hoekman, B. and Messerlin, P. (2002) 'Initial conditions and incentives for Arab economic integration. Can the European Community's success be emulated?' *World Bank Policy Research Working Paper*, 2921.

Horstman, I. and Markusen, J.R. (1992) 'Endogenous market structures in international trade', *Journal of International Economics*, 32 (1–2): 109–29.

Hudson, M. C. (2005) 'The United States in Middle East', in L. Fawcett (ed.) *International Relations of the Middle East*, Oxford: Oxford University Press, pp. 283–305.

Hurrell, A. (1995) 'Regionalism in theoretical perspective', in L. Fawcett and A. Hurrell (ed.) *Regionalism in World Politics. Regional organization and international order*, Oxford: Oxford University Press, pp. 37–73.

Ibn Khaldûn, (1402) *Al-Muqaddima*, French translation by V. Monteil, *Discours sur l'Histoire universelle*, Arles: Actes Sud; English translation by F. Rosenthal, *The Muqaddimah, An Introduction to History*, Bollingen Series XLIII, Princeton, N. J.: Princeton University Press, 1967.

ILO (2009) *Key Indicators of the Labour Market*, Geneva. KILM is a database published by the International Labour organization http://www.ilo.org/empelm/what/WCMS_114240/lang--en/index.htm.

Illahi, N. (1999) 'Return migration and occupational change', *Review of Development Economics*, 3 (2): 170–86.

IMF (2003) *World Economic Outlook. Growth and institutions*, Washington D.C.: International Monetary Fund.

International Energy Agency-IEA (2012) *Key World Energy Statistics 2012*, Paris.

IOM *(2002)* 'Moroccan migration dynamics: prospects for the future', *Migration Research Series*, 10.

IOM (2010) *World Migration Report 2010. The future of migration: building capacities for change*, Geneva: International Organization for Migration.

Iqbal, F. (2006) *Sustaining Gains in Poverty Reduction and Human Development in the Middle East and North Africa*, Washington D.C.: The World Bank.

Isin, E. (2008) 'Social citizenship and the voluntary sector: Ottoman Awqaf, a pious foundation', *Social Policy Review*, Spring: 13–14.

Ivlevs, A. (2005) 'Migration and Foreign Direct Investment in the globalization contest: The case of a small open economy'. Unpublished paper.

Ivlevs, A. *(2008)* 'Are ethnic minorities more likely to emigrate? Evidence from Latvia', University of Nottingham *GEP Research Paper*, 11.

Jacoby, W. (2001) 'The imitation-innovation trade-off. Does "borrowing dull the edge of husbandry"?', *Comparative Political Studies*, 24 (3): 265–93.

Jawad, R. (2011) 'Social policy in the Middle East', *Brown University, Global Security Programme Seminar*, 2011–10–27, Rhode Island.

Jovanovic, B. and Rousseau, P. L. (2005) 'General Purpose Technologies', in F. Aghion and S. N. Durlauf (eds) *Handbook of Economic Growth, Volume IB*, Amsterdam: Elsevier B V, pp. 1181–224.

Jütting, J. (2003) 'Institutions and development: a critical review', *OECD Development Centre Working Paper*, 210.

Kapur, D. and Webb, R. (2000) Governance-Related Conditionalities of the International Financial Institutions, G-24 Discussion Paper Series, 6.

Karajah, S. (2007) 'Civil society in the Arab world: the missing concept', *The International Journal of Not-for-Profit Law*, 9 (2): 35–46.

Karshenas, M. and Moghadam, V. M. (eds) (2005) *Social Policy in the Middle East Economic, Political, and Gender Dynamics*, London: Palgrave Macmillan.

Keller, J. and Nabli, K. M. (2002) 'The macroeconomics of labour market outcomes in MENA over the 1990s: how growth has failed to keep pace with a burgeoning labor market', *ECES Working Paper*. 71.

Khoury, P. S. and Kostiner, J. (eds) (1990) *Tribes and state formation in the Middle East*, Berkeley: University of California Press.

Knack, S. and Keefer. P. (1995) 'Institutions and economic performance: cross-country test using alternative institutional measures', *Economics and Politics*, 7 (3): 207–27.

Kolodko, G. W. (2004) 'Institutions, policies and growth', *Rivista di Politica Economica*, Maggio-Giugno, 45–79.

Korany, B. (2005) 'The Middle East since the Cold War: Torn between Geopolitics and Geoeconomics', in L. Fawcett (ed.) *International Relations of the Middle East*, Oxford: Oxford University Press, pp. 59–76.

Korpi, W. (2001) 'Contentious institutions: An augmented rational-actor analysis of the origins and path dependency of Welfare State institutions in the Western countries', *Rationality and Society*, 13 (2): 235–83.

Kugler, M. (2005) 'Migrant remittances, human capital formation and job creation externalities in Colombia', *Borradores de Economia*, 370, Banco de La Republica, Columbia.

Kumar, K. B. and Matsusaka, J. G. (2004) *Village versus Market Social Capital: An Approach to Development*, paper presented to Econometric Society Meetings in San Diego, CA.

Kuran, T. (1997) 'Islam and underdevelopment: an old puzzle revised', *Journal of Institutional and Theoretical Economics*, 153: 41–71.

Kuran, T. (2003) 'The Islamic commercial crisis: institutional roots of economic underdevelopment in the Middle East', *The Journal of Economic History*, 63 (2): 414–46.

Kuran, T. (2004) 'Why the Middle East is economically underdeveloped: historical mechanisms of institutional stagnation', *Journal of Economic Perspectives*, 18 (3): 71–90.

Kuran, T. (2012) *The Long Divergence: How Islamic Law held back the Middle East*, Princeton: Princeton University Press.

Kuznets, S. (1967) 'Population and economic growth', *Proceedings of the American Philosophical Society*, 111: 170–93.

Lahouel, M. H. (2007) 'The success of pro-poor growth in rural and urban Tunisia', in T. Besley and L. J. Cord (eds) *Delivering on the Promise of Pro-Poor Growth. Insights and lessons from countries experiences*, Washington: Palgrave Macmillan and the World Bank, pp. 199–218.

Laipson, E. (2002), 'The Middle East's demographic transition: what does it mean?', *Journal of International Affairs*, 56 (1): 175.

Langlois, R. and Robertson, P. (1995) *Firms, Markets and Economic Change: A dynamic theory of business institutions*, London: Routledge.

Lapidus, I. M. (1990) 'Tribes and state formation in Islamic history', in P. S. Khoury and J. Kostiner (eds) *Tribes and State Formation in the Middle East*, Berkeley: University of California Press, pp. 25–47.

Lapidus, I. M. (2002) *History of Islamic Societies*, Cambridge: Cambridge University Press.

Lawson, F. H. (2008) 'Comparing regionalist projects in the Middle East and elsewhere: one step back, two steps forward', in C. Harders and M. Legrenzi (eds) *Beyond Regionalism? Regional cooperation, regionalism and regionalization in the Middle East*, Aldershot: Ashgate, pp. 13–31.

Lee, R. (2003) 'The demographic transition: three centuries of fundamental change', *Journal of Economic Perspectives*, 17 (4): 167–90.

Leukert, A. (2005) *The Dynamics of Institutional Change: formal and informal institutions and economic performance*, University of Munich.

Lewis, W. A. (1954) 'Economic development with unlimited supply of labor', *The Manchester School*, 22: 139–91.

Limam, I. and Abdalla, A. (1998) 'Inter Arab trade and the potential success of AFTA', *Arab Institute Working Papers*, 6.

Longva, A. N. (1999) 'Keeping migrant workers in check: the *Kafala* system in the Gulf', *Middle East Report*, 211: 20–2.

López-Cálix, J. R., Walkenhorst, P. and Ndiamé D., (eds) (2011) *Trade competitiveness of the Middle East and North Africa, Policies for export diversification*, Washington D.C.: World Bank.

Luciani, G. (2005) 'Oil and political economy in the international relations of the Middle East', in L. Fawcett (ed.) *International relations of the Middle East*, Oxford: Oxford University Press, pp. 79–104.

Lutwak, E. (1990) 'From geopolitics to geoeconomics. Logic of conflict, grammar of commerce', *The National Interest*, 20: 17–23.

Lynch, L. (1991) 'The role of off-the-job vs. on-the-job training for the mobility of women workers', *American Economic Review*, 81 (2): 151–6.

Maddison, A. (1991) *Dynamic Forces in Capitalist Development: a long-run comparative view*, Oxford: Oxford University Press.

Makdisi, G. (1981) *Rise of Colleges: institutions of learning in Islam and the West*, Edinburgh: Edinburgh University Press.

Makdisi, S., Fattah, Z. and Limam, I. (2007), 'Determinants of growth in the MENA countries', in J. Nugent and H. Pesaran (eds) *Explaining Growth in the Middle East*, Amsterdam: Elsevier, pp. 31–60.

Malik, A. and Awadallah, B. (2011) 'The economics of Arab Springs', *CSAE Working Paper*, 23.

Malthus, T. R. (1798) *An Essay on the Principle of Population as it Affects the Future Improvement of Society, with Remarks on the Speculations of Mr. Godwin, M. Condorcet, and Other Writers*, Harmondsworth: Penguin Classics (1982).

Mansfield, E. D. and Milner, H. V. (1999) 'The new wave of regionalism', *International Organization*, 53 (3): 589–627.

Marchand, M. H., Boàs, M. and Shaw T. M. (1999) 'The political economy of new regionalism', *The World Quarterly*, 20 (5): 897–910.

Markusen, J. R. (1983) 'Factor movements and commodity trade as complements', *Journal of International Economics*, 14 (3–4): 341–56.

Martin, I. (2007) 'In search of development along the Southern borders: the economic models underlying the Euro-Mediterranean Partnership and the European Neighbourhood Policy', in A. M. Ferragina (ed.) *Bringing the Gap: the role of trade and FDI in the Mediterranean*, Naples: CNR, pp. 115–41.

Martin, P. L. and Taylor, J. E., (1996) 'The anatomy of migration hump', in E. Taylor (ed.) *Development Strategy, Employment and Migration: insights and models*, Paris: OECD, pp. 43–62.

Marx, K. (1999) *Capital. A critique of political economy* (German edition 1867, first English edition 1887), Marx/Engels Internet Archive. See marxists.org.

Massey, D. S., Arango, J., Hugo, G., Kouaouci, A., Pellegrino, A. and Taylor J. E. (1998) *World in Motion: understanding international migration at the end of the millennium*, Oxford: Clarendon Press.

Masud, M. K. (2010) *Civil society in Islam*. Available at <http://www.maruf.org/?p=57>. Date accessed January 2010.

Mattli, W. (1999) *The Logic of Integration. Europe and beyond*, Cambridge: Cambridge University Press.

Mayr, K. and Peri, G. (2008) 'Return migration as a channel of brain gain', *NBER Working Paper*, W14039.

McCormick, B. and Wahba J. (2000) 'Overseas employment and remittances to a dual economy', *The Economic Journal*, 110: 509–34.

McMahon, G. and Squire, L. (2003) 'Explaining Growth: a global research project', in G. McMahon and L. Squire (eds) *Explaining Growth: a global research project*, New York: Palgrave Macmillan, pp. 1–11.

Meltem, D., Murat, G. K. and Koç, I. (2009) 'The impact of schooling on the timing of marriage and fertility: evidence from change in compulsory schooling law', *ERF Working Paper Series,* 470.

Mengoni, L. and Romagnoli, A. (2007) 'Beyond remittances in the Mediterranean: what migration pattern for LED?', in A. M. Ferragina (ed.) *Bridging the Gap: the role of trade and FDI in the Mediterranean,* Napoli: CNR, pp. 557–83.

Mesnard, A. (2004) 'Temporary migration and capital market imperfections', *Oxford Economic Papers,* 56: 242–63.

Meyer, J-B. and Brown, M. (1999) *Scientific Diasporas: a New Approach to the Brain Drain.* Paper prepared for the *UNESCO-ISCU World Conference on Science,* Budapest, Hungary, 26 June–1 July 1999.

Michalopoulos, S., Naghavi, A. and Prarolo, G. (2010) 'Trade and geography in the economic origins of Islam: theory and evidence', *Carlo Alberto Notebooks,* 145.

Mincer, J. (1958) 'Investment in human capital and personal income distribution', *The Journal of Political Economy.* 66 (4): 281–302.

Miniesy, R., Nugent, J. and Yousef, T. (2003) 'Intra-regional trade integration in the Middle East. Past performance and future potential', in H. Hakimian and J. Nugent (eds) *Trade policy and economic integration in the Middle East and North Africa. Economic boundaries in flux,* London: Routledge, pp. 41–65.

MIREM, (2008) *Return Migrants to the Maghreb Countries,* General Report, Florence: European University Institute.

Mokyr, J. (2008) 'The institutional origins of the industrial revolution' in E. Helpman (ed.) *Institutions and Economic Performance,* Harvard: Harvard University Press.

Moseley, K. P. and Wallerstein, I. (1978) 'Precapitalist social structures', *Annual Review of Sociology,* 4 (August): 259–90.

Mundell, R.A. (1957) 'International trade and factor mobility', *The American Economic Review,* 47 (3): 321–35.

Munshi, K. (2003) 'Networks in the modern economy: Mexican migrants in the U.S. labor market', *The Quarterly Journal of Economics,* 47 (3): 321–35.

Munzele, M. S. and Passas, N. (2004) 'The regulation and supervision of informal remittance systems', *Small Enterprise Development,* 15 (1): 53–69.

Nabli, M. K. and De Kleine A. I. (2000) 'Managing global integration in the Middle East and North Africa', in B. Hoekman and H. K. El-Din (eds) *Trade Policy Development in the Middle East and North Africa,* Washington D.C.: The World Bank.

Nassar, H. (2007) 'Population dividend and its implications for the labor market in Egypt', *Second Population Report, UNFPA,* Cairo.

Nelson, R. and Sampat, B. N. (2001) 'Making sense of institutions as a factor shaping economic performance', *Journal of Economic Behaviour and Organizations,* 44: 31–54.

Noland, M. and Pack, H. (2007) *The Arab Economies in a Changing World,* Washington D.C.: Peter Peterson Institute for International Economics.

Nordman, J. and Gubert, F. (2008) *Return Migration and Small Enterprise Development in the Maghreb,* Florence: European University Institute.

North, D. C. (1990) *Institutions, Institutional Change and Economic Performance. Political economy of institutions and decision,* Cambridge: Cambridge University Press.

North, D. C. (1993) 'Institutional change: a framework of analysis', in S.-E. Sjöstrand (ed.) *Institutional Change: Theory and Empirical Findings,* New York: M.E. Sharp, pp. 35–48.

North, D. C. (2005) *Understanding the Process of Economic Change*, Princeton: Princeton University Press.

North, D. C. and Thomas, P. T. (1973) *The Rise of the Western World: A New Economic History*, Cambridge: Cambridge University Press.

Nunes, A. B. and Valèrio, N. (2001) 'Three paths to capitalism: an agenda for research', in C. M. A. Clark and J. Rosicka (eds) *Economic Transition in Historical Perspective*, Aldershot: Ashgate, pp. 101–13.

Nunnenkamp, P. (2004) 'Why economic growth has been weak in Arab countries: the role of exogenous shocks, economic policy failure and institutional deficiencies', *Journal of Development and Economic Policies*, 7 (1): 2–18.

O'Rourke, K., and Williamson. J. G. (2005) 'From Malthus to Ohlin: trade, industrialization and distribution since 1500', *Journal of Economic Growth*, 10 (1): 5–34.

OECD (2003) *Regionalism and the Multilateral Trading System. The role of regional trade agreements*, Policy Brief, August.

OECD (2004) *Employment outlook 2003 – Towards More and Better Jobs,* Paris: OECD Publications Service.

OECD (2006) *International Migration Outlook,* Paris: OECD Publications Service.

Ogilvie, S. (2007) 'Whatever is, is right? Economic institutions in pre-industrial Europe', *Tawney Lecture 2006, CESIFO Working Paper*, 2066.

Okeahalam, C. (2005) 'Institutions and financial market development in the MENA region, *Progress in Development Studies*, 5 (4) 310–28.

Olesen, H. (2002) 'Migration, return and development', *International Migration*, 40 (5): 125–50.

OPEC (2012) *Annual Statistics Bulletin 2012*, Organization of the Petroleum Exporting Countries, Vienna.

Ouchi, W. G. (1980) 'Markets, bureaucracies, and clans', *Administrative Science Quarterly*, 25 (1): 129–41.

Owen, R. (1981) *The Middle East in the world economy: 1800–1914*, London: J. B. Tauris.

Page, J. (2007) 'Boom, bust and the poor: poverty dynamics in the Middle East and North Africa: 1970–1999', *The Quarterly Review of Economics and Finance*, 46: 832–51.

Page, J. and Van Gelder, L. (2002) *Globalization, growth and poverty reduction in the Middle East and North Africa, 1970–1999*. Paper presented at the fourth Mediterranean Development Forum: Amman, Jordan.

Pande, R. and Udry, C. (2005) 'Institutions and development: a view from below', Yale University, *Economic Growth Center Working Papers*, 928.

Parent, O. and Zouache, A. (2008) *Determinants of Growth in Africa and Middle East: how to implement geographical features and institutional factors?* Paper presented to the ERF 15th Annual Conference, Cairo, 23–25 November.

Pedersen, J., Pitlykova, M., and Smith, N. (2004) 'Selection or network effects? Migration flows into 27 OECD countries, 1990–2000', *IZA Working Papers*, 1104.

Person, P. (2000) 'The limits of design: explaining institutional origins and change', *Governance: An International Journal of Policy and Administration*, 13 (4): 475–99.

Pissarides, C. A. and Véganzonès-Varoudakis, M. A. (2007) 'Labor markets and economic growth in the MENA region' in J. Nugent and H. Pesaran (eds) *Explaining Growth in the Middle East*, Amsterdam: Elsevier, pp. 137–57.

Platteau, J. P. (2008) 'Religion, politics and development: lessons from the lands of Islam', *ERF Working Paper Series*, 434.

Polany, K. (1944) *The Great Transformation*, Boston: Beacon Press.

Portes, A., Guarnizo, L. E. and Haller, W. J. (2002) 'Transnational entrepreneurs: an alternative form of immigrant economic adaptation', *American Sociological Review*, 67 (2), 278–98.

Potts, J. (2000) *The New Evolutionary Microeconomics*, Cheltenham: Edward Elgar.

Pryor, F. (2007) 'The economic impact of Islam in developing nations', *World Development*, 35 (11): 1815–35.

Putnam, R. D., Leonardi R. and Nanetti R. Y. (1993) *Making Democracy Work: civic traditions in modern Italy*, Princeton: Princeton University Press.

Quadrio Curzio, A. (2011) 'For the development of Middle East and North Africa sovereign wealth funds, European Union, Arab League and others', *Economia Politica. Journal of Analytical and Institutional Economics*, 28 (2): 171–84.

Rahman, A. (1986) *Muḥammad Encyclopedia of Seerah*, London: Seerah Foundation.

Ranis, G. and Fei J. C. (1961) 'A theory of economic development', *American Economic Review*, 51 (September): 533–58.

Rashad, H. and Osman M. (2001) 'Nuptiality in Arab Countries: changes and implication', in S. N. Hopkins (eds) *The New Arab Family*, Cairo: The American University in Cairo Press, 20–44.

Regnault, H. (2002) 'Quale futuro per il regionalismo euro-mediterraneo? (English translation: What is the future for the Euro-Mediterranean regionalism?'), *L'Industria*, 23 (3): 479–95.

Richard, H., Adams, Jr. and Page, J. (2001) *Holding the line: Poverty reduction in the Middle East and North Africa, 1970–2000*, draft, The World Bank Poverty Reduction Group.

Richard, H., Adams, Jr. and Page, J. (2003) 'Poverty, inequality and growth in selected Middle East and North Africa countries', *World Development*, 31 (12): 2027–48.

Richards, A. and Waterbury, J. (2008) *A Political Economy of the Middle East*, Boulder CO: Westview Press.

Richardson, G. and Bogart, D. (2008) 'Institutional adaptability and economic development: the property rights revolution in Britain, 1700 to 1830', *NBER Working Paper*, 13757.

Richter, S. (2012) 'Regional trade integration in the Middle East and North Africa: lessons from Central Europe', *The Vienna Institute for International Policy Studies, Policy Brief*, 14.

Rodinson, M. (1966) *Islam et Capitalisme*, Paris: Éditions du Seuil.

Rodrik, D. (2000) 'Institutions for high-quality growth: what they are and how to acquire them?' *NBER Working Paper*, 7540.

Rogan, E. L. (2005) 'The emergence of the Middle East into the modern state system', in L. Fawcett (ed.) *International Relations of the Middle East*, Oxford: Oxford University Press, pp. 17–39.

Romagnoli, A. and Mengoni, L. (2009) 'The challenge of economic integration in the MENA region: from GAFTA and EU-MFTA to small scale Arab Unions', *Economic Change and Restructuring*, 42 (1): 69–83.

Rostow, W. W. (1960) *The Stages of Economic Growth: A Non-Communist Manifesto*, 3rd edn. 1991, Cambridge: Cambridge University Press.

Ruiz, S. and Zahrnt, V. (2008) 'Regional ambition, institutions, social capital -regional cooperation and external actors, in C. Horders and M. Legrenzi (eds) *Beyond Regionalism? Regional cooperation, regionalism and regionalization in the Middle East*, Ashgate: Aldershot, pp. 51–67.

Sachs, J. and Warner, A.M. (1997). 'Sources of slow growth in African economies', *Journal of African Economies*, 6 (3): 335–76.

Safadi, R. (1996) 'The impact of the Uruguay Round on multilateral trade negotiations and their effects on ESCWA members', *ESCWA, 123–178,* Amman.

Said, M. and El-Hamidi, F. (2008) 'Taking technical education seriously in MENA: determinants, labor market implication and policy lesson', *ERF Working Paper Series*, 450.

Saidi, N. (2004) 'Arab economic integration: an awakening to remove barriers to prosperity', *ERF Working Paper Series*, 322.

Salehi-Isfahani, D. (2010) 'Human Development in the Middle East and North Africa', *Human Development Research Paper*, 2010/26.

Sayed, H. F. (2006) *Transforming education in Egypt. Western influence and domestic policy*, Cairo: The American University in Cairo Press.

Schiff, M. (1996) 'Small is beautiful: preferential trade agreements and the impact of country size, market share, trade policy and smuggling', *World Bank Policy Research Working Paper Series*, 1668.

Schiff, M. (2006) 'Migration, trade and investment: complements or substitutes?', *CEIS Research Paper Series*, 30 (89).

Schiff, M. and Winters, L. A. (1997) 'Regional integration as diplomacy', *World Bank Policy Research Working Paper* 1801.

Schiopu, I. and Siegfried, N. (2006) 'Determinants of workers' remittances: evidence from the European neighbouring region', *European Central Bank Working Paper Series*, 688.

Schultz, T. P. (1994) 'Human capital, family planning, and their effects on population growth', *The American Economic Review*, 84 (2): 255–260.

Schultz, T. W. (1961) 'Investment in human capital', *The American Economic Review*, 51 (1): 1–17.

Schumpeter, J. A. (1955) *The Theory of Economic Development. An inquiry into profits, capital, credit, interest, and the business cycle.* (German edition 1926, translated in English in 1934), Cambridge MA: Harvard University Press.

Screpanti, E. (2001) *The Fundamental Institutions of Capitalism*, London: Routledge.

Searle, J. R. (2005) 'What is an institution?', *Journal of Institutional Economics*, 1 (1): 1–22.

Sen, A. (1999) *Development as Freedom*, Oxford: Oxford University Press.

Shackmurove, Y. (2004) 'Economic development in the Middle East', *Penn Institute for Economic Research Working Paper, 022.*

Shafik, N. (1992) 'Has labour migration promoted economic integration in the Middle East?', *World Bank and Georgetown University Discussion Paper*, 1.

Shakoori, B. (2005) 'Demographic transition and its implications on employment and international migration', *UN/POP/MIG-FCM/2005/07.*

Shihata, I. F. I. and Sherbiny, N. A. (1985) 'The OPEC aid phenomenon in perspective', *OPEC Review*, 9 (4): 323–350.

Shotter, A. (1981) *The Economic Theory of Social Institutions*, Cambridge: Cambridge University Press.

Simon, J. L. (1981) *The Ultimate Resource*, Princeton: Princeton University Press.

Sirageldin, I. (2002) 'The elimination of poverty: challenges and Islamic strategies', in M. Iqbal (ed.) *Islamic Economic Institution and the Elimination of Poverty*, The Islamic Foundation, Leicester UK, pp. 25–46.

Smith, A. (1776) *An Inquiry into the Nature and Causes of the Wealth of Nations*, London: Methuen & Co., Ltd.

Sombart, W. (1951) *The Jewish and the Modern Capitalism* (German edition 1911–1928) English translation by M. Epstein, New York: The Free Press.

Stalker, P. (2002) 'Migration trends and migration policy in Europe', *International Migration*, 40 (5): 151–79.

Stark, O. (1991) *The Migration of Labour*, Cambridge, MA: Basil Blackwell.

Stark, O. (1995) *Altruism and Beyond*, Cambridge, MA: Basil Blackwell.

Stern, R. (1999) 'Dynamic aspects of Euro-Mediterranean Agreements for the MENA economies', The University of Michigan *School of Public Policy Discussion Paper*, 437.

Stiglitz, J. E. (1998) *Towards a New Paradigm for Development*, UNCTAD, 9th Raùl Prebisch Lecture, Geneva.

Streeten, P. (1999) 'Ten years of human development', in *Human Development Report 1999*, UNDP.

Sweezy, P., Dobb, M. and Reinmuth, H. S. (1976) *The Transition from Feudalism to Capitalism*, London: Left Books.

Taboutin, D. and Schoumaker, B. (2005) 'The demography of the Arab World and the Middle East from the 1950s to the 2000s. A survey of changes and a statistical assessment', *Population (English edition)*, 60 (5): 515–605.

Taheri, M. R. (2000). *The basic principles of Islamic economy and their effects on accounting-standards-setting*. Available at <http://panoptiction.csustan.edu/cpa99/html/taheri.html>. Accessed 17 July 2001.

Tawney, R. H. (1926) *Religion and the rise of capitalism. A historical study*, London: A Mentor Book.

Taylor, J. (2004) *Social Indicators for Aboriginal Governance: Insights from the Thamarrurr region, Northern Territory*, CAEPR Research Monograph, 24, Canberra: ANU E-Press.

Taylor, J. E. (1999) 'The new economics of labour migration and the role of remittances in the migration process', *International Migration*, 37: 65–87.

Tétreault, M. A. (2008) 'The political economy of oil' in J. Schwedler and D. J. Gerner (eds) *Understanding the Contemporary Middle East*, Boulder: Lynne Rienner, pp. 255–79.

Thomas, V., Wang, Y. and Fan, X. (2001) 'Measuring education inequality: Gini coefficients of education', *Middle East and North Africa Working Paper Series*, 2525, World Bank.

Thompson, W. R. (1970) 'The Arab sub-system and the feudal pattern of interaction: 1965', *Journal of Peace Research*, 7: 151–67.

Thompson, W. R. (1973) 'The regional subsystem: a conceptual explication and a propositional inventory, *International Studies Quarterly*, 17 (1): 89–117.

Thorvaldur, G. and Zoega, G. (2001), 'Natural resources and economic growth: the role of investment,' *CEPR Discussion Paper*, 2743.

Todaro, M. P. (1976) *Internal Migration in Developing Countries. A review of theory, evidence, methodology and research priorities*, Geneva: ILO.

Todaro, M. P. and Smith, S. C. (2012) *Economic Development*, Boston: Addison-Wesley.

Tzannagos, Z. (2000) 'Social protection in the Middle East and North Africa: a review', in H. Handoussa and Z. Tzannatos (eds) *Employment Creation and Social Protection in the Middle East and North Africa*, Cairo: The American University in Cairo Press, pp. 121–71.

UNCTAD (2009) *Handbook of Statistics*, New York: United Nations.

UNDP (2002) *Arab Human Development Report,* New York: United Nations.

UNDP (2011) *2011 Human Development Report. Sustainability and Equity: A Better Future for All*, New York: United Nations

UNECA (2001) *The State of Demographic Transition in Africa*, Economic Commission for Africa Publication. ECA/FSSDD (2001) *The State of Demographic Transition in Africa*, Addis Ababa: Economic Commission for Africa Publication.

UNESCO (2010) *Towards an Arab higher education space: International challenges and social responsibilities*. Beirut: UNESCO Regional Bureau for Education in the Arab States.

UNHCR (2010) *2010 UNHCR Country Operations Profile – Turkey*, Ankara: UNHCR.

Vertovec, S. (2002) *Transnational Networks and Skilled Labour Migration*. Paper presented to the *Ladenburger Diskurs on Migration*, Ladenburg, February 2002.

Viner, J. (1950) *The Custom Unions Issues*, New York: Carnegie Endowment for International Peace.

Wahba, J. (2004) 'Does international migration matter? A study of Egyptian return migrants', in *Arab migration in a globalised world*, Geneva: International Organization for Migration, pp. 179–200.

Wahba, J. (2006) 'Preliminary analysis on internal and International Migration, (Preliminary results of ELMPS 2006)', *World Bank and Georgetown University Discussion Paper*, 1.

Wahba, J. (2009) 'An overview of internal and international migration in Egypt', in R. Assaad (ed.) *Egypt's Labor Market Revisited*, Cairo: The American University in Cairo Press, pp. 157–76.

Wallerstein, I. (1976) 'From Feudalism to Capitalism: transition or transitions?', *Social Forces*, 55 (2): 273–83.

Weber, M. (1930) *The Protestant Ethic and The Spirit of Capitalism*, (German edition 1904–5) English translation by T. Parson, New York: Charles Scribner's Sons.

Weber, M. (1978) *Economy and Society*, Berkeley: University of California Press.

Weiss, D. (1995) 'Ibn Khaldūn on economic transformation', *International Journal of Middle East Studies*, 27 (1): pp. 29–37.

Whalley, J. (1996) 'Why do countries seek regional trade agreements', *NBER Working Paper*, 5552.

Williamson, J. G. and Yousef, T. M. (2002) 'Demographic transition and economic performance in the Middle East and North Africa', in I. Sirageldin (ed.) *Human Capital, Population Economics in the Middle East*, London: J. B. Tauris.

Williamson, O. E. (2000) 'The new institutional economics: taking stock, looking ahead', *Journal of Economic Literature*, 38: 595–613.

Wilson, R. (2012) *Economic Development in the Middle East*, 2nd edition (first edition 1995), London: Routledge.

World Bank (1999) *Education in the Middle East & North Africa: A Strategy Towards Learning for Development*, Washington D.C.

World Bank (2002a) 'Identifying conflict-related obstacles to development', *Social Development Department, Dissemination Notes*, 5.

World Bank (2002b) 'Republic Yemen: Poverty Update', *Poverty Reduction Strategy Papers*, December 11.

World Bank (2002c) *Building Institutions for Markets*, Washington D.C.

World Bank (2002d) *World Development Report 2002. Building institutions for markets*, Washington D.C.

World Bank (2004), *Unlocking the Employment Potential in the Middle East and North Africa, Towards a new social contract*, Washington D.C.

World Bank (2005) *Economic Developments and Prospects, Middle East and North Africa Region*, Washington D.C., World Bank.

World Bank (2006) *Economic Developments and Prospects. Financial Markets in a New Geography of Oil*, Washington D.C.

World Bank (2008a) *Economic Developments and Prospects, Middle East and North Africa Region*, Washington D.C.

World Bank (2008b) *The Road Not Traveled. Education Reform in the Middle East and Africa*, Washington D.C.

World Bank (2009) *From Privilege to Competition: Unlocking Private-led Growth in the Middle East and North Africa*, Washington D.C.

World Bank (2010a) *Economic integration in the GCC*, Washington D.C.

World Bank (2010b) *Economic integration in the Maghreb*. Washington D.C.

World Bank (2010c) *Economic integration in the Mashreq*, Washington D.C.

World Bank (2011) *Enterprise surveys database*, Washington D.C.

World Bank (2011) *Poverty and Inequality database*, Washington D.C.

World Bank (2011a) *Reducing Conflict Risk. Conflict, Fragility and Development in the Middle East and North Africa*.

World Bank (2011b) *World Development Indicators*, Washington D.C.

Wrobel, A. (1962) 'Regional analysis and the geographic concept of region', *Papers in Regional Science*, 8 (1): 37–41.

Yousef, T. M. (2004) 'Development, growth and policy reform in the Middle East and North Africa since 1950', *Journal of Economic Perspectives*, 18 (3): 91–116.

Yousef, T. (2006) *The origin of the governance gap in the Middle East*. Paper presented to the IMF/AMF Seminar *on Institutions and Economic Growth in the Arab Countries*, Abu Dhabi, UAE, December 19–20.

Zarrouk, J. E. (1998) *Arab free trade area: potentialities and effects*. Paper presented at the *Mediterranean Development Forum*, Marrakech, Sept 3–6.

Zarrouk, J. E. (2003) 'A survey of barriers to trade and investment in Arab countries', in A. Galal and B. Hoekman (eds) *Arab Economic integration, Between Hope and Reality*, Cairo: ECES, pp. 48–60.

Zarrouk, J. E. and Zollio, F. (2000), *Integrating Free Trade Agreements*, Unpublished paper.

Zubaida, S. (2001) *Islam: the People and the State: Political ideas and movements in the Middle East*, London: J. B. Tauris.

Zucherman, W. (2003) 'On networks and markets', Rauch and Casella (eds), *Journal of Economic Literature*, 14 (2): 545–65.

Index

For Product Safety Concerns and Information please contact our EU
representative GPSR@taylorandfrancis.com
Taylor & Francis Verlag GmbH, Kaufingerstraße 24, 80331 München, Germany

* 9 7 8 0 3 6 7 8 6 5 7 1 9 *